THE
LITTLE GIANT™
ENCYCLOPEDIA
OF
*Dream
Symbols*

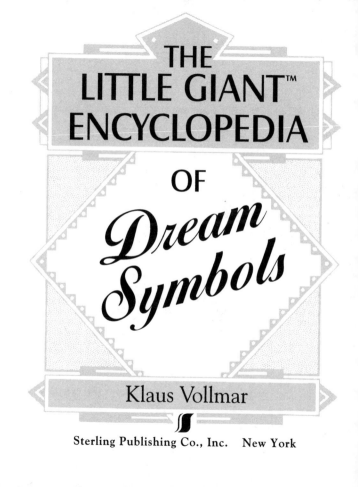

THE LITTLE GIANT™ ENCYCLOPEDIA

OF

Dream Symbols

Klaus Vollmar

Sterling Publishing Co., Inc.   New York

Translated by Elisabeth E. Reinersmann

Library of Congress Cataloging-in-Publication Data

Vollmar, Klausberndt
  [Handbuch der Tram-Symbole. English]
  Little giant encyclopedia of dream symbols / Klaus Vollmar
    p.   cm.
  Includes index.
  ISBN 0-8069-9787-7
  1. Dream interpretation—Dictionaries. I. Title.
BF1091.V65   1997
154.6'3'03—dc21   97-27939
                                                   CIP

10   9   8   7   6   5

Published by Sterling Publishing Company, Inc.
387 Park Avenue South, New York, N.Y. 10016
Originally published in Germany under the title
Handbuch der Traum-Symbole and © 1992 by Konigsfurt Verlag
Translation © 1997 by Sterling Publishing Co.. Inc.
Distributed in Canada by Sterling Publishing
c/o Canadian Manda Group, One Atlantic Avenue, Suite 105
Toronto, Ontario, Canada M6K 3E7
Distributed in Great Britain and Europe by Cassell PLC
Wellington House, 125 Strand, London WC2R 0BB, England
Distributed in Australia by Capricorn Link (Australia) Pty Ltd.
P.O. Box 6651, Baulkham Hills, Business Centre, NSW 2153, Australia

Sterling ISBN 0-8069-9787-7

Contents

Introduction

*"In a very curious way a dream teaches us how easily
our soul is capable of penetrating every object while—
at the same time—becoming that object."* —Novalis

The book presented here is a unique, modern dictionary
for contemporary people who want to gain a more
detailed insight into the images of their dreams. What is
new is that I start with the assumption that each dream
image always has more than one meaning. In this way, a
dream symbol is different from, for instance, a mathe-
matical symbol. Each dream symbol and image is not
only dependent upon the content of the whole dream,
but also on the personality of the dreamer. For that reason, I have departed from the practice that originated
in Egypt with *The Hierarchical Book on Dreams*, which is
the oldest dream book, having been handed down to us
from the Egyptian Middle Kingdom in approximately
2000 B.C. This practice, which is still used in other
dream books, assigns to each symbol *one* distinct meaning. In this sense, this is not a book where different
dream symbols have merely been categorized.

This book also challenges the belief that a lexicon of
dream symbols is wrong simply because there is no *one*

definitive interpretation for each symbol. Carl Gustav Jung, in his seminars on dreams, developed between 1936 and 1942, stated repeatedly that it is possible to understand the meaning of dream symbols and images even without knowing the dreamer. What human beings have in common from the very beginning are many basic and very similar life situations, and images of them have found their way into our dreams in the form of symbols. While "dreamscapes" called forth by these primeval experiences are surely reshaped, varied, and made concrete by each individual dreamer—according to the age and culture of which he is a part—in the last analysis the images remain the same. These thoughts led me to this attempt to capture specific dream images in their many-faceted meanings.

1. Each dream image in this handbook is explored from several different angles:

a. An image can be seen as a challenge as well as a validation. As a challenge, a dream image may offer new insights and new ways of behaving of which previously the dreamer had been unaware. The dreamer may be shown in a dream what is missing in his everyday life. C. G. Jung called this "the complementary function of a dream," because it expands the dreamer's view and way of life.

This method of evaluating a dream assumes that the

image appears because the dreamer is receptive to its message and the experience that is associated with it.

b. Each dream image represents an object or a situation in the outside world, as well as being a symbol from the inner life of the dreamer.

A dream image or symbol may point to the connection with a particular object, or it may address some part of our psyche or body for which the object serves as a symbol. For instance, when we dream about a house it may mean a "real" house—our parents' house, or a house we may want to own or in which we live, and so on—but it may also represent our psyche or our body, both of which are often symbolized by the image of a house. It would be useful if the dreamer could take both points of view into consideration. C. G. Jung—distinguishing between the images—calls one the "objective stage" (the object taken for what it represents) and the other the "subjective stage" (the object referring to the dreamer specifically).

2. This handbook also points out how different cultures and psychological methodologies vary in their interpretation of dream images.

Along with each dream image, I have provided references that are routinely employed in depth psychology, and—whenever useful—in other cultures. In an attempt to make the handbook as easy to use as possible, I have included only those interpretations that still seem relevant today, and that are useful in advancing the work of dream interpretation.

Today, in this age of so-called sexual freedom, we are less likely to sexualize our environment, because sexual experiences are less of a taboo. However, Sigmund Freud's interpretations are also given here. They not only have cultural-historical value, but are often accurate, particularly if the dreamer happens to be in a situation where living out his or her sexuality is not possible.

3. In describing individual dream images and symbols, I did not—as has traditionally been the case since Freud—start out with the assumption that a dream image is necessarily an indication of a pathology in the psychological development of a person. In my experience as a therapist, dream images usually appear so frequently because the dreamer is particularly open to the message and is able to incorporate it into his or her life. This means that I do not see a dream only in connection to the past, but also as being relevant for the future.

4. As far as possible, and for ease of orientation, I have also tried to add practical tips in my description of each dream image. Most of the time I have done this by posing different questions in order to direct readers to the concerns they have in their everyday lives. I do not believe in pushing my own interpretations onto anybody else. On the other hand, however, we all need to be stimulated so that paying attention to our dreams can become part of our everyday experience. Dream interpretations are only complete when the message and the lesson of a particular dream have been assimilated into the dreamer's practical life.

Tips on How to Use This Encyclopedia

"I always have been—and am to this day—a dreamer. But who cares, as long as dreaming is a tool for searching?" —George Sand

If you are unable to determine the meaning of one or more of the images in your dreams (including your daydreams), look under the key word and let yourself be inspired by the meaning that is expressed there. The interpretations and explanations are formulated to guide you to new ideas, insights, and emotions.

In addition, reading this dream-symbol encyclopedia can be useful even with those dreams that pose no particular difficulty. Looking up symbols—even if they seem to be "obvious"—might help to deepen your understanding of and insight into your dreams. It may make you aware of other ways of interpreting certain images, which in turn will help you to look at your dreams more creatively and openly.

It may also be useful to browse through the book without a specific dream in mind, because it will not only stimulate your dream activities, but also help you to deal with your dreams more imaginatively.

An additional advantage of reading about the many

different symbols is that you will become more familiar with the history of dream interpretation. Many of those involved in dream research have understood the same images to mean totally different things. When we realize this, we not only learn something about the times and cultures during which these interpretations were formulated, but we also gain a greater understanding of the complexity of our dreams. Seldom does a dream image have only one meaning. Rather, it points in many different directions at once, and at least a few of them have been recognized throughout history.

Sigmund Freud probably was right that underneath almost every dream symbol is an underlying, repressed, often infantile sexual desire; but C. G. Jung was just as correct in stating, 20 years after his break with Freud, that every dream image represents a creative process that relates to the collective archetype of the soul. Without doubt, people in antiquity who worshiped Asclepius, the god of healing, were correct in assuming that dream images, which they believed were sent them by the god of mental and physical wholeness, had healing powers.

Dream symbols have always been interpreted as forecasts of individual or collective events. In ancient Greece and Rome, dream images were so firmly believed to have prophetic powers that it was customary to report certain dreams to the government.

Each dream has many faces—some more varied than others—and many of them surely will find their way into your own dreams.

It is important for you who use this encyclopedia to find your own, relevant and complex meanings among all the possible interpretations. The interpretations presented in this book are meant to introduce new—and up until now unknown—possibilities, assisting in the exploration of your dreams.

—*Klaus Vollmar*

DREAM
SYMBOLS

Abbey: See **Cloister**. Even though the abbey or cloister has no real meaning in today's world, in a dream it points to the fact that the person is looking for something. The Latin word *monasterium* points to "mon aster"—your own star, your own self (that Jung compares to God). Peace, spiritualization, meditation, and quietness lead you to self, but so does discipline. You have discovered your path and must follow it.

Abbot/Abbess: Bishop, Monk; the archetype of the priest comes to the fore, a person of authority (male or female), who is austere and dignified. Romanticized **Father/Mother** figure, particularly with very religious people (consciously or unconsciously). The dreamer is often longing for a leader—a priest or minister—or perceives himself to be one.

Folklore: Declining health.

Abduction: Repressed urges, similar to **Bomb, Attack, Surf, Explosion** and **Electricity, Defloration, Flames, Violence, Greed, Harem, Skin Rash, Wire (High-Voltage),** and **Hooker/Prostitute.** Longing to be rescued from a situation, but the strength to do something is missing.

Folklore: Your own circumstances will improve noticeably.

Aborting: See **Toilet**.

Abortion/Miscarriage: Emotions are facing reality. Also, you want to discard inner conflicts, as in

Sewage/Waste. Fear of accidental pregnancy. Physical changes. Separation from a loved one or a favorite. Unhealthy (neurotic) behavior.

Abscess: Need for cleansing—similar to **Sewage/ Waste**. A negative attitude needs to be overcome. Expression of disgust towards one's own body, or physical self-cleansing.

Folklore: Health, or quick recuperation. A behavior or attitude that takes on unhealthy or overwhelming proportions.

Abundance: It symbolizes excess—be content with less. But it may also suggest being in the flow, where everything needed is forthcoming.

Abyss: Precipice. This dream usually appears when we are in crisis, or when a crisis has almost been overcome, making room for its deeper meaning. Difficulties in life, critical situations, require decisions. You are looking for help. A challenge to look deeper inside, accepting your own deeper soul.

As a nightmare: Feeling overburdened, fear of the difficulties ahead. Descending into an abyss means paying attention to the unconscious, because that is where the reason for the present difficulties resides. Falling into an abyss is usually accompanied by feelings of depression, similar to those connected to **Ashes**, **Murder**, and **Trap**. Turning away from an abyss is often a sign of having turned a blind eye to the facts; it points to emotional grief.

Accident: Often a sign of dealing emotionally with real accidents. A warning that mirrors fear. Also a suggestion of being inattentive towards everyday affairs. This could also be a "preventative dream" that emotionally replaces troubling events or experiences in the real world—difficulty and problems that you feel you cannot handle. An accident may also be a symbol for orgasm. According to author Jack McGuire, there are four different levels or stages of this symbol:

1. Tendency towards self-punishment.
2. The feeling that life or a specific situation is out of control.
3. An expression of rage and fear.
4. Mistrusting the situation in the dream that led to the accident.

Acid: Is something nagging and eating at your insides? Has the relationship with yourself or others gone sour?

Acorn: Precaution; well-known phallic symbol.

Acrobat: The desire for, or fear of, risky endeavors. It is the image of modern man's fight for survival. The dreamer is looking for validation, **Applause**.

According to Freud, this dream image appears to those who, as children, have witnessed sexual intercourse among adults. Even if it does not necessarily always address a question of sexuality, it clearly refers to the body and physicality. How are you treating your own body? How agile do you feel? This image can appear when you are not physically active enough.

Actor: See **Theater**. You are pretending to be something that you are not. You want to be the center of attention and admiration. Also, you are trying to discover your own potentialities. See **Exam**.

Adam: Returning to the origin of masculinity, this is often the symbol for **Father**. As the first **Man**, you also want to be the "top man." Be more vigorous in shaping your life. This symbol rarely occurs today, as is the case with most religious symbols.

Address: It is important whether it is your own or

somebody else's. Your own address may point to the fact that you are too self-absorbed; some other person's address, that you should become more aware of others. A "good" address means social advancement, a "bad" address social demotion.

Administrator/Public Servant: Often appears in a dream when you are suffering from lack of self-worth. Also addressed here is the dreamer's "responsibility to govern," which means facing the problems and developing the capabilities to manage his own issues. In that sense, it addresses self-determination. Such concerns are surely influenced by the dreamer's attitude toward power and acceptance. Freud is said to have dreamed as a young man that he was a public servant, which might help explain his ambitions.

Admiral: See **Captain**, a symbol of manliness, like **Abbot**, **Athlete**, and **King**. A person of authority. Authority over **Water**. **Water** relates to the emotions, compulsive tendencies, or, less often, being particularly sensitive. A leader and example, but the Admiral also represents masculinity that has rejected aggressiveness. The dreamer is very self-confident, able to steer the ship of life (although sometimes aggressively). There is a sexual connotation here, since a ship is generally thought of as female. One wants to rule and own women. After all, the **Admiral** is a seafarer, and a symbol of unrestricted sexuality.

Folklore: A very important event is about to take place.

Adoption: Taking on something foreign—giving aid. Longing for the "child within." Here you should always ask what is missing that would make you happy. What would you like to take on?

Adultery: See **Stranger, Other, Intercourse, Sexuality**. Also **Friend, Foreign Language**.

Adventure: Being unsure about one's surroundings; or fearful of a risky relationship while—at the same time—yearning for it. Life is becoming boring; you are looking for adventure and daring in a world that is perceived as being empty. Opposite of the working routine.

An adventure dream may also refer to a chance to become more intimate with oneself. Be glad about the dream; you are gaining self-knowledge and getting closer to your goal!

Determine what kind of adventure it is and what

your feelings are. And do remember that adventure may sometimes take place in the internal rather in the external world.

Advertisement: A long-overdue situation needs to be resolved; otherwise it will become public. Or it is absolutely necessary to make it public. Let the world know about your wishes and longings.

Too much self-congratulation and advertising of oneself, but also creativity and inspiration.

Advice: Searching for direction and support from the outside. Friendship and help.

Africa: The dark continent, our own shadow, our own hidden side and our own urges/drives. (See **Primeval Forest, Jungle.**) It is the continent of hunger and of chaotic political situations, chaos, **Heat, Thirst.** That which is black, dark, and from which all female creativity originates.

Age (Old Man or Old Woman): Happiness and satisfaction have been reached. On one hand, you are fascinated by age, because it implies maturity, experience, and the ability to judge. On the other hand, it represents fear of getting old. Are you afraid of being less attractive? It is the archetype of wisdom.

The question here is: What is really important in your life and where do you want to go from here? How do you see yourself? In practical terms, this is mostly a question of taking life and its problems and fears more calmly.

The old man/old woman is and always has been the symbol of the teacher. Often, it also represents the grandfather or grandmother of the dreamer or even the dreamer him/herself. This image may also express a desire for greater peacefulness. Standing at the outside of society looking in, like the **Alchemist**. Gaining freedom since one has nothing to lose.

Agent/Spy: Points to too much fantasizing. Wanderlust, being shallow. Make inquiries before coming to a decision; search for the truth first. This is a frequent dream symbol when life is boring and has no excitement. But this symbol may also be a general sign of searching. Ask yourself what it is that you are looking for (and what it is that you want to find).

Also addressed here may be a life lived intensely and dangerously. It is the image of the male hero that appears when the dreamer is showing little masculinity, and in rare instances, also, when much masculinity is present in a woman or man).

On the other hand, this dream image also appears when the dreamer has an unconscious suspicion that, in most cases, is unfounded. It is helpful in such cases to adopt a positive attitude to life (positive thinking).

Air: Symbol of essence and awareness. Insight, ideas, imagination, and creative thinking, as well as a rich intellectual life. Effortlessness, but also a warning not to be a "happy-go-lucky" sort of person. Air is also a symbol of opportunities in the future. Thick, muggy, smoky, and bad air have negative meanings; fresh, morning, or spring air mean youth and well-being.

Airplane: See **Flying.** Airplanes and flying are considered symbols of far-reaching thoughts, ideas, and new insights.

According to Freud, the plane is a phallic symbol. It is able to rise against gravity.

Airplane Crash: Illusions and unhealthy attitudes need to be discarded.

Airport: See **Flying.** The starting point of the flight. Freedom and travel.

Alarm: Something needs to be activated; something must be done immediately (a dream of warning or a dream of war). Are you showing tendencies of too great a separation between conscious action and unconscious feelings or wishes? It could also be a reactive dream, after your alarm clock has gone off!

Albatross: Bird. Elegance, ease, good control.
Folklore: Good news is "on the way." Everything will turn out okay.

Alchemist: Pharmacist, Chemist. Spiritualization. Inner strength is solidifying; character ennoblement. Also: **Adventure.** Warning: Look out for too much romanticizing.

Alcohol: "Muddying the water," lack of clarity, unscrupulousness, intoxication, emotionalizing, melodrama. It may be a concrete warning of too much alcohol consumption. The symbol may also be a challenge from the unconscious, demanding more clarity and deliberation. Is life lived in a fog? Are important problems being repressed? In another sense, this symbol may be pointing to positive social skills and communication, as well as the healing aspect of euphoria.
Astrology: Symbol of Neptune.

Alligator: Fear of being swallowed up by tasks and work. Pay attention to your animalistic aggressions.
Folklore: A warning that an enemy is arriving.

Almond: An erotic symbol. Bitter almonds mean disappointment; sweet almonds mean good luck.

Alphabet: Wholeness and complete spiritual richness is realized. Order. Highly oriented toward the abstract, as also when dreaming about numbers.
Folklore: A friend is returning.

Altar: Well-known holy place; a place of power, spirituality, personal growth, and development. Ideals that are held dear are addressed and should be either elevated or sacrificed. The altar is the place of transformation and ascent.

Amazement: Good things are going to happen to those who did not expect anything.

Amazon: Strained relationships with women or towards the feminine in oneself. Desire for, or fear of, female aggressiveness. For women: a desire for more strength and independence from the masculine.

The dream image of the Amazon always includes the **Horse**, because Amazons were considered "wild horse women." The unity between rider and horse is the image of the unity of the feminine and the animalistic.

Implied is a delicate balance between controlling one's own "wildness" and still "living to the full," as well as embracing the joy of "wild passion" and "urges."

Astrology: The astrological sign of Sagittarius.

Amber: Petrification, narrowness (restricted lifestyle), as in: **Siege, Elevator, Village, Cage, Trap.** A warning about arrogance. Also jealousy, like all types of jewelry (gems).

Amphitheater: A challenge to become active, to produce, even if it is risky. Fights and risky self-portrayal, as in **Adventure, Athlete, Arena**, and **Circus.** Points to the importance of presentation (the show). Social criticism. Tourist attraction, vacation.

Amputation: Losing something of oneself. Always restricted and needs are ignored (see **Abortion, Funeral, Divorce,** and **Death**). Expression of fear of loss and an invitation to discard nonessentials. Important: Which limb is being amputated?

Amulet/Talisman: Need for security, desire for magical powers, which points to regression. Unconsciously wishing for a stronger personality and individuation. It is important what the amulet looks like and what it is to protect. *Talisman* in Arabian means "magic picture," and in a dream it can also point to one's having illusions and false hopes.

Anchor: A symbol of security, as in **Family**, **Home**, and **Notice-of-Intention-to-Marry**. The desire to be grounded in spite of all the emotions. Self-confidence, but also standstill.

Anesthesia: Calming, unconsciousness. But often also anguish, and a defense against anything lively and spiritual.

Angel: See **Flying. Messenger** from God. In a broader sense, angels are messengers from the higher self who is guiding the dreamer. Or a woman or man we love is being placed on a pedestal.

According to Jung: *Animus*-figures often represent still unfinished, not yet understood, but surprisingly new intellectual gifts, power of reasoning, or character ideals.

During the night of November 10, 1619, René Descartes had three consecutive dreams during which the angel of truth appeared to him. On the basis of this revelation, the 23-year-old Descartes developed his philosophy. **Lightning.**

Opposite: clear counterimage of **Devil.**

Folklore: Luck in love (you are given the gift of an angel); desire for harmony and purity.

Animal: The animal, compulsive nature of human beings. Instincts, according to Freud and most other dream interpreters, removed from awareness (*animus*); or awareness removed from instinct (*anima*) in human beings. The image of the suppressed or of the shadow, suggesting a chance for integration.

The type of animal in the dream is important. Jung suggested that we find out more about the innate character of the animal we have dreamed about. According to Freud, small animals always symbolize children and siblings, while wild animals are a symbol for sexually excited or exciting people, evil urges, or passions.

Antelope: Elegance. Symbol of vivacious women, desire, eroticism.

Antlers: Aggressive, physical male drive, as in **Rifle**, and all other weapons. Unfaithfulness. Antlers mounted on the wall are reminiscent of sexuality (fertility) in the past.

Ants: Classical example in psychology of a disturbed nervous system. It is necessary to reevaluate your obligation to the community. Become more actively involved. There are tendencies to isolation. Patient and persistent work will bring benefits, or you may be too much of a busybody. It may also be a sign of too much turmoil, excitement, and nervousness. A possible warning signal: Unwind, make time for self-contemplation. Ants are also considered a sign of intelligence.

Anvil: Resistance. Toughness, also becoming passive endurance. May also point to a sadomasochism that is not expressed. Also: a romantic look back at the period when craftsmen flourished.

Ape: Developmental difficulties. Points at the same time to increased rigidity. You need to allow yourself to be more playful and happy. Leave room for the animal side of you (the ape is considered one of the most sexual animals). The ape is the shadow of the ego, the soul of instinct, the most ancient and most human creature.

It is a symbol of imitation, which points to self-ridicule as well as a lack of autonomy. Pay special attention to the type of ape that appears in the dream.

Apothecary: Emergency situation, calling out for help; **Medication**. Symbol for what is expensive. See **Pharmacist**, **Alchemist**, **Chemist**.

Applause: Approval. Vanity based on fear of rejection or success. Often a sign of avoiding criticism.

One is surrounded by envy and jealousy. A warning not to be so vain. Also an expression of the need for recognition. You should compliment yourself and others. In any case, you want others to pay attention to you. What are you doing to make it happen?

Apple: Health and naturalness; also renewal of life and the symbol of immortality (the golden apple). Seduction and sexual symbol for breast. (The ideal in the Middle Ages was to have breasts like little apples.) Something that turns into something good (and deservedly so—for instance, William Tell's apple) or, less frequently, something that turns into something bad (see the Apple of Paris).

According to Freud, the apple, like almost every other **Fruit**, is the symbol for breasts, particularly when there is more than one apple. In psychoanalysis apples are generally considered a typical sexual symbol. According to C. G. Jung, they are a symbol of life, an ancient fertility symbol, as are the pomegranate, fig, and quince).

Application: Desire or **Fear** of making one's needs known and/or to plan for them. Manipulation by others, or wanting to manipulate others. Relationship proposal: yearning for a long-term relationship.

Looking for something that is not easily obtained. What are you applying for? Are you confronted with new tasks that require talents you don't know you have?

Apricots: Female sexual symbol, well-being. One of the most common erotic symbols for skin, often used as a metaphor in contemporary pornography.

Folklore: Being lucky in love.

Apron: See **Veil**, **Curtain**. Protection and domesticity, as in **Baking**, **Roast**, **Cooking**, **Iron**, **Hen**, **Pillow**, **Porcelain**. Also a symbol for transformation (it was in St. Elizabeth's apron that food for the poor was transformed into roses). The apron is also connected with the image girls and women hide—the secret of motherhood. According to Jung, the apron also has sexual meanings. Loss of an apron symbolizes the loss of virginity.

Aquamarine: Purity, healing, spirituality, noble thoughts.

Aquarium: Artificial living space. Unnatural, deep (repressed) desires for a more natural lifestyle.

Arabian: Longing to be "wild." May also appear as a symbol for the masculine world and misogyny. Fanaticism and danger of war, but also romanticism (Lawrence of Arabia). This symbol also, and always, addresses the dreamer's own urges (in the case of women, the masculine side).

Arch: On one hand, a well-known symbol for security, protection, and home, as in **Family** and **Anchor**. On the other hand, it often points to restriction and confinement, as in **Cage**, **Prison**. From mythology we know about the practice of leaving an infant in a basket. Here it indicates a special child who has been abandoned or disowned, and in spite of a hostile world is making its way successfully. A very specific point is being made here: it is possible to survive and overcome early childhood suffering.

Archer/Arch of a Bridge: Tension, overcoming contradictions.

Arena: A room where the ego is placed in the center, as in **Amphitheater**. Struggle, the determination to achieve, and striving for success. If you are in the center of the arena, it is necessary to be active, self-promoting, and bold. If you see somebody else in the center, you are too passive.

Aries: The image of the creative energy of the dreamer. See **Lamb, Sleep**.
   Astrology: The meaning is "I am."

Aristocrat: Inferiority complex. You feel inferior in your social environment. Symbol of self-worth, wanting to advance but feeling your shortcomings. Sign of romanticizing social status by holding on to ideals uncritically, even those that should have been discarded long ago. What do you really want out of life?

Arm: Basics for action, reaching for or getting something. Wanting to accomplish something ("the arm of the state," for instance). Also see **Beggar**.

Armament: Separation and disarmament, distancing, which may be positive or negative. Protection from emotional pain. See **Knight**.

Armchair: Resting, being peaceful, as in **Evening**, **Worship**, and **Prayer**, but less religious in meaning. It may, however, also be a sign of laziness or boredom, and point to the fact that you act like a ruler.

Arrest: You feel your life is exciting, seen and lived like a detective story, but you are feeling guilty. Certain habits need to be changed immediately if you want to avoid complications. You have caught the "culprit" that was residing inside of you, which means that you have met yourself, your motives, and intentions, and have understood the consequences.

Arrival: Beginning. Obvious meaning: one part of life is completed; something new is about to take place. A goal is reached. See **Adventure**.

Arrow: Focus and concentration on a goal. This image is a "point of reference," and suggests the way you have—or should have—developed. In addition, the arrow is a male sexual symbol and a symbol of aggression.

Arteries: See **Blood**, **Red**. Life is in motion, as is your circulatory system.

Artichoke: Luxury, well-being and driving out bad moods. Vacation memories.
Folklore: Artichokes are said to drive out demons.

Artist: A well-known symbol for a life lived freely and creatively.

Ascension: The obvious meaning is success through effort. Where do I want to go? Is the goal worth the effort? See **Stairs**, **Ladder**.

Ashes: Something has come to an end, has been completely dissolved. Ashes often signify weakness, the loss of vitality, and act as a reminder to enjoy life and have fun. Symbol of the **Phoenix**, the **Bird**, who, after total self-condemnation, sets himself on **Fire**, only to be born again by rising from the ashes. In that sense, the ashes are a sign of rebirth, transformation and, in the last analysis, of **Birth**, and **Death**.

One feels burned out, with no interests (depression, as in **Abyss** and **Murder**). Insults, disappointments, **Illness**, and the **Death** of a loved one can create such dreams. Guilt, blame, and atonement for transgressions (**Ash Wednesday**, the mark on the forehead). Glowing ashes point to self-reflection and purification.

According to C. G. Jung, ashes were in the olden days seen as protection from demons, particularly against the ghosts of death. In addition, ashes are the product of cremation. The physical shell must be completely destroyed before the soul can become free.

Ash Wednesday: Suffering after pleasure, carrying one's own **Cross**. Also, all suffering is over. ("On Ash Wednesday, everything comes to an end.") Contemplating the essentials.

Asparagus: Not only Freud considered this a phallic symbol.

Ass: See **Buttocks**.

Assassination: Hopeless situation; it is essential that something be done. Fear of political instability, **Ruler**. Greater attention needs to be paid to everyday occurrences.

Assaults/Attacks of illness: Breaking out of what is considered the norm. Repressed drives. See **Termination, Surf, Fire, Electricity, Abduction, Defloration, Flames, Violence, Greed, Harem, Skin Rash, Wire (High-Voltage)**, and **Prostitute**. In the form of ecstasy, it has a sexual meaning. If your dreams are about severe seizures (particularly when specific organs are involved), consider seeing a psychologist.

Astrology: Cosmic connnectedness, ancient and profound wisdom, or superstition, relinquishing responsibility for oneself. Search for one's own star.

Astronaut: Expanding consciousness; seeing and being given much news. Exploring the hereafter and other realities.

Asylum/Exile: Having committed a crime against society; bad conscience, often due to tax evasion.

Asylum/Homeless Shelter: Fear of difficulties, fear of becoming destitute. (See also **Beggar**, **Charity**, **Rags**, and **Counterfeit Money**.) Fear of those people and things that are different.

Athlete: Symbol of sexual masculinity, the **Hero**. Masculine power, as in **Bear**. Frequently appears as a dream symbol when one is feeling weak.

Advice that one ought to get involved in fitness. Often, also, the dream symbol for simple-mindedness.

Atlas: Orientation in the world. He who carries the weight of the world on his shoulders: troubles and burdens. Longing to travel to foreign lands and have new experiences.

Atom Bomb: Bomb, Explosion. Worry about humankind or at least about the immediate surroundings. Fear of death and war as in **Shot**. Recommends taking greater responsibility for the larger questions of life and asserting greater influence upon things affecting society and the community.

Attaché Case: Money, wealth, image of what is owned. Since the attaché case is always taken along, its loss may point to a loss of identity.

Attack: Similar to **Being Run Over**, only more aggressive, and accompanied by the fear of losing property.

Attic: The place where forgotten goals and expectations are hidden. According to Jung, the place of the first sexual experience, as in the fairy tale "Sleeping Beauty," where the princess is pricked by a spindle in a room under the roof of the high tower. Here in the attic are the intellectual taboos, the sexual ones, and the taboos of independent conscience. In the attic are the thoughts that we don't dare explore and the attitudes we don't dare express.

Poverty, perspective, advancement.

Folklore: Engagement (since the attic is a romantic place).

Attorney/Lawyer: A need for fair and proper self-treatment and self- analysis. The search for what is "proper." You are making demands. A symbol of fair treatment for the self.

Call for help, or business problems. Points to career difficulties. Question of fairness, or the opposite of it, is being addressed. Points to powerlessness, or unused persuasive skills.

Auction: Something is coming your way. Or pay attention to business and make fast decisions. Wanting to own something of worth (usually art or antiques) in bad economic times. According to Erich Fromm, it points to a "have-mode," as in **Attaché Case, Booty,** and **Stock Market.**

Audience: This may symbolize the way you portray yourself. In the extreme, it represents exhibitionism. Often what is hiding behind this dream is the desire for fame. On the other hand, it is the image of a search for your own world and a real Self. It also points to a manipulated secondhand experience that is, like television, often a substitute for reality.

August: Vacation time, harvest time, relaxation. Also heat, laziness, and eroticism.
   Folklore: Unexpected news.

Aunt: As with every female symbol in the dream of a man, it is a symbol of the man's feminine side. In the case of a woman, the image of the aunt in a dream often refers to her own shadow; only in exceptional cases would it represent an ideal. The feminine to which one feels attracted. The aunt, as is the case with the **Uncle**, often symbolizes "wholesome common sense."

Folklore: Good omen.

Author: Independence. A person who is creating his/her own life. The smart man or smart woman is not necessarily the wise man or wise woman! Here is the need to be productive and produce something of intellectual value. Everybody has something worthwhile to say. Communicate it and express yourself. Maybe you have to speak up more often, and more clearly? Do you want to give somebody a piece of your mind, openly and honestly?

Autumn: Time for harvesting and utilizing, a time of becoming aware about life, reaching new goals. Allow yourself peace and quiet, reflect on your circumstances. Harvest, maturity, success, and prosperity.

Awakening: You are becoming more aware of yourself or certain characteristics. Or your fear of waking up to something dreadful (a bad surprise). Reflects a positive development in awareness, new perspectives, desire for something new, a new beginning, as in **Opening, Baby, Birth.**

Axe: Ability to assert oneself, desire for control, often carried too far, bad behavior. The image of the axe also points to chopping wood and, with its rhythmical movement, carries a sexual connotation that implies aggression. The meaning here could be crudeness, but it may also express the joy of sexual vitality. In addition, chopping wood always is connected to chopping trees, clearing the way to create farmland. The soil is prepared for something new, is cultivated, which is a reference to the intellect, the power to divide, as in **Sword**. It could also be a reference to strength and usefulness or to something that is being chopped down. Here the question is: What are you being separated from? Or what is it that you must let go of?

In a famous dream of Nebuchadnezzar, the king of Babylon sees himself as a tree that is later chopped down and the tree stump left exposed to the weather and without protection. This depicts the King's haughtiness and admonishes him to let go of his arrogance.

As with all tools, the axe, according to Freud, has a sexual meaning, which here is easy to see.

Folklore: Danger.

Axis: Movement of life, the wheel of life (or Wheel of Fortune). You are concentrating on your center—"navel-gazing."

Baby: See **Child.** A dream known to be good, good news, success, and advancement. A wish is fulfilled, a childhood wish. Or, it may suggest that the dreamer is childish and immature, wanting to be taken care of. Often this image corresponds to a feeling of helplessness. This is also the symbol for a loved one ("my baby," "sugar baby," etc.).

If the baby is perceived as a threat, the dreamer might be afraid of an accidental pregnancy, as in **Abortion.** Also, it may suggest fear of letting go of one's children.

In another context, longing for rebirth and a new beginning. Always ask yourself what you would do differently if you could start over again.

Folklore: A child in a dream always promises good luck and happiness, unless the baby is not feeling well, which means bad luck in love.

Bachelor: Possibly a hint that, at least during the period while you are dreaming, it would be better to remain single. See **Companion, Hermit, Invalid.**

Back: If you see a person only from the back, in addition to lack of knowledge of him, it also may express opposition and distance. Rarely will you see yourself from the back, but if that should happen, it is an indication that you have become aware of your shadow. A dream about a back is a symbol that we are searching for our own hidden energies and weak points.

According to Jung, the unconscious begins at the

back; every magical influence or cruel attack comes from behind. This was the original reason that people everywhere wore amulets around their neck, hanging down at their backs. (Today they hang down at the front.)

Back Door: To a large degree, similar to **Backyard.** Frequently, the way to escape.
  Folklore: Bad omen.

Backpack: See **Luggage**. The burden that you are carrying around with you, or relaxation and moving about in nature.

Backyard: Hidden place, secrets. Poverty and the unconscious.
  Folklore: Engagement.

Bacon: Conscious or unconscious wishes to get something or someone. Also "Bring home the bacon."

Bad Luck: Points to trouble. On the other hand, it might be a sign that you can make good connections and have someone you can rely on. Always remember that what appears to be bad luck in the beginning often turns out later to be good luck.

Badge/insignia/decoration: A symbol of belonging, of which you have dreamed repeatedly, from which you feel rejected. How was the sense of belonging demonstrated? Was the badge given/awarded for something?

Badger: A lot of work is ahead of you. Occasionally, but rarely, a sexual dream symbol.

Bag: The symbol of the unknown and the surprises that life has in store. Because it is similar to a *surprise package*, the bag is often a symbol for secrets ("letting the cat out of the bag"). On the other hand, it might also point to obstacles and burdens. It is the image of the burdens that you are carrying. It is important to pay attention to what is inside the bag.

Bag (as in handbag): Important what is inside the bag. A bag filled to the brim indicates egocentricity; an empty bag, inner emptiness.

Bagpipe: Remembering vacation; androgyny, because of the Scottish kilt.
    Folklore: Relationship difficulties.

Baker: Baking, Cooking. The domestic male, the practical and creative male.

Baking: Like **Cooking,** this image is connected to transformation. See also **Alchemist, Apothecary.** Urge for domesticity. Being contented and convivial, as in **Communion.** Often refers to creativity.

What are you baking and from what recipe?

Balcony: Command, focus, and planning. A symbol for female breasts.

Folklore: Points to hurdles/obstacles.

Balcony (railing): A feeling of security based on intellectual control, or a longing for security and intellect. Often overemphasizes intellect and exaggerates the need for security.

Baldness: Intellectualization (the crown chakra). Also brutality, or effects of radiation. Intellectual failure. According to 2nd century dream interpreter Artemidorus, loss of relatives or objects.

Folklore: Either bad health or problems in love.

Ball (Dancing): Dissatisfaction with the social situation (similar to **Aristocrat**), or enjoying social recognition. A ball also is considered the place where one is introduced to social/cultivated passion.

Ball (game): Symbol for letting go, as in **Water, Brook/Stream.** Playing ball represents self-expression. However, a ball, as in football and handball, also expresses aggressive penetration, forging ahead.

Here, the reference is to the masculine side of pleasure in man as well as in woman. Often an expression of the pleasure men and women derive from submission. In rare cases, this symbolizes fear of aggression.

According to analytical psychology, it is a symbol of wholeness, of concentrated psychic energy. In depth psychology it is connected to experiences with one's own sexuality. If you yourself are the ball (in the game), it refers to a lack of willpower, steadfastness, and purpose.

Ball/Globe: See **Circle**. Completeness, wholeness. The dynamics of the psyche that bring contradictions into harmony. The symbol of the all-encompassing "completeness of the cosmic soul." You are on the path of individuation and able to view it from many perspectives. The glass ball (hollow inside) is like the soap bubble. Since the Middle Ages it has been a symbol of impermanence. A solid globe made of glass or a crystal ball is a symbol for all-knowing, or the pretense of being all-knowing.

Balloon: Flying, weightlessness. Being or having often been depressed, now is the time to conquer depression. But this is a warning that you are losing ground. It is also a symbol for arrogance, or the desire for social advancement, similar to **Aristocrat, Auction.** Less often a symbol of ideas. Is the balloon flying or bursting?

According to Freud, a phallic symbol (particularly in the case of a Zeppelin).

Banana: Fruit. Generally, a well-known phallic symbol. As monkey food, a symbol for delighting in silliness and boisterous nonsense.

Bandage: Support, help and security, as in **Apothecary, Medication. Fight** (protective bandaging), shackled and handicapped.

Band-Aid: Part of the body is injured and needs to be protected (with a Band-Aid), held together, or "hidden."

Bank (Savings Bank): Fear of losing money, a warning against being wasteful, but also power, recognition, and energy. See **Money, Wealth.**

Bankruptcy: Fear of loss, making excuses, freeing yourself of debt. Often a feeling of being at the end of your rope, not knowing what to do next, usually due to exhaustion and denial, instead of facing the situation. Desire to come clean and start all over again. What would you like to do differently?

A warning dream. Important to be more careful how you use your energies. A need to tell the truth to others and to self.

Banquet: Inner nourishment, a social event. Often a desire for social advancement, similar to **Aristocrat, Oyster, Ball.**

Baptism: Deliverance, rebirth, official opening. See **Bath, Spring**.

Bar: Erotic place, forbidden place; relaxation, similar to **Armchair, Bench** (sometimes with erotic meaning).

Bar (Chocolate): See **Sweets.**

Barbed Wire: Boundaries or injuries. See **Sting**.

Barber/Hairdresser: The way you care for your hair shows your attitude toward your own sexuality. Vanity, as in the case of all jewelry.
Folklore: Economical difficulties.

Barefoot: See **Foot**. Being grounded. Asceticism, health, frequent vacations.

Bareness: Naked, Stripping. A frequent dream symbol when you want to hide something. Or search for the "naked truth."

Barking: Warning that danger is lurking. Aggression.

Barn: Making use of your own abilities. Success and well-being, but also a place of adolescent sexuality.

According to Jung, the barn is a place where demons and ghosts reside, but also a place of protection against rain and cold.

Barrel: A full barrel points to abundance; an empty barrel indicates bad times ahead.

Barricade: Dream about obstacles. Logical boundaries or self-limitation.

Barrier: Restriction, limitation, or establishing boundaries. A frequently occurring dream symbol when feeling confined and unable to move forward. Also see **Amputation**, **Cage**. Balking at something, holding back. Sign of social force. Taboo.

Difficulty in making social or business contacts. To have hit a brick wall. Usually points to a challenge.

Basement: House. A scary place where, according to Jung, we lose our soul or rediscover it. It is the unconscious, the dark, the impenetrable, that which we repress.

The foundation of your life. A longing for greater security.

You are coming into contact with your unconscious.

Basket: Container. Warmth and marriage. The contents of the basket are important. Symbolically, the basket is connected to the element Earth, the same way the chalice is to water. In that sense, the basket always is connected to being grounded. Ask yourself if you are doing all right in your everyday existence. Do you have reason to be dissatisfied, or are you looking for security and more acceptance? According to psychoanalysis, the basket represents the female sexual organ in a man's dream.

Bat: The symbol for **Vampire**, sucking out, being sucked dry. Dull, compulsive, dangerous emotions. On the other hand, this dream symbol expresses great sensibility, having radar-like skills and useful instincts.

Bath: Suggests cleansing (possibly a ritual cleansing, from sin). This type of washing usually refers to "cleansing of the soul." It often also refers to relaxation and recuperation. At the same time, the image of a bath is always connected with the "fountain of youth." The symbol is similar to **Shower, Sauna, Soap.** Cold water means trouble; and so does hot water—"getting into hot water." Water that is too hot means unconsciousness.

Bathroom/Bathhouse: A place for cleansing, as in **Bath.** An erotic place where clothes are taken off (see **Physician**). Often refers to the psychoanalyst's office, particularly during sessions. A place of emotion.

Baton: See **Rod**.

Battle: Erotic symbol, overstimulation, and overwork.

Bayonet: Well-known phallic symbol. Fear of sex and war, as in **Helmet, Shot,** and **Atom Bomb**. A symbol for distance, masculine aggressiveness.
  Astrology: A symbol of Mars.

Beach: The border between consciousness and the unconscious; or a desire for vacation and relaxation.

Beaker: See **Mug, Cup, Goblet.**

Bean: Symbolizes, as do all things that germinate, female sexual organs; but also masculine sexuality and, in general, everything to do with nutrition. Today, it is a frequently occurring dream symbol about doubt, or searching deeply in order to overcome unconscious obstacles.

Bear: Particularly in the case of men, tremendous vitality (strong as a bear). For our ancestors, the bear represented a real danger and threat. Those who wore a bearskin became attackers and experienced a tremendous increase in energy and vitality.

Can also be a person who is a little stupid but good-natured. The symbol often indicates disappointment or that one is about to disappoint somebody. Often a symbol of the neglected inner animal (extinction).

According to Jung, symbol of the negative side of masculine strength.

In Nordic mythology the bear usually symbolizes female attributes. Also, the followers of Artemis called themselves *arktoi* (bears). Since ancient times, the bear has been depicted as a motherly, earthbound animal that represents the female drive.

Astrology: The bear corresponds to Taurus.

Beard: Symbol of the ruler, of male strength and vitality, of aid from a wise man; wisdom increasing with age. Nurturing your masculine side. Indicates male superiority and authority (the beard of the prophet). A beard being cut off almost always means loss of vitality and fear of impotence. However, there is also another side to the image of a beard being cut off—exposing the face, approaching the world with openness. In this context, shaving off a beard in today's setting might also mean an increase in potency.

Astrology: Symbol of Saturn.

Beauty: In fairy tales, as in dreams, the image of beauty is another expression of truth and honesty. At the same time, it symbolizes vanity, good luck, and great success. In the Oriental tradition, it is the most sought-after dream for luck.

Bed: Longing for domestic bliss and quiet, also erotic encounters. Often points to sexual problems; if that is the case, the type of bed points to the sexuality of the dreamer. In the *I Ching*, the bed always stands for intimacy (see #23 "Splitting apart").

According to Jung, bed is always a place of security and caring, also the symbol of **Sleep**, and the unconscious. The place where people are born and die; the symbol of the circle of life.

Bedcover: Protection against cold (in life and the emotions). It is important to note who is with you under the covers! It is also, more often than not, no more than a fighting over the covers during sleep.

Bedroom: A place of relationships, their problems, and their beautiful moments.

Bee: An industrious person. As with all insects, positive social behavior and the desire for personal development. A bee also points to honey, as sweet nutritious food (and the slang expression for a girl or boy friend). Do you need to do something nice for yourself? Being threatened by a bee means tension in your life (you are asked to conform to society); also, it often refers to problems with teamwork.

Astrology: The sign of Virgo.

Bee Keeper: See **Honey, Bee.** Getting along with nature.

Bee Sting: Sexual intercourse. In ancient Greece and Rome, when a girl dreamed of a bee sting she was said to be in love.

Beer: Alcohol. Happiness, social life, and either fogginess or inspiration.
Astrology: Symbol of Neptune.
Folklore: Monetary loss.

Beggar: Symbolizes the fight for existence, inferiority complex, fear of poverty. Somebody is giving you a gift. Do you need to learn to ask for something or demand it?

Beginning: A new beginning, like: **Arrival, Baby, Child**.

Being Chauffeured: Great wealth. Archetype for clergyman.

Being Hoarse: Something is taking your breath away.

Being Run Over: This may point to an inferiority complex or a feeling of being overwhelmed.

According to Freud, this image, particularly in men's dreams, appears when sexual intercourse is problematic and can't be actively lived out.

Bell: Steadfastness, trustworthiness, joy, and harmony. The bell is inseparably tied to time. This dream poses a question about what hour has just been tolled.

Hearing a bell ringing means that something new is happening. The sound of the bell is often thought to be the sound of a "heavenly message." "Wanting to hang something on the great bell" means that you either have arrogantly exaggerated about something because of your craving for admiration, or you need to make something known that you rather would hide.

Since the beginning of the 15th century, bells have

been a symbol for the **Fool** and, at the same time, for Vanity.

Bellow: Stimulating drive and vitality. More "fire" is needed. Puffing yourself up, pumping yourself up.

Belly: Determine if real intestinal problems exist. The belly represents the kitchen of the body, the place of transformation **(Alchemist)**, but also the place of desire and physical urges. It can also stand for wealth that belongs to the dreamer.

Often points to a connection between the will and the emotions, conscious and unconscious needs. A flat belly often points to unfulfilled sexuality; a fat belly of too much sex (or substitution for sex) and excess. The medieval Swiss philosopher Paracelsus said everybody has an alchemist in his belly.

Belt: The belt indicates the place where love and beauty (and the fascination with it) reside. The belt (waist), as a physical expression of the connection between the conscious and unconscious, asks us to decide if we want to walk the path of physical urges and drives or the path of the spiritual. Ideally, both paths lead to harmony and balance between body and soul. This image also asks how we deal with sensuousness and the pleasures of life. The image, however, usually appears when we feel restricted and bothered by something. If that were not the case, our unconscious would see no reason to produce such an image. For that reason, the belt usually points to restrictions imposed by the spouse (often the wife). The belt is a symbol of power, strength, and the influence of the woman (as in the *Nibelungen Ring*—the belt of Kriemhilde—or the belt of the Queen of the Amazons in Greek mythology). In today's terms, the belt is clearly a sign of repressed emotions, particularly sexual repression, for men as well as for women. If the belt appears in the dream of a woman, it is usually a symbol of virtue and purity; in the dream of a man, it is energy and fertility.

Bench (Park Bench): Resting, tranquility, as in **Armchair, Worship.** A long bench points to procrastination.

Beret: See **Hat.** Finding your spiritual identity. Protect yourself from intellectual influences and mental manipulation.

Berries: You are having fun and pleasure. Having a

desire for berries is often an expression of sexual desires. But it may also be a warning that you are becoming careless. (This interpretation was already known in ancient Persia.) A yearning for health and nature, as in **Farmer, Farm, Ear (of corn), Sowing.**

Bicycle: Getting ahead under your own power. Individualism and independence—you are pursuing your own path. The type of bicycle points to the personality of the dreamer: if a kid's bike—childlike or childish; a sports bike—fast, vigorous; an old bike—you feel old. Trouble-free riding: you are pursuing your own path and have no problem with it.

Folklore: Important decision.

Billiards: Finding success around several "corners." Fun and relaxation. See **Ball.** The ability to set something in motion. Fertility.

Binoculars: Don't get into a panic about every little thing; don't make everything you see larger than it is. Or bring something closer toward you, including something you want to remember. This might also refer to searching for access to your subconscious. To see more clearly what is not visible.

Birch: Young, slender girl. The birch combines black and white in its bark, implying contradictions.

During the Middle Ages, magic protection against witches and evil spirits.

Bird: See **Raven, Owl, Dove.** Spiritual content. An attempt to get a better perspective. This symbol also has an erotic meaning. In addition, it may imply that you want to be different, as in the myth of Icarus.

A flock of birds has a special meaning, since they seem to represent the intelligence of nature in their movement, an intelligence that is completely different from humans'. They express group will, in contrast to the will of the individual. In the ancient Welsh epic poem *Mabinogion*, the goddess Rhiannon is described as a flock of birds, since she symbolizes female wisdom in nature. However, a flock of birds, like a colony of insects, may also appear dangerous, as in Hitchcock's film *The Birds*.

Bird Woman: A creature of myth, symbolic of excitement and temptation, the *anima* in her heavenly and at the same time animalistic role threatening and destroying. Also a symbol of the wise woman (for instance, night owl) and a symbol of death.

Birth: First, this image expresses actual birth, maybe your own, that of your children, or others'. Wishes, fears, pain, and the joy of becoming "a human being" may be expressed here, as well as the dreamer's interaction with his or her children. In addition, the beginning of a generally promising, creative time. Creating something new. Complete state of happiness and clarity. On the other hand, often a longing for rebirth, in the sense of personal changes. This image also appears frequently just before or just after having started a new project. Occasionally, it also may express a resistance to letting go of the old, to maturity and completion. With this symbol the question is: What do you want to do with your life and where do your desires lead you? See **Child.**

Birthday: A common symbol for luck in any form. The birthday is a magical time when wishes are fulfilled, but where somebody could also cast a spell over you ("Sleeping Beauty"). Important are the gifts, the kind of celebration, and how old you became. Gifts usually represent characteristics of the dreamer or the person whom the dreamer is meeting and are an indication of how rich your life is because of them. In addition, a birthday is a celebration of your personal existence and your individual characteristics are the gifts. They are worthy of being honored. Pay attention to the overall flavor of the birthday party. How did you feel?

Bishop: Symbol of masculinity, as in: **Author, Pope, Father, Wise Man.**
 Folklore: Poor health, similar to **Abbot.**

Bite: Aggression ("sharp tongue"), chopping up. Often points to the animal side in humans. Vicious personality, social inhibition, in many ways related to the acceptance/rejection of one's own "animalistic" side. Also, on another plane, reference to eating habits, with the ability to chew. See **Eating, Teeth.** Who is biting whom? Being bitten by an animal: contact with one's own drive. See **Animal, Vampire, Bite.**

Black: A symbol of emotional stagnation or a depiction of the unconscious or the unknown. Grief and death, but also magical power and fertility. In earlier books about dreams, black animals are always seen in an unfavorable light, while white animals are always considered positive images.

Blackberry: Connected to nature. All **Berries** have a sexual connotation (clitoris).
 Folklore: Bad omen because of the dark color.

Blackbird: See **Bird**. Subtle sign of hope. If the bird is singing, happiness and the need to be more casual. Points to the carefree life of birds: they neither sow nor reap.

Folklore: A bad omen.

Blackboard: Memories of something repressed. Points to fears and difficulties during your time in school. At issue here is knowledge and being tested. See **Table**.

Blade: This dream symbol often appears when you are dealing with important decisions. The blade stands for the ability to make distinctions (to divide the material). However, the symbol of the blade also points to risks: "Something is balanced on the edge of the knife." **Knife**, **Sword**.

Blaze/Flames: Fire. Emotional purification. Psychological and physical energy (flame of life), will. Devastating dangers, destruction, depletion, and transformation. Sexual passion up to and including addiction ("my old flame"); or intense passion. Need for togetherness, or the power to consolidate or remove contradiction. Cremation is said to assist resurrection (See **Ashes**).

According to the *I Ching*, fire is that which bonds and radiates. The fire that Prometheus steals from the gods is seen as a creative act of the human, as is the flame of the Easter candle that is the symbol of God's power.

According to Germanic mythology, if consciousness fails to rule, the world will be set ablaze and consumed by a great fire. Purification, on the other hand, takes place in the fire in purgatory. It separates the sin from the sinner.

According to the alchemists' interpretation, it is God Himself who glows in divine love in the flame of the fire. Also, according to Jung, hell is fire, since everything is destroyed there. The fire in hell is a symbol of eternal pain; the fire in purgatory is the fire of purification. In Frazer's *The Golden Bough* are many references to cleansing, **Light**, and fertility, related to the powers of fire.

For the Mayans, fire is the mother of the gods, residing in the center of the earth. The image of the "fire mother" can be found in many cultures. According to Jung, fire is the true symbol of life, the center of life, the place where it is warm and light, where people assemble; that's where you can warm yourself and cook something. It gives protection; it is the essence of being home. Fire is the primeval component and vitality of human beings.

As a male symbol, fire is brightness, the connection to the light, the **Sun**, and, in particular, to **Lightning** (Zeus and Wotan). Fire symbolizes the power of passion and action in the archetypal man and woman.

According to Freud, it is often connected with bed-wetting.

Folklore: A serious warning to be careful.

Bleeding: Life, passion, courage, or disappointment, as in **Blood**. Also giving in and going with the flow, as in all **Water** symbols. Dreaming about menstruation. Injury or shock. The secret of life. Is the bleeding accompanied by pain?

Blending: Illusions, usually of grandeur. Too much sun, too little shade, overexposure; a challenge to illuminate your own dark side.

Blindness: Danger! You are not seeing something or you're avoiding taking responsibility for something or reflecting on something. You are unaware. Appearance gives no clues. Are you looking for new insights?

Blood: Red. "Blood is a very special liquid," (Goethe: *Faust, Part I*)—it is that which is alive, the driving substance, expressing fire and passion (something that Freud and Jung agreed on). Life, love, and passion, but also injury and disappointment. Blood also—and often—points to **Mother**, and can symbolize soul and will. When the "voice of the blood" is speaking, a very special sensibility or domination of one's urges is being addressed.

Exchanging blood (or drinking blood) represents a joining of life forces (brotherhood). The blood of Christ is symbolically served at communion; it has a universal healing power.

Loss of blood usually means loss in love; blood transfusion corresponds to the strengthening of vitality. See **Menstruation, Bleeding.**

Blossoms/Blooming: As in **Spring,** joy, abundance, physical aspects of the emotional life, sexuality (particularly female sexuality).

According to Freud, a reference to female sexuality. White flowers mean sexual innocence; red flowers mean sexual maturity.

Blue: Points to faithfulness and deep emotions, but also to the desire for relaxation. It is the symbolic color of the soul, since blue also symbolizes the depth of the sea and the expanse of the sky. It also stands for the unconscious, as well as isolation, expanse, and infinity. It stands for pure, clear **Water**, distant mountains, and sky. Blue symbolizes nature that has been saved. Pay attention to the degree of brightness!

The color blue may also indicate fogginess (like drunkenness); see also **Alcohol.** It is also a symbol of depression ("I am feeling blue"). And last, but not least, a symbol of cold (particularly metallic blue).

Blue can also, as in the case of "blue mountains," symbolize the connection between heaven and earth—spirit and nature. Blue coats were worn by wise women, pointing to our connection to water, mist, and heaven.

Blue is also the color of the cape worn by Mary; the womb that bore Christ is a symbol for the "sacred vessel."

In alchemy, blue is the color of the moon, standing in for silver, and blue is also the color of the soul.

As opposed to **Red**, blue indicates a soothing, cool state (in color therapy, blue is considered relaxing).

In the Orient, blue is the equivalent of black and is considered the color of the underworld.

In Egypt, the underworld of Osiris is depicted in blue or black.

The Sufi (a mystical circle, followers of Mohammed) saw blue as the center of a flame, the expression of the highest form of passion. A reflection of blue as an expression of passion is also found in our culture in the phrases "the blue hour," and "blue movies"; also the "blues" in music.

Astrology: A symbol of Neptune.

Boar: Animalistic male instincts, as in **Buck** and **Bull.**

Board: That which is flat, smooth, and connects. The function of the board is important.

Boat: See **Ship**.

Body: To see one's own body in a dream implies a tendency toward narcissism, being in love with oneself. Or you have lost contact with your body, and the forgotten body is making itself known in your dream.

Boil: As in **Abscess**, points to an inferiority complex. A symbol for disgust. However, this dream might also show that poison is leaving the body literally or figuratively, and that the disgust felt represents a wrong attitude toward life, constitutes repressed emotions, and is unwarranted. Always be glad when unacceptable parts of you (the shadow) find expression. That which is expressed cannot control us or remain to bother us again.

Bomb: See **Atom Bomb**. Aggression and destruction, fear of war, as in **Bayonet, Siege**. Frequently indicates that you are being too domineering and aggressive, or need to be more so. In psychoanalysis, a bomb explosion symbolizes orgasm. The picture of an exploding bomb also points to an act of freeing oneself and of unloading. Addressed here is removing and shattering boundaries.

Bones: Referring to life experiences, the spiritual and emotional backbone of life, but also "ossification."
  Folklore: Usually implies poverty; when in the form of a skeleton, **Death** or wealth.

Book: Being well-read and wise is an obvious interpretation. Also, a suggestion that one ought to turn more often to the "real world." In the "Book of Life," one's own inner wisdom is written, which means that we find here the script for our life. The content of the book is important and its title and the color of the cover. Compare also **Author**.

Boots: Being grounded, mobile, and getting ahead. A symbol of something new. A sexual symbol.

Booty/Loot: Getting something through one's own efforts and trouble. A state of "Have-Mode," according to Fromm, as in **Auction, Stock Market, Attaché Case.**

Bordello: See **Hooker.** New experiences. One is doing something for money that would be better left undone. Expression of calculated sexuality. Desire for or fear of licentious sexuality. Usually symbolizes wanting to break conventional boundaries and a search for new ways of expressing lust.

Border: A frequent dream symbol for those who are being restricted and are feeling a lack of possibilities. You need to overcome the obstacles in your path and, at the same time, be reminded that it is limitation that brings forth the master. Experiencing restrictions. See **Hedge.**

Boredom: See **Snake, Time, Haste.**

Bottle: See **Container.** Male and female sexual symbol, but according to Freud, it is always female. What kind of ghost or spirit is bottled up inside? See **Glass, Vase.**

Boulder/Piece of Rock: Mountain. Intellectual, physical, and/or emotional strength. Hardy. Something is in your way.

According to ancient Egyptian interpretation: if you climb a rock, you will be confronted with obstacles. According to Freud, a phallic symbol. Modern interpretation: You are striving for something higher, but it is not going to be easy.

Bowling: On one hand, you may want to take it easy, look for relaxation and fun; on the other hand, bowling expresses power and agility. Last, but not least, this symbol could point to hidden aggression, if a powerful throw "bowls over" the pins.

Folklore: Disappointment.

Box: See **Container.** Love affair and relationships, but also your own burden. What is inside the box? Also female genitalia.

According to Freud, a symbol of the female body, as with all musical instruments and **Church.**

Boxing Match: Ability to assert yourself. Aggression. A frequent symbol for work/profession or marital situations, but it can also point to a positive fight.

Braiding: See **Thread.** The act of connecting the threads of life, meaning different situations and personal characteristics.

Brakes: Obstructions; lack of mobility and inhibition. Often, this dream symbol is an incentive, but also a compulsion to be more accurate, more moderate. It is important to establish what is putting on the brakes and what is being held back. On rare occasions, it is a sign of security.

Branch: Twig, Tree. Looking for help, support (Don't saw off the limb you sit on). Symbol of the back, or at least the shoulders. Connected or being close to nature.

Does the tree have leaves or are they already on the ground? If it is a broken or sawn-off branch, you have too much on your plate.

Brass: See **Metal.** Usually points to a desire for success and prosperity.
Folklore: False friends.

Brawl: Repressed aggression, and a desire for physical closeness.

Bread/Rolls: Life-sustaining food, strengthening, nurturing substance. Economical security, as in **Bureaucrat**, but not as materially oriented as **Shares**, **Auction, Attaché Case**. Because of its shape, often the symbol for female genitalia. In addition, this symbol also relates to everyday life ("Give us this day our daily bread"). Pay attention: Are they big or small rolls? According to Jung, the womb. A frequently appearing symbol when sexual urges remain at the pre-intercourse stage (oral sex). Freud calls this a regression into the oral phase.

Breakdown: An obstacle dream, gloating. **Bad luck, Embarrassment**.

Breakfast: New beginning, good beginning.

Breast: Longing for connectedness, tenderness, rest. Those you take to your bosom become related. According to ancient Germanic law, families gave their members names of body parts in order to indicate how closely they were related. Somebody with the name "bosom" was a close blood relative.

Breath: Life energies (Prana). An exchange with the environment.

Breathlessness: Exhaustion, having a lot of staying power, patience.

Briar: Problems and difficulties, as in **Bush,** often between partners.

Bricklayer: Building something, a challenge to be more productive.

Bride/Bridegroom: See **Marriage.** A specific event concerning your own development. A desire for a partner, for bonding, or looking for balance between internal and external contradictions. Are you seeing your dream partner? Such a dream partner often depicts the ideal of your soulmate. Rarely, it signifies a warning of unwanted pregnancy. See **Baby.** An unhappy or ugly bride or bridegroom often points to conflicts with your partner.

Alchemy sees these symbols as a connection between opposites. According to Jung, the images connect the masculine and feminine parts of the soul and are a symbol of light and fertility.

Folklore: Surprisingly, a bride and bridegroom in a dream always mean accident and great disappointment, particularly when you yourself are the bride or bridegroom.

Bridge: A frequent symbol in dreams and mythology, the bridge spans an abyss. It is often a place of danger and of falling; you are crossing a boundary. In the Catholic faith, the protector is Saint Napomuk, patron saint of bridges. Uniting, re-establishing relationships; contradictions are bridged. If the dreamer has self-confidence, the fear of the abyss may be going away, but although the bridge becomes wider and is safe, it is still a place of danger. The condition of the bridge is important. How are you feeling on the bridge? When you have crossed the bridge, you have done a lot of inner work. Changes have taken place (you have reached the other shore).

In the Koran, the bridge over hell is as thin as a thread and can only be crossed by the righteous. In Celtic lore, there exists a bridge of horror that is also as narrow as a thread. The bridge always spans an abyss in which spirits, the devil, or God resides. Often in the dream one must bring a sacrifice in order to cross the bridge. For that reason we often see chapels on the bridge where the sacrifice has to be offered. Jung related the symbol of the bridge to the unconscious. He saw the unconscious as different islands in the sea. For him, the bridge connected these islands and is therefore a symbol of working toward a strong consciousness.

Bristle: You are obstinate. Or this may reflect your ability for self-assertion. You are crawling into your hole and shutting down.

Brooch: As with all other jewelry, it refers to vanity or cultivation in life. You want recognition, to amount to something, or to receive a gift.

Brook/Stream: See **River, Water.** Flowing emotions, allowing oneself to let go and give in, as in **Cliff.** Should you go with the flow, or are you just drifting about? Similar symbols are **Flying, Sled, Parachute.** Longing for quiet and nature. Also, keep in mind that the movements here mainly refer to the emotions.

Broom: Cleansing, as in: **Bath, Trash Can.** Popular symbol for a witch. Pointing to a problem that needs to be resolved. Phallic symbol, magic wand.

Brother: In the case of a man, the second ego. You are dependent only on yourself; you walk unaided; or your masculine side needs to be strengthened. In the case of a woman: Strengthen your masculine side.

Brown: Nature, nature-connected, vitality, groundedness. Also vacation and sunshine. Clay, mud, feces. It also might point to subjugation.

Buck/Ram: Well known symbol for earthbound vitality, lechery. The buck and the rooster have been allegorical since the Middle Ages for male—but also witchlike—horniness and carnal lust, the animalistic and the wild; but this symbol also stands for stupidity. The task is to make the buck into a gardener, which means to allow growth and development and to give him human qualities.

Buckle: Holding something together. Something is connected, understood.

Bud: Refers to energy that should be used for your own development. The same as in **Tuber, Flower, Fruit.**

Buffalo: A well-known symbol for male sexual urges as in **Bull, Buck.**

Bug: How you view the bug depends on your personal relation to it. As a germ or virus, it does not seem to offer any great threat. As a slang expression—"to bugger someone"—it has a sexual connotation.

In Egypt, the scarab (black dung beetle) symbolizes rebirth; later it became a symbol of luck. In our culture today the June bug is generally a symbol of luck.

Building: See **House.** According to Freud, Jung, and some current dream analysts, a building always represents the dreamer. The condition of the building is important, as is the atmosphere in and around the building, and where it is located.

Building/building a: A building, like a **House,** almost always symbolizes the human body and personal identity. Pay attention to the type of building you see in the dream. The process of building usually points to independence—rebuilding oneself during hard times.

Bull (wild): The bull/steer and **Tiger** are always personifications of drives and urges. Running after a bull in a dream means you are in conflict with your drives. You must always confront the bull or the tiger in your dream, because both have something important to say.

The bull is a symbol of masculine (originally feminine) strengths, fertility, and potency. Also indicates that animalistic urges have been mastered. See **Buffalo, Buck**.

Bulldozer: Energy for pushing something out of the way; or are you feeling pushed away?

Buoy: Aid used for orientation; hope and security, as in **Anchor, Arch,** but also **Family, Notice-of-Intention-to-Marry**, and sometimes **Bureaucrat**.

Bureau: See **Office, Bureaucrat**.

Bureaucrat: Symbol of a steady, secure human being who is serving the public, with the emphasis on "serving." Rigid, conventional and secure, as in: **Shares, Anchor, Arch, Notice-of-Intention-to-Marry, Sidewalk, Parents' House, Family**. Boredom, similar to **Office**. Economic fears.

Burglar: The need to get something on the sly. Greed (you are "breaking into" yourself). You can't trust people around you. Somebody is violating the dreamer's boundaries—emotionally or physically (another person is breaking in). Something new is coming, and there is fear of loss (as in **Thrush**) through changes. What has the burglar taken from you?

Burial: See **Funeral, Corpse.**

Burning: A frequent warning dream when risks are too great. See **Flames, Fire, Light**.

Bus: Moving forward quickly on the road of life, but, in contrast to **Car**, it is oriented toward the community. You want to force your way to your goal alone—something that is not always a good idea. Less force and more patience would be better. It is reminiscent of the collective, the power of many. Going on a trip, changing location. What is the condition of the bus? How is the trip proceeding? See **Driving**.

Bush/Shrubs: Secretiveness (hiding behind the bush). Protection from an unreasonable public or fear of openness. Female emotions, penchants, and desires (Merlin being seduced behind the white thornbush by Viviane). Is the bush bare or in bloom? Is something behind or inside the bush? (God was revealed to Moses in the form of a burning bush.)

Symbol of the personality of the dreamer. Hiding place.

According to Freud, the female genitalia.

Business: Usually is connected to present business. You are either too busy or not active enough. As in **Factory**, the image of "business" also represents a symbol for monetary transactions, which, in turn, depend on the interaction of the dreamer's individual characteristics. What kind of business is it? What does the business sell, what is your role in the transaction?

Businessman: This dream image refers to the masculine side of men and women. It is either the result of feeling self-confident or points to the need to become more self-confident. The businessman stands for the exchange between people. He is the one who guides the flow of goods and, in that capacity, is the negotiator between nature and people. The property of the businessman points to the talents of the dreamer, as do the goods that he sells. The way in which he is moving the goods may be an indication of how the dreamer uses his energies.

Busy Dreams: These are usually a sign of much activity

during the day (less often, a suggestion to be more active). In contrast, being an observer in the dream means to be less passive. These dreams may also point to too much stress, indicating that your life has become too frantic. Try to determine whether you see yourself as being very active in the dream or if you seem to be disappearing from view.

Butter: A positive symbol: everything is okay. Symbol for nutritious food and refinement.

Butterfly: One's own transformation (from **Caterpillar** to butterfly); also the image of inspired lightness and the soul of the child. The image of the butterfly is that of "spiritus," the connection between mind and soul. In this sense, it is a symbol for enthusiasm and salvation/happiness.

Buttocks: Those who don't "cover their ass" show how vulnerable they are. Or they don't have to hide their disadvantage, such as "The Fool" in early Tarot decks.
According to Freud, infantile sexual symbol.

Button: Buttons usually refer to your emotional attitudes toward society, similar to **Dress/Clothing.**

Buttons hold something together, closing up something that otherwise would be exposed. Are you all buttoned up or not?

Cabbage: Points to simple food (for body, mind, and soul).

As with most types of vegetable, a symbol for female sexuality.

Folklore: Health and long life.

Cactus: Defense, brusqueness, distance, hate-love and, in general, contradictory emotions. This image often comes up in dreams when you are in a situation in which you fear you have been injured. It points to the need for new boundaries and distance. This need for boundaries is often an expression of your sensitivity. Are you often acting irritably toward the world around you? Or, are you feeling overwhelmed by the intensity of your emotions? Take your emotions seriously and look for an appropriate way to express them.

Cafe: Obvious symbol for a place of rest, relaxation, and enjoyment. Meeting place, intellectual stimulation. What did you choose to eat?

Cage: A symbol for narrowness and being deprived of freedom, as in **Elevator, Village.** Restrictions, however, are felt more strongly, similar to **Sewer, Amber, Trap.** On the other hand, this dream symbol can have positive meanings, particularly when the cage is seen from the outside. Then it usually is a symbol of protection and taming (of wild urges). In addition, the cage can also seem like fencing, because fences create protection, giving you the peace you are seeking.

Cake: Reward. Food is often a sign of love that you either receive or give. Emotional and intellectual needs.

Calculation: Pay attention to the symbolic meaning of numbers! Do you want to—or should you—take stock of your life and pay for your deeds, meaning taking responsibility? See **Price/Payment**.
Folklore: A good omen when you can pay your bills, bad if you cannot.

Calendar: Impermanence; fear of age and death; make use of your life (*Carpe diem!*—utilize the day). On the other hand, this dream image may also appear because you fear being mortal; you are afraid of things that could have long-standing consequences; you feel overwhelmed by responsibilities and the burden of them. In the end, this dream is asking you to have a productive life and to enjoy it.

Calf: Youthful inexperience. Childlike, naive.
Folkfore: Good omen for love.

Calling Card: Advancement. Symbol of a desired identity.
Folklore: Secret admirer.

Camel: Adventure, deprivation, travel. Symbol for patience and quiet, but also for stupidity. The ability to "overcome dry periods." In addition, this is also a symbol of the search for what is essential.

Camera: Methodical, technical perspective. Suggests you look at something more impersonally and objectively—look through the objective! You should document something very carefully. The film in the camera refers to the initial screen, the creative power of the soul, where external impressions leave their imprint.

Camping: See also **Tent**. Longing for relaxation and vacation. Sense of community, longing for a simpler life.

Can: See **Container, Tin.** Female sexuality. What is in the can and what can you do with it? According to Freud, cans, containers, and boxes all symbolize the female womb.

Canal: Symbol of the dreamer's psychic energy; a path laid out by tradition. Life is too regulated and artificial. A desire to change. On the other hand, the canal also implies "draining," which makes land productive. There is a desire to be cleansed and rinsed out in order to become productive again. This cleansing also suggests the desire to reduce feelings (water). In the end, this dream symbol represents a matter of "emotional economy."

The condition of the water is important. Clear water is positive and means health and energy. Cloudy water is negative and means illness and depression, as in **Clouds**, **Abyss**, and **Ashes**.

Canary: Happy, comfortable home, as in **Singing**. Being locked up, as in **Cage**.

As with all **Birds**, what is also addressed here is freedom and intellect. A bird flying high in the sky symbolizes sexual ecstasy that, in the case of the canary, is (only now, or already) present in the beginning stages.

Candelabra/Candlestick: Enlightenment. Awareness.

Candle: A symbol of life, particularly a burning candle. May also point to specific festivities. See **Light**.

Already, in antiquity, the candle was a male sexual symbol. Also, according to Freud, a phallic symbol. A broken candle symbolizes impotence.

Cane/Pointer/Baton: See **Rod**.

Canister: Container. What is in the canister is important.
Folklore: A secret is being told to you.

Cannibal: A grabby kind of person whom you feel overwhelmed by. The desire to establish an intimate relationship with somebody. You feel you are eaten up by something, usually a relationship. See **Incest**.

Cannon: Weapon. A symbol for immense, massive energy. This dream image may also refer to your personal drive and power, force, and ability for achievement. Either you carry out your actions too strongly or not strongly enough.

Cap: Hat. Consciousness and thinking. Are you living too much in your head? It also addresses the fact that you keep something hidden or that something seems to be hidden. The verb "to cap" also points to completion, the end of a situation. In fables and fairy tales, the cap often plays a significant role as a magical covering for the head, allowing the person to become invisible. It also points to the fact that you may be too visible. Or that you might pay more attention to yourself and be more outgoing. See **Shadow**.
Folklore: Unhappy love.

Cap (of female): This symbol often appears when the dreamer is longing to get married. It indicates the transformation from a girl to a woman. It points to the head and consciousness. See **Helmet.**

Cape/Cloak: Searching for warmth or a place to hide.

Capital City: This symbol always takes on the meaning of **Ruler** and **Government.**

Captain: A guide that is determining the proper (emotional) course. A person of respect. Symbol for father, or for yourself. Also prosperity, dignity, and worldly experience, in the sense that you know the strength of your own soul.

Car/Driving: One of the most frequently occurring symbols of modern times. It points to the transformation into something new. Individual means of transportation, status symbol, motorized energy—it is also a sexual symbol. In a modern sense, usually a symbol for being on the go every day, and of psychological strength and mobility. As with the "Chariot" in the Tarot, it always presents a question about our road in life and how we are charting our course. As a symbol of environmental pollution, it often points to the need for inner growth.

Are you driving yourself or is somebody else driving you? What kind of an auto is it? For example, a sports car relates to virility, a utility vehicle to control. What color is the car? Are you fixing it up or **Driving** it?

According to Freud, in psychoanalysis a car is often the symbol for treatment. As Freud sees it, a slow car is making an ironic statement about the slowness of the analytical process.

According to Jung, it is a symbol for moving away. See **Wagon**.

Car Key: Key to movement. See also **Auto, Driving**.

Caravan: Symbol of an adventurous trip. You are in search of a pilgrimage. Burdens are being shared.

Cards: Cards can appear in dreams in many different forms—such as postcards, maps, entrance cards or tickets, playing cards, and business cards.

In the case of playing cards, it implies that you do not take life seriously enough and are taking too many risks. It also may be a suggestion to look at life more as if it were a game and to be *less* serious. It is important whether you have good or bad cards in your hand. If you dream about a particular card, find out the meaning by checking out books about reading cards.

With postcards and maps, refer to the place or area pictured on them. If you can't make any connection with the picture, postcards and maps may be an expression of a desire for travel and vacation.

Tickets and business cards point to areas that are normally unavailable to you. In the case of tickets, the specific area depicted is most important: what you are admitted to is an indication of the direction you should take in your life. In the case of business cards and credit cards it is the person who carries them who is important. A business card shows that you are, or want to be, successful.

Folklore: Quarrels loom on the horizon.

Career: Career dreams often indicate the importance of work in daily life. Such dreams either imply that we take our careers too seriously, or that we should pay more attention to them. In any case, career dreams appear only when tension exists in this area. Less often, the career itself can be seen as a general symbol of wanting to get ahead.

Carnation: An attempt to voice a desire that can only be expressed through flowers.

Folklore: A girl who can be "bought."

Carnival: The time, or the age, or period of development where "anything" goes, where you can be "somebody else." Merriment and being carefree, but also a warning about pretense. A dream about carnival points either to the need to stop pretense, to take off your mask (the *persona*, and show the true Self). Or it could be a message to be more outgoing and have more fun.

The image of the carnival often appears when you feel rigid and cut off from life. Particularly, when, in the dream, you are rejecting the carnival, you are denying your own wild and carefree side. Furthermore, carnival is also always connected to the **Fool**, a symbol that combines the absurd and the wise, and represents freedom. On the other hand, the fool is also somebody who, in a conventional sense, is unable to organize his everyday activities.

Folklore: Advancement.

Carpenter: See **Wood**. Architect, builder of the roof—in other words, consciousness, intellect, and the mind. One who builds knowledge and awareness.

Carriage: See **Auto, Chauffeur, Wagon.** A symbol of personality and status. What kind of carriage is it?

Folklore: Loss.

Cartoon, Animated: You are trying to get through life by hook and by crook. You have the ability to find what is comic in every situation.

Cash Register: See **Money.** The image of a cash register often means limited access to the world around you, which is blamed on money. You would rather *have* more than *be* more, indicating greed.

On the other hand, the cash register is a place where money is kept in an orderly fashion, protected and saved. In this case, **Money** is a symbol for your abilities and talents.

Folklore: Good omen, prosperity.

Castration: Loss of masculinity and vitality. As a dream image, it is almost always a sign of repressed physical urges. Castration dreams refer mostly to inferiority complexes and feelings of guilt. In rare cases, castration points to a deep-seated denial of masculine sexuality. At the time of Sigmund Freud and Carl Jung, castration dreams were relatively frequent. Now, they happen relatively seldom, since our attitudes to sexuality have changed. A woman is not likely see herself as a castrated man, and aggressive masculinity is today accepted by man and woman as an important part of themselves and does not need to be punished with castration. Castration dreams today are mostly seen as referring to work and vitality. Also, castration dreams dreamed by women and men are often a reference to their relationship. If a relationship is problematic and a partner feels restricted, fantasies and images about castration are normal. Castration dreams, in rare cases, may also have a positive side: one is liberating oneself from burdensome tasks. See **Donkey, Genital Organ, Sexuality**.

Cat: The emotional side of the dreamer, as well as the unconscious willpower of the dreamer. On one hand, it is a symbol of deception and cunning. It always refers to a woman, since the cat is connected to the archetypal female. On the other hand, the cat is a symbol for independence, lust, and self-will, again exclusively referring to women. It is a symbol of female sexual organs (pussy) and sexual aggression. But it is also a sign of physical agility, orgasm, and freedom. If a man or a woman is having a cat dream, it always addresses the feminine side (*anima*).

Caterpillar: See **Worm**. Caterpillars only eat what is not complete. They are greedy and fat. On the other hand, a butterfly was once a caterpillar. Therefore, the caterpillar stands at the beginning of transformation. This symbol almost always points to the process of transformation.

Cathedral (Dome, as in "House of God"): Holy place, self-contemplation, quietness in times of unrest, as in **Chapel** and **Church**, only stronger because of its size and more intense. Nostalgic, remembering old times. Structuring one's own life, great works, correlating many different strengths, fulfilling one's calling.

Security and a place of quiet. It often suggests the need to take time out for contemplation.

Folklore: Viewing a cathedral from the outside is positive; from the inside, negative.

Cauliflower: Its shape is reminiscent of the brain. Think more; taking more deliberate actions will bring results, comfortable home and, as with all vegetables, good health.

Cave: See **Grotto, Barn.** Womb of the mother, uterus, and security, as in **Family** and **Dam.**

According to Freud, a symbol for vagina; protection and femininity. The original dwellings in which human beings lived, with their animal drives. According to Jung, a reminder that human beings developed from animals.

Ceiling: Limited in your thinking and ideas. In the dream, the ceiling is either falling on top of you, creating a feeling of being confined or crushed, or the ceiling is immensely high and you are trying to stretch out in order to reach it. In one case, more intellectual effort is called for; in the other, you are overextending yourself intellectually.

Cello: Harmony, as in **Choir**. Depth, being grounded, and movement into the unconscious. Are you playing or are you listening?

According to psychoanalysis, the female body.

Cement: Inflexible, without feeling, rigid. Ugly and withdrawn. A character that is armored.

Cemetery: Funeral, Death. Longing for rest and relaxation in times of overwork and stress. A classical place for ghosts.

Center/Middle: You are looking for your own center, the quiet pole in your life. Ideal and balanced.

Chain: Close ties, in a positive sense. Chains have been the symbol for shackles and bondage as far back as the second century.

Chair: Need for rest.
   Folklore: News from an absent friend.

Chalice: Important here is how you categorize this object: **Mug, Goblet, Glass,** or even Grail. Different terms refer to different moods and points of view and lead to different interpretations. If seen as a chalice, it always indicates something extraordinary (it is not just a simple mug or a glass used every day!). It may either represent suffering or death (the "hemlock cup" of antiquity, for example) or the search for a higher goal (legend of the Grail and the magnificent interpretation by Emma Jung in her book *The Legend of the Grail As Seen in Depth Psychology*). A chalice holds the liquid that is the equivalent of our emotions and needs. The image of the chalice implies that these emotions and needs are spiritual in nature. Figuratively speaking, it is a matter of nurturing the soul and cultivating the emotions. That was precisely the task of the search for the Grail in the Middle Ages. In Christianity, the chalice is connected with the heart and blood of Christ.

Chalk: Usually points to school and learning. Also debts being written on a chalkboard.

Chamois/Antelope: Skillful, with modest requirements and shy.
Astrology: Corresponds to the sign of Sagittarius.

Champagne: See **Sparkling Wine**. Advancement, happiness; be good to yourself, treat yourself. Longing for luxury, as in **Oysters**. At the same time, it is a warning not to be too extravagant. Taking a bath in champagne is considered a symbol for titillating sexuality and decadent luxury.
Folklore: A sign pointing to unhappiness in love relationships (the partner is unfaithful or wasteful).

Chance: If something happens by chance in a dream, it is usually a message that you can attain something without expending great effort, or that a situation will resolve itself without extra effort.

Chapel: A place of quiet and contemplation. Particularly in times of stress it points to reflection. Romantic place.

According to Freud, a symbol for women, as in **Church**.

Charity: Improved financial situation for the giver, worsening financial situation for the receiver (see **Beggar**). On rare occasions, this can also mean the reverse. It points to hard times to come, or fear of poverty (see also: **Asylum**, **Rags** and **Counterfeit Money**). A warning about being petty and stingy, and about self-deception.

Charm/Mascot: See **Amulet**. Make sure you pay attention to what is pictured or written on the charm.

Folklore: Danger, specifically when in a crowd.

Chauffeur: You are not moving under your own power; you are being steered, which can point to a soul or subconscious that is driving you forward. If you are being chauffeured, help from others. If you are the chauffeur, humility is being suggested: you ought to serve rather than rule. Similar to **Basement**. What is the state of your self-awareness?

Check: See **Money**.
   Folklore: Financial loss.

Cheek: The cheek that receives the kiss of friendship as well as the slap in the face. In classical Greek dream interpretation, red, round cheeks meant a full cash register, while pale, white cheeks meant an empty one.
   Folklore: A good omen.

Cheese: Property and prosperity. Or something is not quite right, or something is going to waste. See **Milk, Butter.**

Chemist: Alchemist, Pharmacist. At stake here are new connections, correlations, analysis, and changes. Often a hint of being intellectually one-sided or not intellectual enough. As in **Physician** and **Pharmacist,** the man in the white coat is the pure man (pointing to spirit, represented by the color white). If women dream about a chemist, it is usually addressing her *animus*.

Cherry: Emotions; a symbol of lips and a sign of love, as in **Heart** and **Red**. Virginity.

Chess: Symbol for the fight of the white (affirming)

against the black (rejecting) energy in all of us. The outcome of this battle is determined by our awareness. See **Game**, **Fight**.

Chestnut: Autumn, play, food, fertility.

Chief/Boss: Symbol of male authority, as in **Father**. You are really your own boss. Or the "chief" is a symbol of your own, higher authority. The ability to self-govern. Positive interpretation: positive masculinity, "ruler" over your own affairs. Seeing yourself as a chief is usually a wish-dream or a compensatory dream: you feel inferior and inadequate, or you are not making good use of your powers. According to Jung, it is usually the voice of the domineering, masculine side of us.

Folklore: Dreaming about your chief/boss is a sign of advancement and thereby prosperity.

Child: Either a positive symbol that refers to new possibilities, or a hint that we are resisting maturity and completion. The child represents the essential in us that we want to see mature. We are supposed to tell the truth ("children and fools speak the truth") and be less complicated ("if you become like children...").

If women dream about a child, it is usually because

they are longing to have one, or that they are looking for something new, meaning a change in lifestyle is about to happen.

Also a symbol of the prime of life and continuity. A sick child points to emotional difficulties. Pay attention to what attitude the child has in the dream! These attitudes want to be supported and made conscious.

According to Freud, the child may represent self-regression or one's own genitals ("my little one," my penis). It is still true today that regressive tendencies are involved when an adult dreams about a child.

However, we ought not to dismiss Freud's belief that "reclaiming one's own childlike simplicity" can also be a positive process that allows us in later years to become lively and even revive a sense of eroticism. The symbol of the child appearing in a dream is always connected to vitality, the joy of life, and also sexuality.

Folklore: Growing family.

Chimney: See **Smoke**. Cleansing, but also pollution. A phallic symbol. See also **Column**, **Tree**, **Stairs**.

Chocolate: Often appears when the dreamer is really hungry. Symbol for temptation.

Chocolate, Bar: See **Bar, Chocolate.**

Choir: Fusion, happiness, harmony (heavenly choir), and a sense of art. How can you become part of a group and remain in it? Are you part of the choir or are you a listener?

Church: As in **Chapel, Cathedral.** A debate about the meaning of life. Contemplation is asked of you. According to Freud, it is a symbol for woman.

Church Service: You need to turn inward, as in **Prayer.** Expression of the desire to "serve God," or to serve a higher purpose

Chute/Slide: Sliding down, meaning closing in on the unconscious. Devotion, enjoyment of life, but also insecurity. See **Slipping, Falling.**

Cigar: See **Cigarette.** Phallic symbol and also represents the father.

Cigarette: Once the image of intellectual activity, cigarettes now indicate dependency and addiction. Symbol of taking a break. According to Freud, a phallic symbol.

Folklore: Lighting a cigarette points to having new plans.

Circle: See **Ball**, **Wreath**. A symbol of wholeness, a magic defense against danger: whatever takes place within the circle has special meaning. Ghosts and demons always move in a straight line, meaning that the circle and everything that is round provides protection. The saying is that the devil sits in the corners and can't stay in round places. Circles and everything round always means wholeness.

In ancient Greece, the circle symbolized immortality with no beginning or end, as in **Ring**. In alchemy, the stone of wisdom (lapis) is always depicted as being round.

According to Jung, the circle (archetype of the mandala) is pointing out that you are on the path of being initiated into yourself. Jung considered the circle to be the primary vision, the oldest symbol of mankind, and also the wheel of the sun.

In a few rare cases, the circle also has negative meaning: the endlessness of the circle can indicate monotony and constant repetition. Freud properly characterized neurosis as a need to perform a certain behavior again and again. This going-around-in-circles may be addressed here and be a hint that the "vicious circle" must be broken for the sake of happiness.

Circus: The uncommon, but controlled manner of using emotions, drives, and the body. Traditionally, the image of the circus is the exact opposite of what is taking place in everyday life, as in **Gypsy** and **Actor**.

City: See **Palace, Fort**. On one hand, and as far back as the Middle Ages, the city has been a well-known symbol for Mother, since cities provide protection and resources and are usually surrounded by a wall (uterus). On the other hand, it may also stand for Father and "father state." It is a symbol of progress on the road to self-development, as well as a symbol of the emotional environment of the dreamer. A large city represents a source of contact, a hectic lifestyle, and stress.

According to Freud, a symbol of woman.

City Map: A map of your life.

City Wall: See **City**. Security and protection, as in **Dam**. Sanctuary and positive femininity, as in **Cave** and **Parents' House**. Memories of vacations, taking walks, and relaxation.

According to Jung, the emphasis is on the motherly function and protection.

Claw: The fear of the animalistic. Also, "claw" implies grabbing. It can represent the dreamer's own wild and greedy grabbing for a world that he is either "dreaming" about or is actually living. Is the animal threatening you with its claw?

However, the claw could just as easily be a "healthy" sign if you are very timid. It might, however, suggest that you need to control your greed instead of living it out.

Clay: Being grounded, healing.

Cliff: See **Abyss**. Fear of **Falling**. Falling down the precipice means either fear of difficulties and adversity or a challenge to let go (See **Shot**, **Brook**, **Elevator**, **Trapdoor**). Moving up a cliff indicates that adversity can positively affect the outcome; the situation is improving.

You want to get some perspective on your life. It may also mean that you have difficulty in advancing socially, as in **Climbing**, **Obstacle**, **Exam/Test**, **Summit**.

Climbing: You have high ambitions, but the path is often dangerous and difficult, in contrast to *walking* uphill, where you also want to advance, but the path usually is not difficult or dangerous. See **Career**, **Ladder**, **Stairs**.

Clock: See **Mandala** and **Time**.

According to Freud, the clock is a symbol of menstruation, because it measures cyclical periods. The ticking of the clock, also according to Freud, corresponds to the pulse of the clitoris during sexual excitation. Is it possible to transfer this meaning to the rhythmical impulses of a Quartz watch?

Cloister: On one hand, a place of silence, meditation, and security, similar to **Abbey**, **Chapel**, **Cathedral**, and **Church**. On the other hand, the desire to get away from the world, fear of life. The cloister is also a symbol of sanctuary in times of trouble. This might be a suggestion to learn to deal with discipline—either to exercise more or to be more gentle.

Closet: Possessions. Hiding something. According to Freud, a symbol for the woman's body.

Cloth: Protection and covering/disguise/masking. Pay attention to the color and its symbolism.

Clothing: See **Dress/Clothing**.

Clouds: Illness, sorrow, and grief. They represent the mood of the dreamer. Gentle white clouds in the sky during good weather symbolize happiness and reverie. "Dark clouds on the horizon" point to difficulties ahead. The blending of *yin* and *yang* is interpreted by the Chinese to mean sexual union. When rain is falling from the clouds, it means that the lovemaking has reached its highest point of exaltation.

Clover: The four-leaf clover is a well-known symbol of good luck. The three-leaf clover points to the normal and the everyday. According to Freud, because of the three leaves it is a symbol of masculinity (see also **Three**).
   Folklore: Luck in love.

Clown: Do not take life so seriously. Lighten up, play. Fear that you are making a fool of yourself due to an inferiority complex, or you are demanding too much of yourself and others. The actions and the mood of the clown are important.

Club: The primitive weapon of the **Giant**. Its phallic shape points to undifferentiated drives. You are being hit over the head with something, in the sense of being overwhelmed.

Coal: Energy that rises from the unconscious. As fuel, it points to passion. A well-known symbol for **Money**.

According to Freud, the symbol of libido. According to Jung and the alchemists, a symbol for transformation, since, in the process of burning, coal is transformed into warmth and ashes.

Coat: Protection, defense, and isolation. The type of coat indicates the type of protection.

According to Freud, the coat also stands for a condom, and it is also a symbol for the genitals.

Coat of Arms: Advancement, ambition, vanity, and the need for power.

Folklore: Protection through powerful friends.

Cockpit/Platform: See **Pulpit**.

Cocoa: Sweets. People are laughing at you, or you are laughing at somebody.

Folklore: A good omen for family, not so good for business.

Coffee: Social gathering, mental stimulation, enjoyment of life. May also point to addiction. Coffee also indicates a need to be more mentally alert and have better concentration.

Coffin: See **Funeral, Grave.** Also dowry, inheritance, and a task that needs to be tackled.

Coin: Money. You either need or have money. Coins are always connected to your energies and talents. Fear of impending poverty, as in **Savings, Food.**
Folklore: Good omen if the coins are made from copper (a symbol of Venus).

Cold: As in **Ice, Snow.** Projecting isolation. It is a symbol of an aloof personality and emotional neutrality. Or it could be a hint to exercise more detachment.

Cold, having a: You are in need of warmth. Or you have "had it" and want to tell everybody to "get lost." You are living too isolated a life, as in **Ice.**

Collar: Order, good grooming, advancement.

Color: Psychological experience. It points out specific colors—see **Red**, **Yellow**, and **Blue**. Colors are very important if they are a function of a symbol. According to some modern dream research, people who dream in color are particularly temperamental.

Column: See **Pillar**, and possibly also **Tree**. Support and help.
According to Freud, a phallic symbol.
Folklore: Honor and success.

Comb: Vanity. Search more diligently (combing through). See **Hair**.

Comet: Special event; this image always points to character. The comet may also point to advancement. See **Star**.
Folklore: Success.

Communion (Church Service): Longing for religious rituals, or having an aversion to them. Betrayal by or acceptance into a social group. The 64-million dollar question: "How do you feel about religion?"

In addition, important here is the dual nature of bread and wine, which mirror a duality: the material versus the spiritual world.

Companion: See **Brother, Sister, Friend, Shadow.**

Compass: Focused thinking and acting. Which course do you want to choose for your life? It often poses the question of re-orientation. But with the compass you are sure to find your way. In other words, you can trust your own power and your own fate.

Compass (instrument for making circles): You are running around in circles; but also a sign of completion, as in **Mandala.**

Compulsion: A very important dream symbol that often allows us to see clearly our internal or external compulsions. Should you be more assertive and show more strength? Or should you try not to force things and situations?

Computer: A symbol of mental discipline and the ability to coordinate. Help at work, impersonal perfection, indifferent precision; what is missing is the soul and the emotions. Warning: too career-oriented.

Concert/Orchestra: A desire for harmony, because in a concert many voices create a harmonic whole. In that same sense, out of many experiences, one may create a life of harmony. When dreaming about an orchestra, it usually indicates a longing for a richer, more meaningful life. Are you part of the orchestra, or are you directing it?

Conductor (of an orchestra): Figure of authority, similar to **Chief,** and **Admiral,** only here it is in a harmonious atmosphere. You want to be the guide to ensure that everything is harmonious.

Conductor (of a train): Control. Are you going in the right direction?

Confection/Confectioner: Sweets. Fun and winning.

Confession: Benefiting from communication and honesty. Needing to free yourself from guilt and/or from morals that are too rigid. This symbol is similar to **Punishment.**

Confetti: Fun, lively continuation of archaic shower and fertility magic.

Folklore: Disappointment.

Constipation: Difficult emotional work ahead. The process is faltering.

Construction Site: Building. Planning one's life, creating one's livelihood and personal growth.

Container: Bottle, Box, Vase. These containers symbolize the body of the woman and female sexuality, at least in men's dreams. The male body and male sexuality is seldom, if ever, represented by a vase. If a container symbolizes male sexuality, it appears in the shape of a barrel or bottle. For men and woman alike, though, a vase may represent the innermost part of the person in the sense of the unconscious. But here the image usually appears in the form of a box (Pandora's Box) or a treasure chest.

What is inside the container is important (the spirit in the **Bottle**—the genie). Ever since Sigmund Freud, containers have been seen as referring to sexuality; if the container is empty, impotence. Pouring liquid from a container or removing a cork from a bottle is, according to classical psychoanalysis, usually a symbol for intercourse.

Conversation: Quiet conversation indicates the pleasure of making contact. Openness, in the form of arguments, usually reflects inner conflict.

Conversion/Change: A scene of conversion or change usually points more to mobility and to the hope that a situation can be changed.

Cook (Female): The other "mother" who is not trying to educate and punish, but the woman who cares for you, spoils you, and does not discipline you. In addition, this dream symbol also shows the inner power of the woman and her ability for transformation. See **Cooking, Kettle.**

Cookie: Mental and emotional food. Gratification.

Cookies: Indulging in sweets. In general, the time for sweets is in childhood, but you are still enjoying sweets. Are you longing for your childhood? Do you wish to have the protection and care you had when you were a child? Is "sweetness" missing in your life? Maybe you should make more room in your life for security and childlike enjoyment? According to Freud, cookies with a smooth surface represent nakedness.

Folklore: Be careful in matters of love.

Cooking: Change and emotional development, exactly as in **Kitchen**. May also point to seething/boiling with anger. On the other hand, cooking may mean bringing something to conclusion and maturity. What is being cooked? What are you supposed to prepare? Do you want it well done?

Cooking Lesson: Desire to improve your domestic skills, usually meant as a contrasting symbol to cooking, **Roast**.

Copper: Symbolizes success, sensitivity, and appreciation of life.

Astrology: Symbol of Venus.

Coral: Symbol for the beauty of life. And since the coral is a water creature, emotions are also addressed here. Are you using your emotions as the key to a happy life?

Folklore: Return of the lover.

Cord/Rope: You would like to lasso somebody.
Folklore: Good sign.

Cork: Taking out a cork means intercourse or ejaculation. The corkscrew is usually a phallic symbol.

Corner of a House: A complete persona or a "person with corners and edges."

Corners and Angles: Take a chance on being more open and direct in your communications. It is also possible that somebody is hiding something from you. Or are you hiding something?
Folklore: The devil hides in the corners. Today we might think of the devil as representing unknown danger or unknown chances.

Corn-on-the-Cob: A phallic symbol.

Corpse: See **Murder, Death, Dying.** Disconnected personality or emotions. Warning signal: You are carrying something foreign—something that is dead—around with you. If these dreams appear frequently and are accompanied by fear, it would be a good idea to consult a therapist. This is a frequent dream among women when they are oppressed. On the other hand, the dream symbol may also suggest putting an end to something, letting go of it.

Cosmetic: Points to improving your image—also to vanity. In a dream, it may often be a hint that you are caring too much or too little for your soul.

Cosmic dreams: When people of antiquity had dreams of strange cosmic events, like fire raining down from heaven, comets, etc., they would report them to the Areopagus in Athens or to the Senate in Rome. According to Jung, such dreams meant that the dreamer was being prepared for a position in government.

Couch: Quiet, rest, as in **Armchair**. Couch almost always has sexual connotation. What is the color of the couch and who is with you on it?

Coughing: A negative answer in a very important matter; fear of the future and dissatisfaction. Coughing is almost always connected to an unconscious need for distance and rejection. See **Cold, Lung.**

Counterfeit Money: Dishonesty and pretense. Your

values are too materialistic. Fear of poverty, similar to **Charity**, **Asylum**, and **Beggar**, however not as intense. Here, it is rather a case of not quite trusting your assets.

Country Fair: Vanity and bustling activity, joy and **Feast.**

Court: Bad conscience. You are sitting in judgment of yourself. Don't be so hard on yourself. Search for justice. Are you always trying to get "it" right? Is it important for you to have certainty and a clear direction for your life?

Cousin: That which is familiar, usually your own characteristics.

Cover (as in Bedcover): Protection and warmth, hiding, being secretive. To be under the same cover with someone else indicates intimate connection and trust.

Cow: See **Milk**. A symbol for mother. It appears only very rarely in men's dreams, and only when there is a strong connection to the mother. It has also been a prophetic symbol—of a lean or productive year. Remember Pharaoh's dream about the seven lean and the seven abundant years, as interpreted by Joseph? In India the cow is seen as the earth itself, and in Egypt the cow represents heaven (Hathor).

Cowboy: Adventure, individualism. Exaggerated craving for admiration. Longing for directness and being closer to self. See **Rifle** and **Hunter**.

Crab/Cancer: Often connected with fear of illness. Positive meaning: age-old instincts, and, in addition, hidden and rare wishes and fears. Now they can be more easily identified. The way the crab is moving is important. You are not pursuing your goal in a straightforward line, but coming at it from the side. See **Scorpion**, **Fish**.
  Astrology: A symbol of the emotions.
  Folklore: The crab is considered a messenger that brings bad luck, illness, and death.

Cradle: Baby. If this image is not a desire for a child, it usually symbolizes new ideas. See **Scale**.

Craftsman: Vigor, practical intelligence, and being constructive.

Crane (machinery): To remember something, to find something, to lift and remove something old.

Cream (as in lotion): Points to the "character mask" in everyday life. You want to be more beautiful. However, cream also indicates "balsam for the soul." In a deeper sense, the beauty of the soul is addressed here, and a beautiful soul is, in at least one sense, a true soul.

Cream (food): See **Milk**. Heavy food. Taking pleasure in sweets.

Criminal: See **Burglar**. Loss; moral conflicts, often of the sexual variety.

Cripple: Emotional or mental handicap. In this dream an important part of the shadow is expressed: your own weakness and neediness, for example. This dream symbol often appears when you are feeling overly important and are tending toward arrogance. Often it is a challenge to become more responsible, compassionate, and helpful. In addition, the image of the cripple is also related to **Beggar**, which may point either to becoming more humble or to greed and a hunger for possessions. See **Illness**, **Crutch**.

Folklore: Warning of being unfriendly.

Crocodile: Do you want to swallow up somebody? Or are you biting off more than you can chew? See **Dragon, Dinosaur**.

Crocus: New life is emerging.
Folklore: Luck.

Cross: Symbol for direction and order. It appears in classic dreams, where it is the cross of the victor, the cross of God's praise and honor, and also a sign of victory. According to Jung, it appeared in a dream about agony (cross to bear).

According to Artemidorus, the 2nd century dream interpreter, it is a favorable sign for those who are going on a sea voyage, because ships were made of wood, and the masts took on the configuration of the cross. For non-seafaring people, however, it is a sign of bad luck.

Crossing: Here it is always a matter of weighing alternative solutions. What do the different paths look like and where do they lead?

Crow: Symbolizes misfortune or death because of its

black color. See **Darkness**. It may also be a symbol of an aggressive woman. It was an Early Christian symbol of faithfulness. See **Bird**.

Crowds: A sign that you need more freedom and space, as in **Prison** and **Cage**. You feel crowded (this could be an actual sensation). Are you able in your everyday life to articulate your point of view and assert yourself? Do you need more space?

Crown: Hat. Symbolizes power, fame, and influence. Points to a high level of awareness that is related in yoga to the Crown chakra (*Sahasrara*). See **Head**, **King**.

Since the Middle Ages, a crown made of straw has symbolized impermanence, which still is part of today's dream interpretation. This crown of straw also points to **Harvest**, meaning that experiences from the past can now become useful.

Crutch: Fear of life, inhibitions, and inferiority complexes, or being freed from them. See **Invalid**, **Bridge**.

Crying: Release from pain, letting go. See **Water**, **Tears**.
Crying, according to Freud, meant ejaculation.

Crystal: Harmony and clarity. **Glass, Diamond, Mandala, Star**.

Cube (geometric): Being on the path of individuation. As far back as ancient Greece, geometry was considered the path to self-realization. According to Plato, the cube stands for Earth.

Cucumber: Phallic symbol. Recuperation and health.

Cup: See **Thirst**. Refers to female virtues and emotions, and the needs of the soul. See **Pitcher, Chalice**. According to psychoanalysis, a symbol of female sexuality.
    See **Mug, Beaker, Goblet**.

Curl/Hair: Temptation and youth.

Curse: Great caution is called for. You are getting caught up in guilt.

Curtain: Wanting to hide something. Confusion—"can't see through it." On the other hand, it might be necessary for you to "draw the curtain" for protection.

Cushion: A need for quiet.
  According to Freud, a symbol of the female.

Cypress: See **Tree**. Memories of vacations. Longing for **Warmth**. Slender and graceful.
  Folklore: Troubles.

Dahlia: As with all **Flowers**, you are blossoming. Full of color and openness.

Daisy: Symbol for girl, as in **Goose.** A childlike quality and naturalness that you are missing.

Folklore: Luck.

Dam (as in dike): Repressed, built-up aggression, similar to **Steam.** Controlled feelings and suppressed desires. Also protection and security, as in **Anchor, Arch,** and **Buoy.**

If the dam breaks, aggressive or compulsive discharge. To be on top, being healthy.

Dam (as in railroad embankment): This symbol always points to a road that is certain and predetermined. Also, the dam could possibly have sexual-erotic meaning, as a first sexual experience. The dam is also a term used for the perineum, the area between rectum and genitalia.

Dance/Dancing/Dancer: A frequent dream of women. Expressing joy and sorrow about one's body. The rhythm of life, specifically the female's. To this day, many native peoples depict important life events in dance, and it often happens that a new situation is introduced during a dream in the form of a dance. Similar to **Swimming.**

Dancing with a partner refers to the roles people play in a relationship. Who was leading?

Desire for a partner; dynamic expressions within a relationship (playfulness).

According to Freud, all rhythmic body movements are a symbol for intercourse. According to Jung, a female dancer expresses the principal archetype of the female. See **Ball (Dancing)**.

Darkness: Well-known symbol for our shadow, where a shadow depicts something invisible. Fear of people, emotions, thoughts, actions, and situations we don't understand, since they are in the dark. Ambiguous premonition; not knowing; secrets. Walking into your own darkness, more awareness is called for. The task almost always is to become more aware (**Light**), to shed light on something intellectually, or to deal more consciously with the unknown. Your own shadow is now visible, which is great progress and brings freedom. There are also "light shadows"—**Angel** and **Fairy**—but they are seldom addressed in dreams.

Also, do not lose sight of your path in the dark.

Dashing Up: A symbol for ascending.

Date (fruit): Symbol of female gender. According to Oriental interpretations, a passion fruit, pointing to a passionate love affair in the making.

Daughter: The creative feminine that has many possibilities open to her for development. See **Moon**. This image also represents the dreamer's need for new and unique powers.

Dawn: A new beginning, energy, and youth. Postponing something until tomorrow. You are either waiting to see, or you are simply too lazy to do what you feel you need to do, but this can sometimes be quite proper and healing.

Day: Confidence; infinite possibilities (the whole day lies ahead). Increasing awareness.

Dead Person: In the past, dreams about dead people were rather frequent; today they are relatively rare. The land of the dead is that of the unconscious where the **Shadow** resides. A dead person, according to Jung, is first and foremost a representative of unconscious incidents. See **Death.**

Dead-End Street: You don't know how to proceed, you have no solutions. This can be a positive image if you see yourself turn back. Learn from old mistakes. Often the image appears in fearful situations where you are being pursued. This fear can be overcome if you understand that you need to turn around (or back out) in order to free yourself. If such a fear-based dream image appears, experiment with different behaviors. Changing your behavior almost always leads out of the dead-end situation. The experience of a dead-end street is, from a developmental point of view, absolutely essential.

Deaf: Not wanting to hear something, being uncomfortable. Also, either too much or too little compliance. Not being fully aware of one's environment/surroundings. In rare cases, also real physical symptoms during sleep.

Death/Killing: If it is the dreamer dying, it never has any connection to a real impending physical death. Rather, it is a reference to the need to change one's path in life and allow old attitudes to die. Death usually means that radical change is necessary.

Basically, there are eight different levels of this symbol:

1. An indication that a necessary end has come to a certain phase. It is a transition to something new.

2. The desire to shed something (attitudes, behavior, situation, etc.).
3. A suggestion to come to terms with death and the fear of death, meaning a search for fulfillment and productivity.
4. A limit has been reached and there is an inability to know how to go beyond that limit.
5. A suggestion to take better care of one's health.
6. Something is dying inside.
7. A close connection with somebody deceased.
8. A desire for peace, solitude, and harmony ("the death of fear").

According to Jung, dreaming about death means letting go of something that has died; it is a symbol of transformation and a new beginning.

Debris/Rubble: Internal debris, a challenge to start "cleaning up" and recognizing the gifts and the chances that are hidden behind existing problems.

Debts: An obvious reference to material that burdens you and to real debts and mortgages. Your life is out of balance, meaning you are confronted with guilt feelings in order to resolve them. Also, unconscious punishment for actual financial burdens.

Decapitation: You are "losing your head" and consciousness, and can't clearly see your present situation. Suggests you either disregard your head—the control center—or be reasonable again.

Deceased: See **Death**.

Deception: A symbol of the unconscious. It is a suggestion to become more alert and more clear; or have you been engaged in (self-) deception lately? If that is the case, this symbol shows that you are already more conscious, more alert, and more clear.

Points to sexual inhibition, angst. Who has betrayed whom?

Deck: Ship, Travel, relaxation. Are you on the upper or lower deck? This would tell you whether you are centered more in the head or the belly.

Deer: A symbol for a woman or girl.

Astrology: According to teacher Johannes Fiebig, a traditional symbol for the zodiacal sign of Cancer.

Defense: See **Fight, War, Armament, Jewelry, Attorney**.

Defloration: To be deflowered. See **Flower**.

You are either losing your innocence, or you are opening yourself to the pleasures and joys of life. Something is being pointed out here that cannot be undone. In addition, this dream symbol points to very profound experiences.

Deformed, Being: Emotional wounds that may lead to insecurity and fear. You are unable to evolve fully and have lost your balance. You are longing for your own needs to be fully revealed, and that would again make you beautiful. See **Invalid, Cripple**. This dream symbol may indicate fear of failure. It may also indicate that a possible failure (being deformed) can be prevented.

Delay: Fear of missing something.

Deliverance: Always a longing for freedom.

Demonstration: Were you participating or watching? What were your feelings during the dream? Who demonstrated for what? And the most important question that you have to ask yourself is: What would I be demanding or wishing for? What purpose motivates me?

Dentist: A stressful situation. Is there a reason for you to dream about aching teeth? Fear of illness and pain.

Astrology: A symbol of Saturn.

Depths: Walking into and through the depths is part of growing and developing. Confrontation with one's unconscious.

Descent: This is the world of instincts and physical perceptions. As in **Abyss, Cliff, Diving**, we are talking here about delving into the unconscious. This image often points to the world of the feminine and is a warning that the male archetype is too dominant. Women, particularly, but men as well, will find their center and their own identity deep within themselves.

Social or economic decline. Fear of being destroyed. How did you descend? Where did you end up? Be clear about what you really want and where you can get the energy needed for the task.

Desert/Wasteland: Emotional isolation and loneliness. The place where fear and temptation and ghosts reside. See T. S. Eliot's *The Waste Land*. Withdrawal and asceticism. Symbol of the peak experiences that will lead toward self-realization. But the dreamer has to get all the insights and power from himself; there are no teachers. An illustration of the new and unknown.

Detective: The thrills and dangers of everyday life. This dream symbol often points to your search for your personal, as yet unknown, abilities and possibilities, but also to danger.

Detour: Pursue goals more directly, or a detour is necessary. The detour may represent the quickest road to your goal. (The Chinese say, "If you want to make haste, make a detour.")

Devil: Usually an indication that the shadow needs to be better integrated in the Self, or a reference to a one-sided intellectual attitude like Mephistopheles' in *Faust*. A black devil represents darkness and death; a red devil is the messenger of light and passion, who is keeping close company with the wild. A green devil represents nature, which usually appears in the form of a snake, cat, or goat (all are symbols for the Devil). The Devil symbolizes the animal nature of human beings and their connection to the earth.

Like Ahriman (an ancient Persian version), the Devil is the antagonist of light, descended from the heavens in the form of a snake. In Hebrew he is Satan, representing the picture of evil lust; in the New Testament he is the antagonist of the church, embodying the absence of God among peoples. According to Irenaeus, a 3rd century Greek priest, the Devil is really an angel who has fallen because of his arrogance. As Lucifer (who brings light), the Devil is considered a creature of light. In Dante's *Divine Comedy*, Lucifer has three heads, lives in the darkest parts of the earth, and is the opposite of the Holy Trinity. In the eyes of Christianity, almost all gods of native tribes were considered devils. In that sense the Devil also symbolizes everything that is natural, original, and has the spark of light.

Dew (drops): Almost without exception a symbol of liberated sexuality.

Dialect: If it is the dreamer's own dialect, this image points to identity or psychological rigidity. If it is a foreign dialect, it points to a side of the dreamer that is unknown to him. The connections the dreamer can make to the dialect are important.

Diamond: Archetypal image of the human self and its

transparent and unchanging nature. The diamond stands for the purest **Water** and the cleansed **Earth.** It is a symbol of the wholeness of the soul, of clarity and that which is particularly valuable. Whoever possesses the diamond can, according to Buddhist beliefs, withstand all temptations. On the other hand, this dream symbol also points to vanity (as with all jewelry), to unnecessary harshness and being cold and distant. If you see transparent diamonds in your dream it is a message to honor—without reservation—your own self, in spite of all shortcomings. You might want to ask yourself if you possess enough clarity and strength in your life.

According to *Physiologus*, one of the most widely read books of the Middle Ages, the diamond is a sun stone that can be found only during the night and that won't melt when placed in fire.

According to Jung, the highest development of the earthly body (the resurrected body).

Dictator/Ruler: Person of authority. You desire authority that you either do not have or that you have, but are not using. Consciousness is always demanded when the image of the dictator/ruler appears in the dream. And this awareness involves the ability for self-determination and self-control (you are the ruler of your own life). See **King/Queen**.

Like **Chief**, only stronger and more aggressive. Fear of the **Other**. Are you craving admiration? Compare with **Admiral**.

Dinosaur: Frequently the "great" parent or parents, ancestors, etc. Memories from childhood situations, because, from the perspective of small children, their parents seem very large.

The image points to inherited or early childhood experiences. In the end it is also a fascination with all that is huge and monumental; you either desire to be in command, or you're in love with your own status.

Diploma: You would like to excel intellectually or to be recognized publicly. Or are you craving too much recognition?

Diplomat: Be diplomatic, more careful with the words you use, and with your actions. Often a need for awareness of the world and the self.

Director: Who in your life is the director? Do you feel your life is determined by outside circumstances? In the last analysis, such a dream image points to inner strengths and weaknesses of the ego, which usually directs the course of life. See **Government**.

Dirt: Feelings of being unclean, which are a burden to the dreamer. Frequently, sexual feelings, which parents have told their children are "dirty." What is often addressed is the task of cleansing oneself or cleaning up a situation.

Discotheque: Youth, Dancing. Also a symbol of detached communication while simultaneously longing for contact. Physical acting out. Longing for a more interesting and colorful life.

Discovery: Something new or something you forgot is awaiting you. What has been discovered? These are always personal, often unknown, qualities.

Discussion: Frequently appears during work on unsolved intellectual problems (during the day); it is an unconscious problem-solving strategy, or perhaps a hint that a particular problem can only be solved collectively.

Dish/Jug/Chalice: As in the symbol of the Grail, emotional capacity and the soul itself. What is inside the dish is important. See **Cup, Container**.

Dishes/China: Domesticity. Broken china is commonly considered bad luck (in contrast to broken **Glass**).

Dismembering/Breaking Up: Do you have the feeling that you are falling apart? Dismembering often comes up in a dream when there is a fear of the breakup of a love relationship. In mythology it frequently represents alienation and estrangement, and the dismembered person is then sometimes put together again by the gods. See **Mosaic, Puzzle**.

Disobedience: Symbol of liberation, but also of irresponsibility.

Disorder: Chaos from which everything may evolve. A challenge to put more order into your life.

Diving: Either exploring the depths of the soul, or trying to deny something. Diving is an image of flight. It also means regression into a pre-birth condition and a preparation for rebirth (a new beginning). Diving dreams always deal with an **Adventure** where the dreamer is surrounding himself with **Water** (emotions). Such experiences may be ecstatic or full of fear. In most cases, however, they are an image of liberation. After all, moving in water is easier than on land. See **Fish**, **Submarine**.

Divining/Dowsing Rod: Being grounded, emotional sensibility.

Division: Separation, estrangement, and loss. Depending on the context, this image may also refer to social skills.

Division often points to the individuality of the dreamer, because individuality is indivisible.

Divorce/Separation: Either a desire for or a fear of separation. This symbol also may indicate separating things out—differentiating—which points to your ability to make judgments.

Dock: Groundedness, security, as in **Anchor** and **Buoy**. Being at home, coming home, as in **Parents' House**, **Family**.

Doctor: See **Physician**. Helper, healer, wise man, advis-

146

er, and leader. Symbol of the healing power residing in yourself, which you can trust. On the other hand, "Doctor" as a title points to the appearance that we would like to present to the outside world. If that is the case, this is a message to seek your true self.

Folklore: In general, always speaks of a good omen.

Dog: The animalistic. A symbol of instincts to be used and guided by conscience. The dog may also appear as a guard to protect property and defend against attack. He may symbolize a true friend. The dog is the closest creature that humans come to call "brother." It may also represent part of the dreamer—for instance, the shadow.

The dog as a pet almost always points to our instinct or loss of instinct, particularly when it is a trained dog, which in this case does not imply cultivation, but rather the destruction of instincts. The dog is also one who needs to inspect its environment, who looks for and finds information. In the Tarot the two images of "the Fool" and "the Dog" always appear together. A vicious dog means envy and unscrupulousness. According to Jung, the dog is the undertaker who buries the **Corpse.** The dog with its instincts is seen as aiding the process of dying and resurrection (like Anubis in ancient

Egyptian mythology). According to Greek mythology, the dog from hell, Cerberus, stands on the border between life and death.

Also may point to fear of rejection—"dog" as an unattractive female.

Dolphin: The smart, wise mammal (See **Fish**); highly developed, intellectual emotions.

Donkey/Ass: The obvious meaning is stupidity. But also stubbornness, sexual energy, and vitality. (In the language of the 16th century, "driving an ass" meant to arouse the penis.) Today this symbol is seen differently, since the proverbial stubbornness of the ass can be seen as his strength. He follows his own sense and possesses a sense of what is his. And in the pursuit of his urges, the ass can also be very smart (urges are not always stupid!).

According to the 2nd century dream interpreter Artemidorus: if you see an ass that is carrying a load, a burden is removed from you.

The most widely read book of the Middle Ages, *Physiologus*, relates the ass to the custom of castration.

Folklore: Luck in love.

Door: A new beginning. See **Gate**. In ancient Egyptian dream interpretation, if the door is open, it is a sign that a favorite visitor is coming.

According to Freud, symbol of the female sexual organ. According to Jung, symbol of a transition from one phase to another.

Doormat: You are feeling inferior or stepped on. Everything dirty seems to be unloaded on you.

Dove: The animal without trickery. As with all **Birds**, a symbol of sexuality as well as intellectual euphoria and ecstasy. A symbol of peace and creative thoughts. Doves can also be experienced as spirits or demons that one is unable to shed. In that sense, the dove is also a symbol of fear and disgust.

In the Christian Church the white dove is the symbol for the Holy Ghost and is usually female. According to Early Christian understanding, the dove is also the opposite of the **Snake**. According to Jewish tradition, the dove is the messenger of God. Today the "Christian-influenced" image of the dove of peace is a particularly favorite notion, as described in the best-selling book *Jonathan Livingston Seagull*.

Downhill: Letting go; fear of "going down" (to the depth of emotions, or sexuality, etc.) as in **Falling.**

Dragon: Fear of a woman, usually the partner or mother. Great wealth and luck. The dragon might be threatening and combative (Blake related it to mental battles). Often, as in depictions of St. Michael or St. George and the Dragon, a symbol of desire that needs to be resisted in favor of intellectual development. Pointing to one's own "poisonous" and destructive side. Are you hoarding too much? What do you want to own?

According to dream interpreter Artemidorus, wealth and treasure. The dragon is also a Chinese symbol for luck.

Drapes (opaque curtain): Something is hidden—what is it? Deception and isolation, but also necessary distance. See **Net, Fog,** and **Smoke.**

Draught: Economic loss, suffering. From the Bible: The dream of Pharaoh, seven lean years and seven prosperous years.

Drawbridge: See **Bridge.** It is the connection between consciousness and the unconscious, sometimes being open and sometimes not. Support and help.

Folklore: Unexpected travel.

Drawer: See **Closet**. Image of secrets and possessions.
Folklore: An open drawer is positive; a closed drawer—or drawer full of underwear—points to unfaithfulness.

Drawing: This symbol suggests that you look at something very carefully and realistically. Also, there is a need to be more active.

Dream: It symbolizes the unconscious; awareness is demanded.

Dress/Clothing: An image of poverty. Symbolizes the role the dreamer plays in the world and how he presents himself—"clothing makes the man." The type of clothing refers to the social standing of the dreamer, either the one he occupies or the one he would like to occupy. According to Freud, it points to nakedness, which is hidden under the clothing.

Drink: Images of a drink usually appear when the

dreamer is actually thirsty. It can also relate to taking pleasure in love What did you drink?

See **Thirst, Cup, Glass, Water, Wine, Tears**.

Driver's License: Symbolizes identity. You have been recognized as mature enough to become a **Leader.** You can move freely (symbol of freedom). Loss of driver's license, loss of identity, immaturity. Searching for the driver's license, searching for one's identity.

Driving: Always refers to your life's journey, to the growth you have achieved. Here, particular emphasis is placed on your mobility. What kind of **Vehicle** are you using? How is the trip? Are you driving yourself or are you being driven? Check more closely **Driving a Car, Train, Airplane**, and **Bicycle**.

According to Freud, a symbol for intercourse.

According to analytical therapy, the analytical process itself.

Driving a Car: See **Highway, Moving**. Here it is important to note what kind of vehicle you're driving and what your feelings are as you drive. Is it hectic or pleasant and relaxing? Are you moving ahead fast or did you have an accident? It is important to note if you are starting the car, parking it, passing another car, etc. All of it would be symbolic of how you are moving ahead in life. This image is often a reference to the subjective space in which you are moving. The dream is showing how you move and present yourself to others in daily life, and what the possibilities, problems, and tasks are.

Drowning: Sinking into the unconscious, helplessness, lack of planning in your life. Being washed away by the flow of emotions.

Fear of being swallowed up by the unconscious. As in **Suffocating,** where the issue is to get more air, here it is a matter of being safe in the **Water,** about feelings and (emotional) needs that bring more energy and inner strength.

Drugs: Opium. Murky, foggy; a message to be more awake, more clear, and more focused.

Astrology: Symbol for Neptune.

Drum/Drumming: Movement, something new, excitement. According to the latest research, if a person has frequent dreams about drums in quick succession, it might indicate that the nervous system is in a state of alarm.

Arrogance, exaggerated self-importance, enjoying contact.

Duck: Symbol of female friendship, but also falsehood.

Duel: See **Duet.** Problems with your environment, contradictory emotions. This dream symbol may also have sexual aspects. A frequent dream image when one is at war with oneself: I am torn!

Duet: Contradictory thoughts and feelings, as in **Duel,** but more harmonious. Harmony, particularly in relationships.
Folklore: Domestic bliss.

Dunes: Memories of travels; temporary. Something is fizzling out. **Quicksand, Sand, Beach.**

Dust: Symbol of immortality; everything turns to dust. Also a warning about being too vain.

Dwarf: A fairy-tale figure, a helper, and a symbol for being connected to the earth. Are you feeling small and inferior? Should you be more humble? Also a symbol of the shadow, of what is minuscule and invisible. You *still* feel like a child; or you know how huge the world and cosmos are and feel small, again like a child.

Dying: According to psychoanalysis, wanting to get even with somebody. See **Death/Killing**.

Dying Forest: Often a suggestion that the foundation of the dreamer's life, the unconscious, is disturbed. An exploiting worldview has taken over. The dreamer needs to find and stop the ways he is exploiting himself—and others. See **Forest**.

Eagle: Ancient symbol for rulers and power. The eagle can, like the phoenix, rejuvenate himself and thereby become immortal. The eagle possesses superior viewing power, but there is also a warning connected to the symbol—bold plans and actions can turn dangerous. The eagle is an ancient symbol of freedom. As an endangered species, it symbolizes a rare but also most powerful animal. Like all **Birds**, it points to the connection between heaven (spirit) and earth.

A white eagle is a symbol of happiness and spirituality. With a lame wing, the eagle points to constriction and restrictions, similar to the symbols of **Amputation** and **Cage**.

Freud saw in the eagle a distinctive and powerful sexual symbol. For C. G. Jung, it was a symbol of transformation. For William Blake, it was the marriage between Heaven and Hell. The eagle is also viewed as the symbol of the (high-flying) genius.

Ear: You need to listen better, be more obedient or more understanding, pay attention not only to sounds and tone, but also to voices and indirect meanings.

The ear is also a female sexual symbol that expresses a need for more emotional openness, or a need to be careful of emotional boundaries. Pierced ear lobes mean penetration and therefore defloration, according to most depth psychologists. In the Orient, the ear is the symbol for a married woman.

Ear (as in an ear of corn): Symbol of fertility and well-being, also a phallic symbol. Here it is usually a question of how productive you are—what has grown inside you, what you want to harvest.

Astrology: The sign of Virgo.

Earring: See **Jewelry**. Are you greatly invested in your outward appearance? Or should you listen more carefully, as in **Ear**?

Folklore: Quarrels.

Earth: Being rooted, grounded, protected. Everything grows from the womb of the earth, symbol of motherliness and fertility. The type of earth may also point to the dreamer (for instance, clay, sand, humus, etc.) Memories and ancestors are residing deep within the earth. Also a symbol of a difficulty in digesting reality.

In the *I Ching*, earth represents the dedication to conception, the mother. The food for the people of the Babylonian underworld was earth.

According to Jung, earth and clay are the food of the underworld, because as the earth accepts the dead, the dead eat the earth.

Basis and foundation of a subject.

Earthquake: Enormous event, severe emotional upset;

often hinting at self-destructive energies. Sign of general insecurity.

According to Jung, always a blow to one's point of view or convictions. Something confronting you can only be handled if you totally abandon your old convictions. In that sense, this dream symbol is always a sign of getting another chance and making a new beginning.

Easel: Creativity.
Folklore: Good luck.

East: From the East comes awareness and enlightenment. See also the Bible story of the three wise men from the Orient. The **Sun** rises in the East. A dream about the East is almost always connected with a longing for higher consciousness, greater clarity, and better self-understanding.

Easter: Resurrection, joy, and vacation. See also **Spring**, with people becoming visible again, going outside. Easter is closely connected to the joy of resurrection. This image shows that after any dark period, light and joy will return and you can go outside again and let others see you.
Folklore: Good omen.

Eating: Grounding, taking something in, being touched by sensual pleasures. In the widest sense of the word, it always points to emotional or spiritual food. What do you have to do to nurture your soul?

Ebb Tide: Emotional relaxation, or lack of energy, calming one's emotional life. A poor financial situation.

Ebony: Black, Wood, Beauty. In the fairy tale "Snow White and the Seven Dwarfs," ebony plays a role.
Folklore: Traveling to a faraway place.

Echo: Usually the result of noises in the immediate environment. Otherwise, you ought to pay more attention to the impact of your own words; everything that you send out is coming back to you. Also, it is frequently a symbol of the soul, where everything resonates. You are hoping for a reaction from the world around you. It may refer to remembering something that was said a long time ago, and that now may possibly be seen in a new light.
Folklore: You will hear about a positive event.

Economist/Specialist: See **Villa**.

Edge: Are you on the edge, or is it a bridge to something new?

Eel: See **Snake**. The eel appears often as a dream symbol when you are feeling numb and lethargic. The eel symbolizes activity, and expresses the desire to be like a **Fish**, in **Water**, able to move through life like an eel, smooth and unencumbered. It is also connected with being unemotional (distant). The quality of the water in which the eel is moving is important.

If there is a feeling of disgust when seeing the eel, it indicates a childlike aversion to sexuality. The same holds true when fleeing from the eel. In classical psychoanalysis, the eel is also seen as a phallic symbol and having sexual urges.

Egg: Symbol of beginning. Many mythologies depict the earth as having been developed from an egg. Symbol of rebirth—Easter eggs. Also, that which is fragile. Longing for or fear of pregnancy, as in **Baby, Birth.** In the *Koran*, virgin women are compared to well preserved eggs.

According to Freud, female sexuality and motherhood.

Astrology: Symbol for Cancer.

Eight: Symbol of wholeness, completeness, the eightfold road of Buddha, an octave in music. Grounding, since the dice, as the symbol of earth, have eight corners. In rare cases, a sign of being fixed and motionless. Also: Pay attention!

Infinity—the sign of infinity is a horizontal 8. In rare cases, eight is also the sign of an outcast (ostracized).

Electrical Cord: The energy of the dreamer is addressed here.

Electrical Wire: See **Wire**. Energy transformation.

Electricity (as in power plant): Symbol for energy, supply, and transformation of power; or you may be under tension. If there is an accident in an power plant, and you can't handle internal tension, this indicates repressed urges—see **Termination, Attack, Fire, Surf, Kidnapping, Defloration, Flame, Violence, Greed, Harem, Skin Rash, Wire (High-Tension), Hooker/ Prostitute,** and in part **Elf.**

Elephant: Perception of your own power; or you are not letting anybody near you. The power of the unconscious is not available to you, and you are afraid of it. Points to thick-skinned people who are unaware of their destructive powers (the elephant in the china shop). Warning of one's own repressed sexuality. A need to be more patient (thick-skinned), or perhaps you have too much patience. Tusks and trunk are sexual symbols. The image of a sick or weak elephant points to emotional injuries. If it is a peaceful elephant, you are handling your unconscious comfortably.

According to early Christian belief as described in *Physiologus* , one of the most widely read books of the Middle Ages, the elephant has no sex drive and is a powerful enemy of **Snakes.** Elephants' hair and bones were burned inside the house as a protection against evil spirits.

Elevator/Lift: See **Ladder, Stairs**. Emotional changes, and the degree of those changes is expressed here. Caution, remaining aware of reality. If the lift is moving up fast—advancement, high hopes. If the elevator is moving down fast—to the point that it is uncomfortable—fear of letting go. See **Abyss** and **Trapdoor**. If the elevator gets stuck, inferiority complex or strong inhibitions.

A symbol of Kundalini, vitality in Yoga. Advancement and wish for self-affirmation; or, fear of **Falling,** and **Shooting**. Being constricted, as in **Siege**, **Amber**, **Village**, and **Trap**, except not so extreme. Emotional transformation; becoming more aware without effort.

Elf: Helpful spirits, figures of light. As a complementary symbol, it often points to inner tension and imbalance, as in **Electricity (as in power plant).** Elves represent emotions and situations in everyday life and are friendly toward human beings. Such dream images also may point to flight into the world of fairy tales and away from reality. In this case, the dreamer is shown something that is foreign to him—lightness, being carefree and selfless.

According to Jung, the elf is the guide of the soul.
Folklore: Looks on the elf as having no soul, and the dance of the elf is seen as a sexual temptation.

Elk (reindeer): Being in nature. Points to the basics of life and longing for freedom and simplicity; if held captive, you are unable to live out your physical urges, your male instincts, your need to roam about. The image of the elk is also connected to the sense of wide-open spaces that is usually expressing a longing for mental clarity and openness. As a mighty animal, the elk elicits awe about the nature of passion.

A symbol of self-development and redemption. Also

masculine power and superpower. In myth, it corresponds to the "Hubertus Elk," a white elk with a cross between his antlers. To see him is considered a sign of special grace.

Folklore: Erotic meaning.

Ellipse: As in **Circle,** but with two focal points—a double center.

Emaciation: Thin. Loss of substance and not taking up much space, or taking up too much space. Trying to compete with the ideal of beauty. This image often points to the fact that you don't want to work as much as you have been working.

Embarrassment: On one hand, admitting imperfection—not being what you would like to be. On the other hand, breaking through limiting conventions. This dream may also point to the end of long-standing behaviors and/or attitudes. See **Puddle.**

Indicates the inability to communicate and express your needs clearly. Part of the Self is lost or was put aside and is not being lived.

Embers: Emotional stability, inner warmth, intense

inner energies. Symbol for the center of life, the eternal spark, standing for life's energies, willpower, and the power of intuition. Also, however, it stands for the power of stress—"midlife crisis," for example—that indicates change. Pay attention: Is the ember dying out or turning into **Fire**?

Embrace: The desire for closeness, but fear of restriction and boundaries. Problems in bonding. It's important who is being embraced.

According to Freud, desire for sexual union.

Embroidery: If you are doing embroidery, it indicates that you may need to calm your nerves.

Emerald: One of the hardest gemstones, the emerald symbolizes the character or the innermost soul.

Folklore: Good fortune in business or separation from loved ones.

Emergency Room: Ambulance, fear of accident; you are looking for help.

Folklore: Your wishes will be fulfilled quickly.

Emigration: Trying to find a new field of

activity/employment, but also fear of necessary reorientation. Could also be interpreted, as in **Giving-Up/Getting Out**, and **Foreign Countries/Abroad**, as a warning for being unrealistic. **Asylum/Exile.**

End-of-the-Line: You are either at the end of your rope, feeling exhausted, as in **Blindness,** or you have reached your goal.

Enemy: Contradictory ideas, attitudes, and aspects within the self. Often that which you want to deny. See **Ruler.**

On an objective level: people in your surroundings whom you reject. On a subjective level, one's own characteristics and mistakes.

Engagement: See **Marriage**, **Wedding**. Symbol of at least a temporary union. An unknown side is integrated. It is symbolically important whom you have become engaged to.

Folklore: A bad omen.

Entrance: Openness. Sexual meaning seems apparent.

Entrance (as in performing): Often fear of success or a

more generalized fear of failure (particularly when stage fright is part of the dream). "Where do I have to appear?"

Envelope: See **Letter, Post Office.** Are you expecting an important announcement?

Environmental Pollution: 1. Dealing with real problems and quality of life.

2. Problems of "inner pollution"; emotional burdens and uncertainties.

3. A positive intention to create your own environment, an expression of realizing or ignoring complex personal needs and wishes. See **Earth, Fire, Air, Water, Garbage, Spring, World.**

Envy: Internal tension and guilt feelings.

Eraser: To undo something, to get rid of something, to repress and forget facts. Faulty and indecisive actions.

Erection: Erections during a dream are normal, but here we are talking about a dream of erection. Symbolically, this points either to fear of impotence or to the joy of masculine power. This symbol is about willpower and vitality within men and women. It almost always poses the question of how goal-oriented and focused your actions are. For men as well as for women, this dream can be interpreted as the need for hetero-, auto-, or homosexuality.

According to Freud, women dreaming of erection indicates penis envy.

Escape/Flight: Repression, particularly when you are afraid of examining your own shadow (thoughts and feelings that you are unaware of), as is often the case in dreams about flying. Are you running away from part of yourself? You might have good reason for it! However, in a dream, escaping is a sign that whatever you are running from wants to be understood and accepted—otherwise, it would not appear in a dream. Whenever you are fleeing, you are also *looking* for something. Ask yourself what your goals are.

Evening: Time for reflection, a comfortable, peaceful time. Often an expression of the need for rest when being overwhelmed. This symbol frequently appears when the person is in a stressed or out-of-balance situation. It may also appear after a stressful period. The evening as the "twilight of one's life," or taking a rest at the end of a day's work, is often a sign of life lived with purpose and accomplishments (you may rest on your laurels).

The evening is, in part, a sign that you are reaching deeper layers of the unconscious. Less frequently, the image of being at the end of the day may also be expressing a painful loss.

Evening Gown: The image of evening dress combines enjoyment and culture, a cultivated passion that one can either experience or long for. See **Suit, Ball, Dress**. The color of the evening gown has great symbolic importance.

As a "wishful dream": a longing for social advancement. It may be that there is happiness about reaching it, or a failure to know how to handle it.

Folklore: The more beautifully the woman is dressed, the worse the omen.

Evening Meal (Dinner): Longing for or fear of happy **Family** and a cozy **Home** appear often when all of this is being missed, or when it is simply too much to cope with. Enjoyment of the retirement years **(Evening)** indicates a zest for life and sensuality.

Folklore: News about a **Birth**.

Exam/Test (university): Difficulty at work. Passing a test points to ambition; failing a test points to inferiority complexes. Also, a symbol of differentiation and self-testing. According to Freud and Adler, memories of childhood misdeeds and punishment that are never forgotten. Today in psychoanalysis, the test is more indicative of life struggles.

One of the most common dreams is failing an exam. In the dream one is not prepared for the exam. In a variation, one is onstage and doesn't know the lines. Both situations refer to a fear of failing in public. The dreamer should examine his self-esteem. In the exam situation, usually the subject—or question one doesn't know how to answer—gives an indication of the field in which one feels insecure. Onstage, the play or scene is sometimes a key to the field of fear.

Excavation: Old emotions (submerged/buried) need to be brought to consciousness; psychological work on self. Similar to **Taking Apart.** Self-determination is asked for. It is important to note what it is that is being excavated (a submerged potential?).

Freud looked on the process of psychoanalysis as an act of excavation.

Excavator: Strong or destructive power. Something has to be dug up from deep down. Uncover the foundation and dig for the treasure that is buried deep. Occasionally, this is a dream symbol for something colossal, as in **Monster.**

Execution: Don't panic when you have such a dream. This is a symbolic expression and not a threat. In some cases, the image of an execution can be particularly positive, because something is finally dying that has bothered you for a long time. If you are the one who is being executed, this symbol indicates strong negative emotions, self-doubts, and guilt feelings. If somebody else is being executed, it symbolizes the **Other**—usually characteristics or behavior that you must urgently discard. See also **Death.**

Psychological and mental re-orientation. Changes need to be made.

Exile: Feelings of estrangement and abandonment. Longing to belong. Or are you seeing a part of you that you have "condemned into exile"? Repression. See **Hermit** and **Asylum/Exile.**

Folklore: Luck.

Explosion: Emotional outburst, intense (inner) conflict. Repressed urges, as in **Electricity, Attack, Surf, Abduction, Defloration.** You really should allow yourself to "explode" now and then! It is important to look at what is exploding, and what form the explosion takes.

Express: Stress, hurry, and importance.
Folklore: Pay attention to your superiors.

Eye: Mirror of the soul, window of vitality and willpower. Since the eye, symbolically, also represents the image of the **Sun,** this dream points to vitality and courage. Here, body, mind, and soul are synonymous with heart, consciousness, and emotion. Often a sign of inner restlessness. Fear of missing something or being left out. Being aware of something but not wanting to see it, or simply being curious. Become a better and more thorough observer. Greed ("eating" with the eyes).

The color of the eyes and its symbolism is important.

In our culture, green and blue eyes are very much eroticized. In Islamic countries, people protect themselves studiously from the "evil eye," but being stared at in a dream is considered a good sign: it means being considered an important and interesting person.

Freud and Jung both considered the eyes—because

of their shape—to be a female sexual symbol (the self-destruction of Oedipus is a castration symbol).

Looking yourself in the eye in a dream means self-knowledge; it is a challenge to have courage and see yourself as you really are. It is important who is looking, in what manner, and what direction. Open eyes show recognition and openness; downcast eyes mean a weakening of the willpower.

Eyebrows: Vanity. Eyebrows joined above the nose are, according to folklore, a sign that physical urges dominate. During the Middle Ages, it was seen as revealing a pact with the devil. Important is the motion of the eyebrows as, for instance, raised eyebrows.

Eyeglasses: Help, or an obstacle to seeing something more clearly. Refers to your own perception and the courage to hold to your own subjective convictions. Insight, vision, perspective, as in **Eye**, and sometimes **Bird**, but with assistance. Also an expression of your own emotions that are either endangered, protected, or sharpened. Sunglasses point to summer, vacation, and **Blending**. Also "seeing the world through rose-colored glasses." Protective glasses point to work.

Eye Specialist/Ophthalmologist: See **Eyes**. One ought to take a closer look and seek help in obtaining objective insights. See **Physician**.

Fabric: Everything is connected to everything else. Fabric symbolizes the "thread of life," a suggestion to "weave" together the threads of experience and your own personality to create a whole. See **Thread**. The type of fabric is often a mirror of your emotions.

You either want to hide something or you want to present something in a favorable light. Pay attention to the symbolic meaning of the colors.

According to Freud, symbol of the female body.

Facade: A matter of social status and the way that you portray yourself to the outside world. According to Freud, the upright human body. According to Jung, that which, in society, we pretend to be.

Face: Facial expressions stand for the emotional situation of the dreamer, for the way he respects and judges himself. They are a symbol of the dreamer's identity, willpower, and power of intuition. A disfigured face reflects rage, aggression, fear. A distorted face indicates internal turmoil. An uneasy or inscrutable face expresses the search for identity. Is the face a **Mask**, is it made-up, or is it open and free?

Folklore: A friendly face is a good omen; unfriendly, a bad omen. Many strange faces mean that you have to move soon.

Factory: Community spirit, team, collective action, integrating well, and, in addition to all this, a symbol for the different parts of your personality working together cooperatively. But also: slaving away, hard work, and being taken advantage of (as in Charlie Chaplin's film *Modern Times*). Also, becoming impoverished, social demotion, isolation, lifelessness. Loss of wholeness, being cut apart. In case of conflicts between people in the factory: poor cooperation.

Folklore: Unexpected events.

Fair/Exhibition: Communication, contact. See **Masses**, **Mall**.

Folklore: Well-being.

Fairy: Desire for advice and help from the outside, as in **Parents**, **Physician**, and **Pharmacist**. Tendency toward childishness. The fairy is a being of the soul.

According to Jung, it points to the feminine side (*anima*) in men and women. The "good fairy" is the liberated female or the fertile mother; the "bad fairy" is the female temptress who needs to be set free.

Astrology: The symbol for Cancer.

Falcon: Eagle, Bird. Freedom, control, and success. A symbol for aggression, as in **Hawk**. Symbol of an aggressive or passionate person.

Falling: A warning not to be such a realist. It might be better to just let go, as in **Abyss, Cliff, Shot, Parachute, Flying,** and be more open to something new. Also fear of being destroyed, as in **Descent**. Points to loss due to miscalculation on the part of the dreamer (see the myth of Dædalus and Icarus) or is a sign of unjustified euphoria and arrogance. This symbol often appears in dreams during times when a person has difficulty achieving orgasm and during acute midlife crisis.

Doubt and insecurity. You need to let go, as in **Brook, Leaf,** and **Parachute**. Dreams of falling often appear if you are in the process of transition to a new stage in life. Particularly when you are trying out something new, you will first, just as in the dream, fall flat on your face. A falling dream happens again and again if you are fighting against your own limitations. It is very helpful to change falling dreams into flying dreams.

According to Freud, falling dreams are always sexual. In the case of women, the question revolves around giving in to erotic desires (fallen women). Freud has dealt with the symbol of falling extensively in his *Interpretation of Dreams*.

Tarot card: The Tower.

Fame: Dissatisfaction and longing for acceptance.

Family: Fulfillment of the need for protection and security, as in **Notice-of-Intention-to-Marry**, **Bureaucrat**, **Tree Trunk**, **Sidewalk**, and **Parents' House**. On an objective level, the "own" family that is often unconsciously experienced aggressively. On a subjective level, needs, emotions, and partly reflecting the characteristics of self. It can also refer to other groups (at work, friends, etc.)

According to Freud, a symbol for secrets.

Farm: Turning toward nature, as in **Field, Ear (of corn), Farmer**. The "innate" side of the dreamer (the instinctive urges). Acceptance and integration of instinctive urges, material success, grounding, and health.

Farmer: For city people this usually indicates a longing for a more natural and simpler life, similar to **Field, Ear (of corn), Farm**. This dream image almost always addresses a person's productivity (in the widest sense of the word), because the farmer plants in order to reap. What do you have to do so that *you* can reap?

Fashion: Personal style or vanity, as in **Jewelry** and **Mask**.

Fasting: Refusal to accept anything from the world around you. Vanity. You ought to take up less space. The motive for the fast is important.

Fat: Too much of a good thing. Often combined with disgust.

Father: Chief, Teacher, King. A person who teaches the laws of life. The archetypal father figure stands for the need for security, order, authority, and achievement (Mars) and awareness/consciousness (Sun).

Having it appear in dreams is often an expression of a bad conscience. If the dreamer has a problematic relationship with his father, the father in the dream would appear as the **Pope**, or as Almighty God-the Father, who guides and controls the dreamer's world.

According to Jung, the image represents the one who generates and creates, the intellectual principle, the one who gives life.

Faucet: Not only in Freud's understanding, a phallic symbol.

Fax: Effective communication, working through information received. The power to communicate, not least about emotional concerns. Perfect symbol for **Transference**, which plays a prominent role in psychoanalytical dream interpretation.

Fear: We are confronted with many different fears in dreams, but they always refer to obstacles that are a mirror of our everyday—often unconscious—fears and insecurities. Nightmares often have physical causes; we have eaten too much, smoked too much, drunk too much alcohol. Often it is fear of illness (hypochondria), that needs to be overcome. It is important to determine what made you become frightened.

Usually, this is about literal fear, or about undoing a mistake. On the other hand, such a dream might also suggest letting go of unnecessary fears. Fear can escalate into nightmares, showing the way to personal development. Fear is also connected to being too narrow, and is usually a sign that the dreamer is in search of a more broad, liberated alternative to his or her present lifestyle.

Feast: Longing for social contact, as in **Communion**. Eating can refer to all kinds of needs that you are trying to satisfy.

Feather: Travel, ease of movement, with which you can let yourself go gently, as in **Leaf.** Compare also **Bed, Pencil/Fountain Pen.** A white feather means innocence.

Fence: Isolation; or feeling secure, or feeling restricted. See **Wall.**

Fern: Recreation and vacation. A good time to bring into reality what you have planned.
   Folklore: A luxurious plant means that nature will be on your side.

Ferry: A sign of transition (sometimes also initiation) that plays a major role in fairy tales, mythology, and dreams. The ferry brings you to the other shore, traveling to another world. See **Bridge.** A new goal for your life's journey.
   Folklore: Warning of danger.

Field (area): Symbol for women—your field of work/profession. (This patriarchal interpretation, which often does not correspond to the dreamer's conviction, is nevertheless appropriate, because our internal attitudes do not change at the same rate as our ideology. Our conscious awareness is much more eager to change than our subconscious).

Fallow or ravaged field: stagnation, grief, and troubles. Green field: work and good compensation, growth. Overgrown field: disorder in the inner as well as the outer world.

Field (as in cornfield): Productive stage in life, particularly when the furrows are clearly visible. It may be the symbol of a fertile woman or mother (Gaia, the earth mother, and also Demeter). Pointing toward work (one has to work the field). Hard, crusty clods indicate problems or paralysis.

For people living in a city, it is often also the symbol of rustic romanticism, similar to **Farmer**, and **Furrow**, wanting to escape from the city, becoming interested in the country for environmental reasons.

Fight: Symbolizes a problematic way you deal with aggression. Behind it is almost always the wish to deal with aggression more effectively and more constructively. Contradictory thoughts and actions.

File: Coming to terms with something difficult that you want to smooth out, as in **Iron**.

Files/Records: A desire for, or fear of, order and consistency. It appears frequently when life is chaotic. This image also points to emotional stress; much has accumulated. Pay attention to how thick or thin the file folder is. It might also be a sign of a compulsive personality, similar to **Admiral**. Do you always have to keep everything in perfect order? Or are you unable to keep order in your life? It could be either a case of your ego (your unconscious) raising its head, or a justifiable symbolic expression of the feeling that either the state (as father symbol) or an institution is placing limitations on you.

Film: Movie Theater, TV. Here the emphasis is on "emotional stories." Possibly the mirror image of the dreamer. Attempt to get away from internal images.

Filth/Dirt: The desire for cleansing (due to a bad conscience), as in the expression "to wallow in dirt." According to Freud, sexuality. This association, however, was mostly relevant during the Victorian era at the beginning of this century.

Finger: Manual dexterity. According to conventional psychoanalytical theory, a phallic symbol.

Folklore: Suggests that looking at your own fingers, in a dream, means you want to fight.

Fire: A frequently occurring dream when fearing or yearning for inner fire or passion. Warning: Be careful, because here, it is always the fire of life that is being addressed. Either it is destroying something or it is giving a signal. Accumulated urges, as in **Termination, Attack, Surf, Electricity, Defloration, Flames, Greed, Harem, Skin Rash, Wire (High-Voltage),** and **Hooker.**

Fire Brigade: The dreamer is fascinated with **Fire,** but not admitting to it. Fear of too much internal fire.

Firefly: Light, extending kindness and help. As in **Spark,** here it can also mean spark of the soul.

Fireplace: Confined physical urges; family; comfortable home; also **Fire.**
    According to Freud, a female sexual symbol.

Firewood: Wood. Impetus, a short affair.

Fireworks: Playing with illusion. Points to how special an occasion is. Blending passion, lust, orgasm, and enthusiasm.

Folklore: Be careful.

Fish/Fisherman/Fishing: See **Angel, Ocean**. Living life from the depths of the soul and emotions, because fish live in the depths of the sea. Feeling like "a fish in water"—being in one's element. One feature of fish is their wholeness, since they live exclusively in water (the emotional sphere). Fish are usually voracious eaters and immensely productive. They have no eyelids, sleep with their eyes open, and are always attuned to the world around them. Some fish change their colors according to the circumstances. They are creatures of high sensibility, but they are also cold and can't be held. In a broader sense, the symbolism of the astrological sign of the fish is also relevant here, where oceanic feelings, trust and mistrust, and the contradictions of willpower and self-defense are at issue. Also, chaos and the absurd belong here, as well as faith—including superstition and disbelief.

If you see yourself fishing, what did you catch? A small fish indicates small **Booty:** a big fish, big booty. The fisherman is trying to catch the content of the soul. Since ancient times, in China fish have been a sign of fertility. As far back as Babylonian times, fish appearing in dreams were considered phallic symbols. According to 2nd century dream interpreter Artemidorus, a dead fish represents lost hope.

The fish is also a Christian symbol. The point when Spring entered the constellation of the fish coincided with the beginning of Christianity. The salmon of wisdom is part of Irish mythology.

In psychoanalysis, the fish is a symbol of male sexuality. According to Jung, if you are the fish, you can renew yourself in the **Water** (emotions). Also, according to Jungian psychoanalysis, the fish is the symbol of wholeness. It symbolizes the total person of the dreamer and, more to the point, the emotional side of sexuality. Jung also believed that fish are like thoughts and hunches, which surface from the unconscious. (In the fairy tale "The Fisherman and His Wife," we find the "wishing-fish.")

Fishing: Repressed aggression, or too little aggression, as in: **Attack, Surf, Fire, Flames, Violence, Greed,** and **Wire (High-Tension).** Feelings of inferiority, repression, as in **Termination, Attack, Harem, Skin Rash,** and **Prostitute.** Fear of war or aggression, but also desperate search for physical or personal closeness.

Folklore: A warning.

Fishing Rod: Being dependent on somebody, or wanting somebody to depend on you, often with sexual undertones (the happy hooker). To reach for something way down deep (**Water**). Quiet and contemplation.

Folklore: Disappointment or reaching for success.

Five: The fundamental human being, a person in harmony, because a person—hands and legs extended—forms a pentagram. Also related to the "five senses." The connection between the female and the male. Five also means "Quintessence," the fundamental sense, the essential. In China, the number of the center.

Flag: Passion, intellect (**Air, Wind**) and idealism; but also war. See **Standard**.

Flame: See **Flames, Blaze**.

Flames: See **Fire**. A positive sign of your vitality if the flame is under control; otherwise, aggression and discharge of physical urges. According to ancient Egyptian dream interpretation, great monetary gain.

According to Freud: A symbol of male genitalia (since the oven is considered the womb of the woman).

Flashlight: See **Light**. One is unable to tolerate the dark side of the Self or others. At the same time, however, it is a light in the darkness, a symbol of insight and hope.

Flea: Overexcitement, stress, as in **Fly.** A hint that you need to pay more attention to the small things in life.

Fleet (of ships): An emotional conflict situation, fear of emotional conflict.
Folklore: In almost all cases, a ship at sea is a bad omen.

Float: Going forward by the most simple means on the **Water** of emotions. The dreamer should not just drift along. This is dangerous, because when you're floating, it is difficult to steer. On the other hand, you may trust that the water will carry you. It is very important how the trip is proceeding.
Folklore: An interesting life.

Flood: Being overwhelmed; an enemy is about to attack. Fear of drowning in emotions; being thrown back into the world of animals; being thrown back into the world of physical urges. The female archetype. The powers of the intellect and reason standing against the assault of nature on the conscious, civilized life. You need to learn how to "swim," which means being ready to swim in the water like a **Fish.** Both meanings are included here: to swim, and to give in and flow with the river of life, staying flexible.

A sign of being very emotional. You are overwhelmed and swept away and, in the dream, you are afraid of this, even if you would really like to give in. Incoming and outgoing tide: the rhythm of tension and relaxation in everyday life.

Feelings seem to be taking over. A feeling of being imprisoned because of physical drives and unconscious needs. Warning of psychotic behavior. If this dream image is accompanied by fear and appears often, psychotherapy is indicated.

Seething emotions. A frequent dream symbol when fearful of one's own emotions.

Floor: External and internal foundation, personal attitude. Always refers to being grounded, as in **Foot** and **Basement.** The floor can also be seen as a barrier between you and the ground. See **Stone/Clay Floor.**

Floor (in the sense of a four-story building): Level of awareness, level of physical presence.

Flower: Traditional symbol for emotions ("Say it with flowers"). Beauty and fertility. Growing and fading away, like life. Expectations of and hope for love and relationships. Important is the type and the color of the flower. Red roses point to sexual love, white roses and other flowers point to innocence, blue flowers to the strength of the soul and emotions. Snowdrops point to overcoming the cold of winter, asters to autumn and death. Picking flowers is considered a symbol of sexual experience.

In the Middle Ages, flowers with broken stems meant sexual intercourse. In India, in dream interpretations, the flower is the symbol of the highest pleasure. In Freud's dream interpretations, the flower is dealt with extensively and symbolizes women, tenderness, female genitals and genitals in general, as in **Blossoms** (see Anaïs Nin's *The Delta of Venus*).

According to C. G. Jung, flowers represent emotions/feelings.

Flowerpot: Domesticity and cultivating nature. The quality of caring and nurturing. On the other hand, this symbol might also point to substituting for the real thing; the flower in the pot is nature being controlled (and is therefore, in reality, a substitute for nature).

According to Freud, the symbol for women, as in **Vase.**

Flowing: To drift, not wanting to control anything, similar to **River** and **Water.** Are you living your life? Or are you swimming with the tide?

Flute: One of the oldest musical instruments, its sound is said to cast spells over people and gods (*The Magic Flute*). Harmony, accord, beauty, and tenderness. Let more joy come into your life. The flute is also a phallic symbol (Pan's instrument) and may sometimes indicate erotic self-absorption.

Fly: Overstimulated nerves. Resistance, nervousness, and slight irritation, as in **Flea.** May also point to **Flying.** Small things that can be very annoying.
Folklore: Sign of an unsurmountable obstacle.

Flying: Overdramatization or fleeing from a problematic situation. Looking for clarification in difficult situations. **Flying** and **Falling** appear in **Abyss, Elevator,** and **Trap,** usually in nightmares; or as in: **Brook, Leaf** and in part **Parachute,** during very pleasurable liberation dreams. In case of teenagers: often a sign that too much is being asked of them and that they are being pressured to succeed. These dreams are often like being intoxicated, having a sense of being elevated, and a lightness: like being in love. Many ancient myths show the connection between flying and sexuality, and while flying today has become a commonplace activity, the old interpretations are still true (see *Fear of Flying* by Erica Jong). Now modern symbolic interpretations of flying include the image of worldliness, expansive ideas, and communications. Flying is also seen as a symbol of creative ideas. This image may also be a warning not to become too aloof and removed from reality through fantasizing. The dream may also be a challenge for either being too earthbound or taking flight into a greater dimension.

In Egypt, dreams of flying were interpreted as fleeing from difficulties. In ancient Greece and Rome, dreams of flying were seen as passionate love.

According to Freud, they were dreams of sexual desire and erection (Freud dealt with this extensively). He saw dreams of flying exclusively as desire for sex. Some modern dream experts interpret flying dreams exclusively as a desire to get away from problematic situations, or to cross one's own boundaries. Some researchers believe that in our dreams we go back to preborn states, make contact with the state of birds, and realize our innate ability to fly. Another contemporary dream researcher, Jack Maguire, believes that most dreams about flying are just a sign that we want to recuperate and refresh ourselves.

Foal: Enjoyment of life.
Folklore: Birth of a child.

Foam/Froth: This image is connected to the Venus symbol, **Water** and **Air** fusing emotion and intellect and representing redemption. The same symbol, however, might reveal a tendency toward unrealistic ideas and plans—"the hot air merchant"—indicating a tendency to blow things out of proportion, to exaggerate; or it may simply point to necessary cleansing.

Fog: Lack of orientation and lack of focus. Here, something needs to be explained more clearly and made conscious. Insecurity and deception. There is something you don't understand or which confuses you. The fog, however, also means creativity—something new is produced.
Astrology: A symbol of Neptune.

Fold: Usually a female sexual symbol. Not everything is going as smoothly as you would like. Do you have something to iron out?

Food: Physical and emotional strength and energies. You are feeding the animal side in you.

Nourishment for body and soul. The kind of food you see is urgently needed for your soul. For instance, dreaming about **Meat** refers to drives and animalistic needs. Chocolate, on the other hand, or other sweets suggest being more open to love.

Food (stored): Fear of deprivation; difficulties, and poverty, as in **Savings, Coin, Counterfeit Money**. You don't trust what you have, or are trying to protect it. But you have additional resources and energies at your disposal.

Fool: Symbol of wisdom. Since the Middle Ages, the Fool has been the personification of sin. In some periods, he was even compared to the devil. The Fool is considered a symbol of carnal sin—a sex-crazed, lecherous person—with such characteristics as a weak will and an obsession with sexual drives. The Fool in early times was thought of as the counterpart and complement to the king. In the Tarot, the number of the card is the "0," implying emptiness and at the same time completion. The wisdom of the Fool is the wisdom of the hour "0," of spiritual virgin land. It is the sense in nonsense. During a dream the Fool often expresses a very strong loyalty to himself. So the message might be that you want to be able to laugh more—about yourself and others. See **Carnival**.

Foot: Leg. Your own point of view. Independence (to stand on your own feet). Always a symbol for being grounded, as in **Basement** and **Floor**.

According to Freud, phallic symbol.

Astrology: Sign of the Fish.

Football/Soccer: Confrontation. The **Ball** expresses concentrated vitality and/or your own center. Here, the question is: Are you kicking *yourself*? Or are you bringing yourself into the game? It is important what position you play: quarterback, referee, fan, and so on.

Foreign Countries/Abroad: The **Other**, the foreigner. The dreamer must deal with the confrontation of something new. A foreign country always is the "foreign land" within ourselves. A trip abroad and vacation when overworked. What does the foreign land symbolize to you?

Foreign Language: The speech of **Other;** also the unknown part of ourselves. Something is not understood, or you are unwilling to understand. Your task lies in the translation and therefore the understanding of the unknown and the foreign. Should you show more understanding? Or are you too understanding?

Forest: See **Tree.** A frequent dream symbol of the unconscious. Walking the forbidden path in the forest might cause us to be swallowed up and swept away by drives and instincts. The forest is a scary, potentially dangerous place where mysterious beings roam. It is also a place of transition (in Dante's *Divine Comedy*, for instance, a forest is found in front of the gates of Inferno, as well as at the end of Purgatorio and at the beginning of Paradiso). On the other hand, this symbol indicates the attempt to make contact with the unconscious. See also **Hiding Place.**

Fork: Usually points to eating (particularly when you're actually hungry during your sleep). The devil and Neptune both carry a pitchfork (the three prongs are a symbol of the ancient trinity that represents Unity; see also **Three**). As a garden fork, to dig down into your own depth, grounding, also work.

As a "fork in the road," it is a symbol for your ability to make decisions and to differentiate.

As a tuning fork, it is a symbol of harmony (the right note) and orientation. Or—what or whom are you "forking" up/over?

Folklore: A sign of a fight.

Fort: Lodge. Protection, search for a home, and being indestructible. Memories of vacation, longing for relaxation. You want or *have to* protect yourself; or you are too protective: you are withdrawing.

According to Freud, a symbol for women and femininity in general.

Fortune: See Wealth. Abilities and talents.
Folklore: The greater your fortune, the greater the effort you have to make in the future in everyday life.

Fountain: Beauty and harmony; a sexual symbol.

Fountain/Waterspout: Water. Fertility, male sexuality.

Four: A symbol of wholeness, according to Jung. The four seasons, the phases of the moon, the four directions on a compass, particularly also the four elements—fire, air, earth, and water—the four limbs, the four functions of the conscience. Four creates order in chaos. It is the symbol for becoming whole and becoming one, in contrast to **Multiplicity**.

For some Native Americans four is a holy number, the number for everything beautiful (for instance, in some traditions a prayer must be spoken four times). In alchemy the process of transformation happens in four stages. According to legend, the river in paradise separates into four rivers.

According to Jung, four always points out that we are on the way to becoming what we really are. Four symbolizes completeness and totality: the four temperaments and, in Christianity, the four directions of the **Cross** and Christ surrounded by four apostles.

Fowl: Ordinary life. Feathered animals could possibly point to the capriciousness of physical urges.

Fox: A lover or lecherous person, a sexy female. Great instincts. Clever, cunning, calculating, and smart. The fox is considered our soul guide and companion on our life's journey. It points to our childhood. A rabid fox means uncontrollable instincts.

According to the 2nd century dream interpreter Artemidorus, bad reputation.

According to early Christian view, the fox is the devil.

According to Jung, a "foxy," cunning old man.

Foxglove (plant): Death and rebirth, medicine, and poison.

Folklore: Usually a sign of good fortune.

Fragrance/Smell: First, check to find out if you were smelling a real fragrance during sleep. Dreaming about fragrances is very rare. If you do, it is usually a sign that you are enjoying life and your sensuality. The type of fragrance indicates how you feel about the subject or object that gives off the fragrance (there are some smells we simply can't stand).

It was not only Freud who insisted that fragrances are very effective in bringing back memories of places and people.

Frame: Limitation or vanity.

Freak: Behavior that is unbecoming. An outsider, as in **Anarchist;** broken. Unlikely romance. See **Fool.**

Freemason: Good connections, power, and secrets, Are you searching for your own principles or your own significance?

Freezing to Death: See **Ice.**

Friend: Favorable news, something lost has been found. Longing for social contact, similar to **Companion.**

Usually unknown aspects of your own personality. Wanting more support.

Frog: Frequent dreams of young girls. Fear of sexuality. At issue is the emotional connection to her sexual partner (as in the fairy tale "The Frog Prince"). Because the shadow—something she is most repulsed by—is dissolved, she is changed. This is partly to be seen as a challenge to overcome our disgust and then to watch what happens. Conquering this feeling usually leads to a sense of self-liberation, particularly in the area of sexuality.

Men seldom experience this dream. Men usually dream of toads. If a man dreams of a frog, it usually indicates cowardice.

Folklore: Business success.

Frost: Suggests making peace with someone. It may be a warning that you are too cold, as in **Ice.**

Fruit: First of all, the fruit of the life of the soul. Erotic sexual needs. A ripe fruit means being sexually balanced and enjoying life. A rotten fruit means an inferiority complex. Eat more healthfully. The body needs fruit and vitamins.

When used in a derogatory way, insecurity about one's sexuality.

The erotic in adventure, success, and luck. A reminder of the sensual pleasures of summer. The first thing that you can and must pick—if you don't, you are missing your chance. That which is juicy and full. Fruit that is unpalatable or rotten points to problems—often illness—and danger.

Ancient Egyptian dream interpretation: Pleasant encounter. Classical interpretation: Personal luck, when fruit is picked or collected.

According to Freud, women's breasts.

Frying pan: Domesticity, as with all symbols that have to do with food and eating.

According to Freud, as with everything that can be put on top of the stove, a sexual symbol.

Funeral: Frequent dream symbol. Something is supposed to die, to be put aside, to be completed to make room for the new, as in **Baby, Birth.** (Here however, the emphasis is more on something "new" being about to happen). This symbol is similar to **Abortion, Amputation.** Differences are being buried, unrealistic wishes or tiresome, improper habits are being cast off. Possibly a relationship is dying, as in **Death, Divorce, Abortion, Goodbye.** If it is your own funeral, it usually means that the old "you" is dying.

Fur: Symbolizes nature and femininity (*anima*), desire to cuddle. See **Furs.**

Fur Coat: Prosperity, luxury, as in **Oysters, Champagne,** and **Aristocrat.** Self-confidence, vanity, and need for admiration. Important what kind of fur it is.

Furniture: The dreamer's qualities, in the sense of the "internal furniture" of the soul and one's own identity. The type of furnishings and their condition is important.

Furrow: A female sexual symbol. Obstacles are in your way. You must reach down and deal with your shadow.

The opposite of plow. A city person's romantic longing for the natural country life, as in **Field, Ear of corn,** and **Farm.**

Furs: If you know the animal the fur is from, it refers to the animal's character. If you don't know the fur's origin, then it means a longing for coziness and warmth.

According to Freud, pubic hair; according to Jung, the animal within.

Future: Often a real forecast when the dream takes place in the future. Also, a time when you are able to consciously experience intuition, fears, and expectations of the future.

Folklore: An old quarrel is being resolved.

Gable (of a roof): Good advice and security, as in **Arch**.

Gag: Restriction and lack of freedom, similar to **Cage**, **Prison**, **Shackles**. Restricted movements are particularly emphasized here.

Folklore: A dream about obstacles.

Gallows: Hanging up your burden. Or if you are being hanged, extreme danger. Drastic, ancient symbol for punishment; however, it need not always be a nightmare. It could be a relief.

Game: A suggestion to take life a little easier, not to be so serious. It is an image of the liveliness and the ups and downs of life. Communication, a warning against being too superficial. Longing for contact. See **Ball (game)**.

Gap/Opening: Female sexual organ, or a symbol of obstacles.

Garbage: Desire for cleansing. A need to discard internal refuse that is burdensome. Similar to **Abortion**. Much has accumulated and must be emptied: emotional garbage and everyday garbage. Suffering because of involvement with the environment (and yourself). You are making an important discovery: it is in the "garbage" that we find the gold of meaning; in the inconspicuous and rejected lies the chance for self-knowledge. As C. G. Jung has stated, in accepting the rejected shadow, we take the first step to individuation.

Garden: See **Field.** The garden is the place where our soul joins nature. It symbolizes longing, fertility, and a satisfying love life. A place of harmony and relaxation (as well as sin, as in the "Garden of Eden"), a place to become grounded and a place of civilized nature, corresponding to a "civilized" inner life. It is the domestic, fenced-in area in contrast to the untamed **Field,** or even **Forest.** Stepping into a garden is like retreating from the harshness of the outside world, looking for protection and relaxation. In Egypt the garden has always been the symbol for woman.

According to Freud, female sexuality.

Gardener: Relationship to a partner or to one's own nature.

Gas: Influences that are trying to poison you. Something obscure (invisible) that creates fear. But there is a positive side to this dream image: you are becoming conscious of something you have been unaware of until now. What could it be?

Gasoline: Physical and emotional energy, drive, nutrition. Impetus.

Gas Station: See **Tank**. A place where you can fill up with new energy. Taking a rest.

Gate: See **Door**. A symbol of transition and a suggestion that something new is coming. See **Threshold**. According to Freud, if the dreamer is a neurotic person, the image has unmistakable sexual meaning (vagina).
Astrology: A Saturn symbol.

Gazelle: Beautiful woman, girl.

General/Colonel: See **Chief**, except more aggressive or authoritarian. See **Ruler.**

Genital Organ: Its obvious meaning concerns sexuality. On the other hand, every actual sexual image points to the present situation of the dreamer. Often other energies, like love or fear, power and money express themselves in the form of sexual symbols. Freud makes a very clear distinction between genital sexuality and general sexuality. On one hand, he took a broader view: "First, sexuality is freed from a much too narrow connection to the genitals and seen in a much wider sense as a pleasure-seeking bodily function, which is only secondarily put to the service of procreation. Secondly," Freud continues in his *Self Portrait*, "sexual stirrings are all those merely tender and friendly emotions for which our language coined the many-faceted word 'Love.'" What this means is that, for Freud, sexuality is pleasure-seeking, all-encompassing, and expressed by the whole body, internally and externally. He was of the opinion that sexual urges and the tender feelings of love are connected and that one part is not to be withheld at the expense of the other. In that sense it is a question of "separating sexuality from the genitals," of sensuality, of saying goodbye to the notion of "always searching for one part only," when so much more is worth having. At the same time, Freud emphasizes the difference between general, unorganized sexuality and genital sexuality. It is only in the genital phase that "the full expression" of all drives/urges (and not only part of them) is achieved. See **Erection, Intercourse, Sexuality.**

Gerbil: See **Guinea Pig/Hamster.**

Getting Lost: Refers to the search for a proper solution in situations that are causing you great confusion. See **Odyssey, Detour**.

Ghost: Here, it usually means the so-called "spirit of life," which makes up a distinctly human life. In addition, it might possibly point to unused or wrongly applied intellectual activities or actions. You are chasing a phantom. This is a warning against illusions and wrong insights. Creatures from the world of fairy tales are always somewhat frightening. They may be helpful or have bad intentions. Ghosts are often an expression of guilt feelings and pangs of conscience. If these images appear continually and are frightening, seek professional advice. The task connected with these dream images is often to find a better understanding and a more creative use of your intellectual powers.

According to Freud, they appear most often as women (in a white nightgown).

Folklore: Times of troubles are ahead.

Giant: An archetypal symbol of an overpowering father figure, but also of the universal beings that usually appear in the plural ("they" have no individuality). They are the antithesis to the gods, with whom they are in constant battle. They know only sensual pleasures and are greedy. See **Monster**, **Dinosaur**.

According to Jung, in a child's dream the giant represents adulthood. In that sense, giants are a symbol of future changes and growth that, in a young person's perception, appear "gigantic."

Gift/Present: Relationships to the outside world should be improved. It is a matter of sharing joy and the joy of sharing. Life as a gift. See **Birthday**.

Gin: Tendency toward addiction.
Folklore: A short life and many changes.

Giraffe: That which is special, faraway, and exotic. You wish for a better view, to stand out among the crowd, or not to be treated as a child. But pay attention to the distance between head and body!

Girl: Often an erotic dream. In the case of women, it points to their feminine side or to childhood. What is addressed here is usually the lightheartedness of a child's life. In the case of both men and women, it symbolizes the feminine side of the dreamer. When the soul appears in a dream in the form of a girl, it usually points not only to the natural lively and innocent side of you, but also to the undeveloped and childish side.

Giving Up/Getting Out: Fleeing or approaching something, as in **Emigration**. Not wanting to be part of something anymore or not wanting to be doing something in a particular way. What's important is what you want to exit from, and what your feelings are.

Glacier: See **Ice**.

Gladiator: Aggression and inferiority complex, compensated for with heroic dreams.

Glass: The vessel of spirit. Transparent, clear, a sign of spirituality. Fragile and sensitive. Glass containers, glass, and a crystal goblet (the Grail) represent being conscious. A broken glass means injury and destruction of innocence—in the sense of **Defloration**—but also luck, as long as it is not a mirror. Occasionally, a glass is a symbol for frailty in the sense of impermanence and bewilderment. In alchemy, the stone of the Wise Men, lapis, is also called glass (*vitrum*), because it was seen as spiritual. See also **Vase**.

According to Freud, glass symbolizes female genitalia.

Glass House: Greenhouse. Protection, as in **Glass Wall**. A message to be more open and transparent. Similar to the **Container** in which transformation and growth takes place, in people as well as plants. **The uterus.** The glass coffin in "Snow White and the Seven Dwarfs." In mythological terms, a glass house is also seen as a sweat lodge, where the transformation of the prince takes place.

Glass Wall: A frequent dream symbol when feeling cut off from others or objects; lack of contact. Something is seen as being unattainable. Re-examine your goals or ask if you have the necessary energies. In some instances, opposite image to **Mirror**.

Globe: See **Atlas, Ball**. Pleasure of traveling. You are looking for universal, global solutions.

Glove: Being detached from your actions. Reserve and an often exaggerated need for security. Fear of direct touch and danger of isolation. A frequent symbol in cases of the irrational fear of AIDS.

Throwing a glove to the ground is an ancient sign of anger and a provocation to fight.

Glue: You want to put together something that belongs together and has fallen apart. Something is being repaired. Are you being held by something or someone, or are you holding on to somebody tightly? The question of **Liability** and **Responsibility** in every form is being addressed here also.

Goal: As in **Target**, this image refers either to very focused behavior, or to a necessary distance. See **Marksman**.

Goat/Billy Goat/Pan: This image symbolizes wild drives and urges and our sexual energies, with all their joys and troubles. See **Buck**. In addition, this is also a symbol for the outsider—the so-called "scapegoat." The female goat, by the way, is a well-known image of a quarrelsome woman; but, strangely enough, it also stands for adaptability and modesty.

Goblet: See **Cup**.

God/Gods: In the form of an actual image, these dreams are very rare. Rather, the feeling of a God presence is a sign that a new state of consciousness has been reached. How are you dealing with authority?

Gold: The sun of the soul and immortality, but it also might point to blindness, **Greed**, and materialism.

According to Freud, usually connected to feces. According to Jung and his successors, a symbol of whatever is most precious to the dreamer, his most prized possession, his higher self. See **Diamonds**, **Money**, **Heart**, **Sun**.

Goldfish: See **Gold**. The special **Fish**. Life in the water of the emotions brings forth the true essence of your personality.

Golf: Wealth and competition.

Gondola: As in the case of **Swing**, a gondola points to playful fantasies in matters of love, and also to adventure. Memories of holidays often indicate it is time to take a vacation.

Goodbye (saying): Changes in the way you live and questions about your responsibilities. Separating from something important—a person, behavior, emotions—is imminent, has taken place, or is necessary. Compare this to **Corpse**, **Death**, **Abortion**, **Sword**, **Divorce**, or **Funeral**.

Folklore: A good sign, because you are letting go of something.

Goose: A young girl, as in **Daisy.** Stupid goose, stupidity. In ancient Egyptian creation mythology, the goose represented—together with the universal egg—a symbol of origin. The Ur god Amun was depicted in the form of a goose. For the Greeks and Romans, the goose stood for vitality and fertility, leading to the term: "silly goose" for a young girl. In addition, the goose was the divine animal of Aphrodite and was sacrificed to the god of fertility. In antiquity, it was a symbol not only of wisdom, but also of marital love. The St. Martin's Day goose is closely connected to the idea of sacrifice and mercy. To this day, a goose appearing in a dream is seen as being connected to love, sacrifice, and fertility. In the fairy tale "Jack and the Beanstalk," the goose that lays the golden eggs is the symbol of something precious, something that we long for. In Celtic myth the goose and the **Swan** are messengers from another world, and for that reason a goose could never be used as food in Brittany. The goose is also an ancient symbol for the initiated.

Folklore: A positive sign.

Gout: Diminished movements, lack of freedom and mobility, as in **Prison** and **Cave**. Also, part of your own nature has remained unconscious and "lacks guidance."

Folklore: Avoid overexertion.

Government: On one hand, the image has the same meaning as **Director**. But attitudes toward authority are also implied. Do you want to control and govern your environment, or do you feel that you are controlled by it? See **Ruler**.

Grain: See **Rye**. Grain in general symbolizes mental/intellectual and physical needs; but it may also—through an association with the "grim reaper"—point to the transforming power of **Death**. This may also address the question of personal productivity. See **Field, Harvest**. Bountiful harvest means self-confidence and health, crop failure the opposite. A field of grain points to the "Fields of Life" and the "Field of Experience." Here is a chance to find out what you have to work on. If you are a city person, the image of peace and quiet indicates a longing for a more natural life and relaxation. It relates to the idea that life bears fruit and brings maturity. Grain nourishes.

Folklore: A sign of luck. Success after hard work.

Grandfather: See **Grandmother**. The all-powerful **Father** or the archetypal father, in contrast to the personal father. The father principle.

Grandmother: Very much like the symbol of **Mother**, but much more oriented to the past. The all-powerful mother, the archetypal mother (the mother principle) in contrast to the merely personal mother. Grandmothers, like **Grandfathers**, are often wise guides and advisers.

Grand Piano: Well-known symbol for harmony and Venus. See **Piano**.

Grapes: Naturalness, a productive life, fertile nature. See **Fruit**, **Wine**.

Grape Wine: A symbol of luck.

Grass: Growth, connection to nature, groundedness. Something that is deeply rooted. The condition of the grass is important. Fresh green grass means health; dried-out, crushed grass means dissatisfaction, illness; grass that is too high and growing wild means unrealistic ideas. Also, as in marijuana, a longing for freedom, enlightenment, and relaxation.

Grasshopper: See **Greed, Loss.**

Grave/Tomb: Fear of life, resignation and giving up. This symbol may refer to ancestors or to burial. What have you been burying? Or what is it that you should bury? Or should you unearth something? Also see **Death.**

Gravel: A dream of obstacles where it is difficult to get ahead. Gravel is part of the **Earth**, and points to matter and material.

Gray: The color of something as yet unconscious and undefined, a color-less mixture where light emerges from the dark. Blending contradictions, as in **Wedding**, where it mixes black (female) and white (male), so it is archetypal. Gray stands on the border between day and night, light and dark, and—in a dream—asks us to draw clear distinctions. Gray here may represent the unassuming; on the other hand, the inconspicuous gray may also point to the conspicuous, the essential, and the real in life. See **Mouse, Shadow.**

Greed: Be more moderate. Or: you think you have been short-changed. Repressed urges/drives. As in

Miser. Also a hint that you are ravenous, which is a sign of unreasonable needs for gratification. See **Wolf**.

Green: Color of nature. Something is growing out of a state of immaturity.

Greenhouse: An artificially regulated and controlled space where aggression is not allowed ("People who live in glass houses shouldn't throw stones"). Are you isolating yourself in order to create a specific result? You may be able to do this successfully for a certain amount of time, but beware! Isolation must not turn into a "prison." See **Glass House**.

Grenade: Images of grenades, as well as bombs and accidents, according to Jung, appear only where the dream represents an actual experience. It is the attempt of the unconscious to integrate the shock psychologically.

Grid/Bars: Separation tendencies, confinement.

Grinding Stone: A symbol for wanting to smooth out something. According to 2nd century dream interpreter Artemidorus, an encouragement to be more refined in your dealings with people.

Groom: Longing for a permanent relationship. A need for connecting with the other side of the Self. See **Bride/Bridegroom**.

Folklore: A warning of false friends.

Grotto: See **Cave**. The female. Grottos are also holy places and in that sense have magical meaning. See **Uterus**.

Guard: Defense and discipline, attention, and insight. See **Hermit**, **Dog**, **Bayonet**, **Lion**.

Guinea Pig/Gerbil/Hamster: Emotional functioning and sexuality are made trivial, diminished, and viewed from a distance. As children are given guinea pigs as pets, and they build up a relationship to them, here guinea pigs represent the beginning stage of the development of emotional functions.

Guitar: Passion and emotion. It often has a sexual meaning, as in **Violin** (female body). A playful self-portrait.

Gym: Do more for and with your body.

Gypsy: The wild and adventurous person within. At the same time, one of the oldest images of the scapegoat in our culture. The term "Gypsy" discriminates against the Siniti and Roma tribes, branding them as outsiders and "second-class citizens." This image in a dream often points to an immature masculinity.

Folklore: Luck, if the Gypsy is offering you something.

Gyroscope: Are you turning around in **Circles**? Points to the days of childhood and **Dance**.

Hail (bad weather): Well-known symbol for fighting.
  Folklore: Difficulty, disappointments.

Hair: Baldness, Beard. A symbol of wealth and fertility.
In mythology, cutting off the hair is the equivalent of

castration. Samson was robbed of his strength when Delilah cut off his locks. Hair for men is a sign of freedom; for women, long hair is a sign of femininity. According to Robert Bly, wild men and wild women are always covered with hair. Those who dream about "hairy" beings are on the way to satisfying their own nature, longing for vitality. This longing for "the wild energies" to be set free is clearly expressed in the musical *Hair*, which depicts the mythology of the sixties generation.

Today, hair often appears in dreams in connection with wanting to create a certain image, one that we would like to present to the outside world. It also may refer to "splitting hairs."

According to an ancient Indian interpretation, hair that has been cut off means grief and sorrow.

Also, hair-dreams are thought to be about close relatives. And, in addition, they may mean spiritual and intellectual property.

According to Freud, hair, as a secondary sexual characteristic, has phallic meaning. Also, according to Freud and Steckel in *The Language of Dreams*, dreaming of hair means castration.

In mythology, hair and beards play an important role. The chiefs of the Masai were afraid they would lose their supernatural powers when their hair or beards were cut. For many primitive tribes, hair was considered taboo. To be protected from danger means never getting your hair cut. Kings in Franconia (Germany) would lose their throne if they had their hair cut. Young warriors of Teutonic tribes could cut their hair and beard only after they had killed their first enemy. Hair, therefore, seems to mean power, strength, and magical vitality.

Folklore: Abundant hair means wealth; little or gray hair, troubles.

Hairdresser: See **Barber**.

Hairpiece: See **Hair, Mask, Head**. An attempt to change part of the personality you would like to hide—and cover your "baldness."

Hairpin: A deadly weapon of Japanese women against their husbands in bed. The hairpin represents order and vanity, as does all jewelry. See also **Hair.**

Hall: Sense of community and communication; or a representation of your head/mind and its intellectual abilities. As a meeting place, the hall symbolizes your sharing and openness to the outside world.

Communication and action. Often it is part of your-self that needs to be opened up. The function of the hall is important, and who is in the hall.

Hallway: You want to escape narrowness and restriction.

Ham: Hearty nutrition, substantial food, and the need for meat (real meat or flesh).

Symbolizes carnal thought; also a symbol for impurity. See **Pig**. Are you afraid of getting sick?

Folklore: Bad omen.

Hammer: Axe. Power, but also constructive endeavor. Vigor and drive, similar to **Hand.**

According to Freud, as with all tools, a symbol of masculine sexuality.

Hamster: See **Guinea Pig/Gerbil.**

Hand: Vigor and human endeavor, as in **Hammer.** Loss or injury to a hand means you're not active enough. According to classical psychoanalysis, the right hand is masculine, the left hand, feminine.

According to Freud, a phallic symbol. (Each finger, in Freud's view, could be a phallic symbol.)

Handkerchief: Security and order. Crying. Grief. With a handkerchief on hand, you are prepared for all situations. It often represents something comforting that one holds on to.

Folklore: Receiving a gift.

Hanging: As in hanging up clothes——cleaning, elevating, clarifying, and so on. If a *person* is being hanged, something must die. See also **Abortion, Amputation**. Something is suffocating or being strangled.

Hangman: You must root out something—guilt feelings, for instance. Do you have to do something? See **Execution, Murder, Death**.

Harbor: Protection from the storms of life. Coping with life during difficult times or anguish. A need for security, as in **Buoy, Anchor, Dam,** and **Family.** Also, inhibitions. A frequent dream symbol in marriage, but also a place of adventure and "disrepute." When a harbor is visited for a short time only, vitality and self-confidence.

Folklore: Happy times, or you are discovering falsehoods.

Harbor Pilot: Receiving help on your life's journey is

important. Or you are ready to take on a leadership role.

Hare/Rabbit: A rabbit needs protection; it is weak and fearful, but a symbol of fertility. It may also indicate a longing for nature, particularly for someone living in a city.

Harem: Repressed sexual urges or inhibitions (see **Rooster**). Desire for erotic sexual experiences and the desire to have one's sexuality accepted. Most of the time the sign of an inferiority complex.

Folklore: Something hidden is finding expression.

Harp: Festivities, contemplation. A symbol for heaven. The kind of music that is being played is important. Are you playing the harp yourself or is somebody else? Are you harping on something? Or is someone else?

Harvest: Desiring recognition, **Success,** and security, as, for instance, in **Shares, Stock Market,** and intellectual wealth. Here questions about your goals in life are raised. What is it you want to accomplish, to "harvest"? Short-term as well as long-term goals may be addressed here. If the dreamer is a city person, the image of an

Ear-of-corn or **Farm** might mean a romantic longing for the country and the simple life. Crop failures usually point to inferiority complexes.

Folklore: Luck (in love).

Haste: In dreams, in spite of hurrying, we usually never reach our goal. You are afraid you're missing something; pay attention to your plans, stop for a moment and deliberate. As with all dream images that have to do with time, remember that "time" is often only another word for limitation.

Folklore: A warning against impending danger, particularly accidents and fire.

Hat: Points to intellect, but also arrogance, as with all other symbols that have to do with the head. Vanity and self-expression, as with all symbols concerning jewelry. The type of hat points to the personality of the dreamer. See **Cap.**

According to psychoanalysis, a hat is a phallic symbol. Today it is more likely a symbol of the condom.

Hatchet: See **Axe.** Either bury it or excavate it. You have, or think you have, an axe to grind.

Hate: Repressed aggression, often due to a lack of boundaries. A lack of self-protection and a weak immune system. Are you afraid of confrontation? Or are you making your points too aggressively? It is necessary to find out what it is that you really hate. If a "hate dream" overwhelms you, and you have it often, consider consulting a psychologist.

Folklore: A sign that relief is in sight.

Hawk: Fear of future loss, or taking something that you are not entitled to. A symbol of aggression, like **Falcon.**

Hay: In the past it was in the hay loft that many people had their initial sexual experiences. Wealth.

Folklore: Very favorable, luck in all areas (for example, "making hay").

Head: Consciousness, a person's wealth. Mind and reason. The head almost always wants to rule. Ask yourself if you are repressing your intellect or using it at the expense of other functions—the emotions. for example. Or are you trying to go "headfirst through the wall"? Is it wise to lose your head, or is it best to prevent that from happening?

Ancient Indian dream interpretation speaks about

the need to be a ruler. According to Freud, the head is a symbol of masculinity. According to Jung, it is the archetypal symbol of self.

Astrology: The head is ruled by Aries.

Heart: Physical vitality, love, and courage; but also the organ of suffering. The heart has been identified as the place where emotions reside for many thousands of years. Are you doing something with your whole heart? In fairy tales and dreams the Wise Women and Wise Men pose this question to a person, animal, or other worldly being in trouble, "Are you coming to me with an open heart?" If the hero or the dream-self reacts with compassion and a good heart, the test has been passed.

Heat: A symbol for passion and drive. You either need more heat or should "cool down."

Heaven: The realm of spirits, thoughts, and intuition. Here, a person is confronted with two worlds, with head pointing toward heaven and feet planted on the ground. In that sense, this dream image points to the necessity of being more grounded; but it might also mean being in a good mood (heavenly feelings). The castle in the clouds is also pertinent, pointing to the conflict between fantasy and reality. Dark, cloudy skies symbolize depressive moods or lack of clarity, which is often about dreams and goals.

According to the *I Ching*, heaven represents the creative and powerful father. According to Freud, it is the place where wishes are fulfilled. According to Jung, it is the world in which one loses touch with the earth and with reality.

Hedge: Isolation, obstacle, but also natural living space. The border between two worlds (in mythology, witches are said to sit on hedges, one leg in one world, the other leg in the other world).

Heel: Your sore or vulnerable point, place of injury (Achilles' heel). Are you well grounded?

Heel (shoes): Being grounded, which makes you appear taller. Losing a heel indicates the loss of being grounded—either the negative "living above your means," or the positive wish to live more simply and easily.

Height/High: You are longing for excellence but are also afraid of overestimating your abilities. Or, don't be satisfied with mediocrity.

Hell: Archetypal symbol for sin, pangs of conscience, and guilt feelings that influence humans to this day. However, today the image of hell is connected to separation from self, a confrontation with the shadow or unacceptable living conditions. Fundamental changes in situations—particularly improvement of financial situations—are predicted. And there is a warning not to sell your soul. The positive aspect of the image of hell is connected to an image of fire inside the earth; this fire is the light that is born out of darkness. If the shadow is experienced in all its power and is endured, it turns to light and to truly mature experiences that can be integrated into your life, leading to a feeling of wholeness.

Hellfire: Repressed drives/urges.

Helmet: Protection of the head sometimes turns around and suggests that the head is the protector. But it also may mean a stubborn hardhead. Symbol for fear of war, as in **Shot, Bomb, Bayonet, Jet, Siege, Rifle.**

Hen: Feminine, maternal feelings, as in Mother, luck, honesty, and domesticity, as in **Baking, Roast,** and **Frying Pan. Cooking,** but also **Flowerpot, Porcelain, Apron,** and **Iron.** Fertility and fear of pregnancy, as in **Egg.**

Herb: According to Jung, herbs are always connected to healing. The herb is the alchemist's elixir, the universal medicine.

Herd: Are you following your inner voice or that of the general population? Symbol for community spirit or opportunism.

Heritage: Inheritance; precious quality. Talent and/or a task that has to do with the preservation of what has been handed down.
Folklore: Don't let others dominate you.

Hermit: Recluse; danger of losing contact with other people. Self-realization, purification, internalization, fleeing from the world; or self-determination and autonomy.

Hero/Heroine: A well-known desire for acceptance and validation, even if you are the hero or heroine yourself. If you see a hero, it would indicate that you are hoping for help, but pettiness is involved. Adventuresome, craving for admiration, exaggerated and immature masculinity and femininity; but also vitality and the ability to succeed, similar to **Hammer.**

It may also mean the opposite—that you feel like a failure—or you must be in control of everything. Dreams about heroes belong usually to so-called "big dreams," which take place in a person just prior to puberty, during midlife crisis, or before dying.

According to Jung, the hero is one of the important archetypes.

Hiding Place: A symbol of the unconscious. Repression and flight from problem situations. Need and desire to find and to be found.

Folklore: Bad news.

Highway: On life's journey, are you moving along fast, or are you stuck in a traffic jam? Are you rushing or taking a leisurely trip? As a traffic symbol, as in **Driving a Car** and **Auto**, it almost always has sexual undertones. Is the highway crowded (I must defend myself against many rivals) or is it empty (I am going my own way)? Are there any complications during the trip, like accidents, breakdowns, or difficult traffic situations? This would always correspond to problems in the present.

Hiker/Hiking: A peace walk, under your own power, moving ahead slowly but steady. Being on a hike also refers to the life's path—the pilgrimage where we learn and move closer to our goal. On the other hand, it implies distancing—the hiker moves away from his point of origin, or moves away from something else.

Hill: Small obstacles, good perspective. A female sexual symbol. A corn, or callus, aging and experiencing pressure. A hardening.

Folklore: Favorable for business.

Hip: Usually refers to being grounded. The hip is the connection between the upper and lower body—of the conscious and the unconscious.

Hippopotamus: Physical urges and emotional energies that have not yet been developed and are in need of differentiation. It could also mean encountering the massive and devouring energies of the unconscious, particularly physical urges and emotions.

The devouring mother or woman; the devouring unconscious, animalistic but also comic.

According to Jung, the monster, the evil, that wants to swallow you up.

Historic Personage: These dreams may be hidden messages and experiences that are influenced by the culture in which the person lived.

According to Freud, the personage is almost always the symbol for a father or mother. According to Jung, if the name of such a person is mentioned in your dream, you should find out about that person—who he was, who was around during his time, and what he did.

Hitting: Aggression. Energy shift and exchange. Desperate need for touch and an attempt at greater closeness. Immediacy and simplicity of method.

Hole: Female sexuality. During fertility rights in honor of the Great Mother, a phallic-shaped loaf of bread was baked and buried in a hole in the ground. In Rome, money was thrown into a hole in the ground that was a symbol of fertility. A deep hole also symbolizes loss, insecurity, and fear of the future. The hole might also represent a blind spot, that area within us (and sometimes in others) that we cannot see.

Mystical place of death and rebirth (lion's den). Graves as holes-in-the-ground.

According to Freud and Jung, it is an obvious female sexual symbol.

Home/Apartment: Area of life. A longing for a relationship that will bring security and a feeling of belonging.

A new home or apartment points to a new area in your life. It is a symbol for the inner Self.

Homeland: Security that originates from a particular place in the world that you have either searched for or found. This image is often related to **Parents,** and is similar to **Parents' House.** However, with increasing maturity, one usually dissolves the link to homeland and parents. Longing for quietness and a feeling of belonging.

Folklore: Prosperity.

Home (of My Own, A): Home and security; but also cutting the umbilical cord; emotional independence. Pay attention to the type of house: it often is the image of your own identity, your own personality.

Homeless Shelter: See **Asylum/Homeless Shelter.**

Honey: An ancient symbol for rebirth. Wealth, food, and, from antiquity to modern times, it has had a special sexual implication. (Mick Jagger's "I Am a Honey

Bee," for example. Honey stands for the term "loved one.") This symbol represents, in addition to sensuality, pleasure, luxury, well-being, and a general feeling of satisfaction. But it may also point to much work ("busy as a bee," needed to collect honey). It may also be a sign of wellness, particularly in connection with milk, as in paradise, the land of milk and honey.

Honeycomb: See **Honey**. Symbol of the desire of love.

Honoring: Recognition, as in **Applause**.

Hook: To get stuck on something and be unable to get away. A frequent dream symbol in cases of addiction. You feel emotionally imprisoned, as in **Cage, Prison**.

Hooker/Prostitute: As in **Bordello**, only more active. Your physical urges are clamoring for attention. This dream symbol appears particularly often when one's principles are too rigid. Desire for wild sex during times of involuntary isolation. Points to the difficulties the dreamer has in integrating love and sexuality. The symbol appears frequently in the dreams of "confirmed" bachelors and men with strong bonds to their mothers, as well as in the dreams of girls who have had a particularly sheltered upbringing. Acknowledge your urges and have the courage to be who you are!

According to Jung, it points to problems with one's shadow. According to Freud, repressed cravings in connection with living out one's sexuality.

Folklore: Winning in the lottery and, in general, luck in games involving money. See **Prostitution.**

Horn (musical instrument): A symbol of changes in life. Its meaning depends in part on the tone of the horn.

Horn (of an animal): The animal horn, in the past, was often connected with the devil. Today it is a sign (more or less) of a "healthy" ability to achieve. Also it may be related to the idea of giving somebody horns or cuckolding somebody.

Horse: Vitality, energy, mobility, and honor. It may mean speed, power, potency, and drive. Dynamism. According to 2nd century dream interpreter Artemidorus, luck in love. Other classical authors see in the horse a symbol for the woman the dreamer would love to possess physically. In late medieval books on dreams, hitching horses to a carriage meant that one had many love affairs.

According to Freud, a life as well as a death wish.

Folklore: Horses can be messengers of death. This shows the influence of Christianity, which stated that, in Celtic religion, God was the "Horse Goddess Epona."

Horseshoe: Well-known symbol for luck. Travel.

According to Freud, the outline of the horseshoe represents the opening of the female sex organ.

Hospital: You feel in need of help in times of emotional trouble. In rare cases, also a sign that you resent the type of help you get because it could be harmful. The hospital also stands for the dreamer himself. If you are the sick person, the type of illness will give insight about the problems you face. If you are the physician, your role as helper is addressed.

According to Jung, the hospital is the place where people are being taken care of, a symbol of mother.

Host/Hostess: In dreams, a host is often a friendly person who mirrors how the dreamer feels he is being accepted by others and how well he accepts himself. He also personifies the talent for creating a home in the world. Longing for social contact, as in **Friend,**

Companion. Wanting to be more socially acceptable and engaged.

In ancient Egypt, Great tasks are ahead. Pay more attention to the people around you and to your friends. However, the task may also be to be kinder to yourself and to be, in a way, your own guest.

Hotel: Symbolizes real or emotional changes; stations on the journey through life, a transitional period. Adventure and restlessness. Hotel personnel symbolize some of our own internal entities. People in the hotel show us sides of our own unconscious.

House: The emotional and physical constitution, characteristics, and body of the dreamer. A place of protection and security, the shelter of the soul. Individual rooms symbolize the different emotional functions. It is important to determine if **Door** and **Window** are open or closed and what the condition of the house is. The house is also a universal female sex symbol.

Compare this to C. J. Jung's 1909 dream in which—while exploring a house—he finds a flight of stairs that leads to the basement, where he discovers bones and human skulls. This dream was important because it led to Jung's idea of the collective unconscious: Attics and basements are places that hold what we repress; rooms in the upper part of a house provide perspective and vision; bedrooms indicate sexual content; the kitchen is the place where alchemy provides transformation; the bath is the place for cleansing; a workroom is the place for everyday situations.

Humor: See **Laughing.**

Hunchback: An old symbol for luck—"The Hunchback of Notre Dame." A period of great stress. You are challenged to become more straightforward, direct. But it may also be a suggestion that you unburden yourself.

Hunger: Physical, emotional, and mental deficiencies; wanting or being in need of **Food** in any form (usually emotional food).

Hunt: Hide. This image is an obvious reference to pursuing your own goals. In Greek/Roman mythology Artemis (Diana), the goddess of the moon and a feminine archetype, is also the goddess of the hunt and, therefore also a masculine archetype. In the past, the symbol of the hunt referred mainly to the masculine side of a woman. Today it is more a matter of emphasis on masculinity, self-worth, and connection to nature. Or you are feeling pressured and under stress. Are you being chased in the dream or are you chasing somebody? If you are chasing someone or something, then it would not be a sign of stress, but rather a reminder that life needs to be more exciting.

Hunter's Lookout: Overview or warning of self-elevation and arrogance.

Hunting Dog: See **Dog.**
Folklore: Bad omen.

Hurricane: Wild times, but they will pass.
Folklore: Bad omen, quarreling.

Hut: Like **House.** Looking for security, comfort or, alternatively, poverty.

Hyacinth: Demands for pleasure, a messenger of a pleasurable life.
According to mythology, the hyacinth grows and blooms at the door to the underworld.

Hyena: Reckless drives, urges, and aggression, pride of possession and unscrupulousness.

Ice: You are too "cool," too distant. Frozen emotions, emotional coldness. See **Iron,** isolation. In rare cases, there is also the suggestion that the water (of the soul and the emotions) can be carried. **Falling** through the ice—danger that emotions are going to crash.

Iceberg: Great strength through discipline. Distance, as in **Ice**.

Ice Cream: Sexual pleasure, summer fun, relaxation.

Ice Skating: See **Flying**. You are stepping on **Ice**. Are you prepared to take that risk? Trust in your own body and elegance of movement, smoothly gliding over the surface.

Icicle: Happiness and satisfaction or emotional coldness, as in **Ice**.

Idiot: Fear of mental overexertion, longing for a simpler, childlike life. A warning to live unconsciously. Also "idiot" in ancient Greece meant the "nonpolitical" common man—in other words, those who were thought to be negative because they didn't care about the community. In addition, today we use the expression "the idiot savant," which raises the question: what does the idiot know?

Folklore: Unexpected fortune.

Illness: Inner, personal arguments point to a heightened need for self-protection, or it could mean self-injury.

Such a dream should be analyzed very thoroughly, because it can provide valuable information about the condition of the dreamer.

Immunization: Warning about illness. Also a well-known sexual symbol (penetration). See **Thorn.**

Incest: Deep bonds with a **Relative** (often a symbol for parts of yourself), whom you see as your idol, or who is or should be a threatening example. As a dream symbol, incest has an extremely positive as well as a negative meaning. On one hand, incest dreams express a longing for a deep connectedness and bonding that is clamoring for expression on all levels (body, mind, and soul). In a dream where the brother or sister is seen as the lover who is similar and related, in that sense, the dream makes possible a complete union of the masculine and the feminine even within one's own soul. On the other hand, this dream symbol may also represent the matter of love versus power. It is important to note who is making love: sister/brother incest may indicate that control is exercised at the expense of the bonding aspect. It is indeed the brother/sister incest act that expresses such a longing for complete devotion, while at the same time adding the attraction of the forbidden, which in our society makes anything sexual so exciting.

In the case of mother/son or father/daughter incest, the same dynamics may also come into play, but there is the added aspect of the unequal power between parent and child. Such dreams always point to an immature sexuality on the part of the adult, who is afraid of a relationship between equals.

At the same time we should always remember with such a dream that a certain kind of masochism is involved—in the form of fear/pleasure—that resides in all of us. And we might want to be grateful when it finds expression in such dream images only! Last but not least, we also need to take into consideration the Oedipus and Electra complexes, where a child desires the parent of the opposite sex. Psychoanalytically, this stage of sexual development needs to be overcome in order to have satisfying sexual experiences with equals.

Index Finger: The finger used for scolding; or a phallic symbol.

Infant: See **Baby**.

Infidelity: See **Marriage**.

Inflation: Psychological overexertion or a rare expression of fear or poverty.

Inheritance: Heritage. Your own assets and resources need to be put to better use. You have much that you can fall back on. You want money that you don't have to work for.

Injury/Wound: Feeling of hurt and being injured, vulnerable and weak. Often a reference to old injuries that want to be healed.

Ink: Symbolizes a responsibility that cannot be changed. What is the color of the ink?

Insanity: Emotional and senseless action that requires more clarity and insight. Pay attention to the reality of everyday life. Often reveals a distrust of Self. See **Fool, Belt, Door, Stairs.**

Insects: Deeply rooted unconscious content. Almost always a sign of nervousness and unconscious fears. Insects behave like mini-robots and, in that sense, this dream image is a warning against living carelessly.

Institution: A symbol of ability and cooperation of diverse interests, which points to intellectual energies. To agree with others or with the different sides within yourself. Herd instincts, as in **Uniform**.

Insult: Dissatisfaction or arrogance, but frequently directly connected to actual insults, either received or given. In most cases, there is a hidden longing for understanding and new insights.

Insurance: Well known symbol for safety, which may point to emotional rigidity. Be more courageous and stand by your feelings!

Intercourse: Desire for, or fear of, intercourse. Climax and relaxation. The image of one's own personal physical sexuality that often points to sex as an end in itself. What is addressed here is not only sexual lust, vitality, and depth, but also a challenge to find your "self," which is only possible through intense communication with the Other. Symbolic meaning of sexual climax reveals (not only in dreams) how we can become centered and engage our personal strength and passions. Other interpretations, as in alchemy and analytical psychology, include a sign of contradictions acknowledged and overcome.

Intoxication: Warning about illusions. Clear awareness is necessary. Or it points to a great deal of rigidity and an aversion to eroticism.

Invalid: Loss of independence. Loss of room to maneuver. Somebody or yourself needs support. Inferiority complex, self-doubt, and anguish. You feel you have been injured. In spite of the obvious meaning, this image has a positive side: it is a reminder that we are also allowed to withdraw from normal activities. In this sense, the dream image often points to being one-sided in relation to work. For instance, you do not have to do everything yourself and always be the best. It is important to accept and to admit helplessness. On the other hand, there is a belief that invalids are unable to act, which might indicate that you are asking too much of yourself.

Invitation: Loneliness, longing for social contact. Or you are inviting a part of yourself.

Iron: Something is in need of improvement or needs to be "ironed out." Are you being too conventional? Domesticity, as in **Communion,** only here, the social meaning is more or less missing; rather more like

Flowerpot, Baking, Roast, and also **Hen, Pillow, Porcelain, Apron.**

Stability, willpower, resilience, hardness, and coldness, as in **Ice.** Also having "your iron in the fire," which points to vitality and transformation (recasting, forming).

Folklore: Difficulties.

Island: Isolation and loneliness that you suffer from, or that you desire. This image often appears when you are frustrated at work. A longing for harmony and peace, wanting to leave the world; vacation. As the "island of dreams," this image is a symbol of self, pointing to a self-directed life, autonomy, and independence. Also, a symbol of the unconscious.

Astrology: A symbol of Aquarius.

Ivory: See **Elephant.** Male sexuality. The prize that is being sought and stolen; but also that which is protected.

Ivy: Old relationships are getting stronger. Also, warning of false friends. You can be smothered (parasites on the plant). Compare this also with **Vampire.** Also steadfastness and stamina (ivy is ever green.)

Folklore: Good health.

Jacket: What image would you like to present to the outside world? Similar to **Shirt**.

Folklore: Hard work and little reward.

254

Jade: Something not highly valued, but still important and precious. Points to too much vanity or to a bright personality. According to Chinese understanding, jade is a lucky stone that keeps you healthy.

Folklore: Fortune through hard work.

Jasmine: Female gender.

Folklore: Great luck.

Jellyfish: Uncomfortable feelings or, in rare cases, a hint that you entertain addictive thoughts. Memories of vacation.

Folklore: Negative omen and loss.

Jet Airplane: Speed of thought, fear of war, as in **Helmet, Bayonet, Bomb,** but more impersonal and technical. Aggression. Such dreams often appear when the airplane noise is real.

Jewel: See **Jewelry.** Emptiness, vanity, and often a suggestion of the treasures that reside inside you. Temptation, because of the glitter.

Jewelry: Well-being. Beauty for women, honor for men, or vanity; but it also implies that an inner **Treasure** has been discovered. Also a desire for acceptance and affection. According to Freud, the symbol of the person one loves.

Vanity or pleasure in one's own attractiveness.

Folklore: In the case of women, ambition; in men, wanting to possess the jewel, the woman. Bad omen.

Joke/Jest: A joke works because it shows situations in a new perspective. Perhaps you should re-examine your rigid perspective. Don't take life quite so seriously, and let the soul be a source of joy.

Joy: Inner equilibrium; or you need more fun in your life.

Judge: A symbol for the superego that is a warning against bold undertakings. Also the desire for justice. See **Court.**

Judgment: At issue here is the attitude toward a very important matter and justice. Earlier dream interpretors believed that the conscience was speaking. **Court, Attorney, Confession.**

Folklore: A journey across the land.

Jug/Pitcher: See **Container**. Symbol for the emotional capacity that takes in joy, grief, tears, fulfillment, and so on. Also, a female sexual symbol, eroticism. What is in the pitcher is important. See **Chalice**. A full pitcher means abundance; a broken pitcher means loss.

Juggling: Are you trying to juggle life by keeping all the balls in the air? If you juggle balls in your dream, it means that you need to keep your energy in motion, be more playful, and keep your goals and desires in balance. On the other hand, this image might also symbolize a fear of making decisions; you are too often undecided.

Juice: Fruit, joy, and health. Juice usually refers to life and energy.

Jungle: Often points to difficulties, particularly when you have to clear your own path in the dream. The jungle is a symbol of the working, everyday world. Frightening or intimidating situations, usually of the emotional type. See also **Primeval Forest.**
Folklore: Financial difficulties.

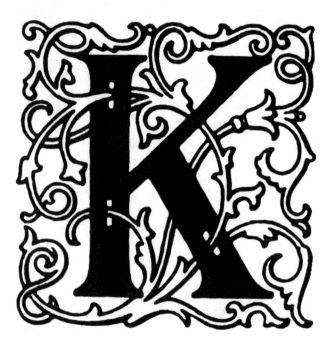

Kennel: See **Cage, Elevator,** and **Prison.**

Kettle: Where cooking takes place and where life is renewed. In the mythology of the Mabinogions (medieval Welsh lore), the kettle was where dead soldiers were brought back to life. The kettle, just like any of the containers in alchemy, is where transformation of matter takes place, and for that reason it is reminiscent of the uterus or the center of the earth. The kettle is almost always a sign of creative energy. Figuratively speaking, it is the kettle where the vitality of the dreamer is transformed into something new. It is the blended pot where emotional energy and the power of the soul are blended together to create the individual personality.

Folklore: Good omen.

Key: See **Lock.** You have the right attitude and are posing the right questions, in the sense of how you are using your personal qualities. Ideas and new experiences.

Locking up something speaks of fear of relationships and of fear of getting involved.

According to Freud, the symbol of the key/lock stands for sexuality. The key is the phallus, the lock the vagina, and the function of locking means intercourse.

Folklore: To lose a key has negative connotations; to give somebody else your key means domestic luck.

King/Queen: Lover. Archetypal symbol for father/mother,

dependency on father/mother. Also always the dreamer himself.

See **Dictator/Ruler**. May also represent the Great Father and Great Mother. The Great Father is the symbol of an aware and elevated consciousness. You are standing with great awareness in the world. In fairy tales, as well as in dreams, the self usually has a royal beginning, from which it is separated in order for it to master the adventures in the world. The king also means wholeness and completeness.

The Great Mother is symbolized in the dream as a queen, always representing the image of wholeness. In the end she represents the integrating power of nature. Furthermore, the image of the queen as the fertile mother always addresses the self of the dreamer. Implied here is the idea that we should rely on our own abilities, care for ourselves, and find a **Home** within ourselves.

Kings and queens also represent one's masculinity (*animus*) and femininity (*anima*). Such archetypes are not only persons of authority, but they also represent the image of a loved one (idealized and elevated masculinity or femininity). According to Freud, often the symbol of parents who are seen as overly powerful.

Kiss: Uniting, connecting, and good luck. Intimate closeness, intellectual communication, desire for closer contact, maybe making up after a fight. Rarely is a kiss a sign of betrayal (the kiss of Judas).

Kitchen: See **House**. Refers to housewife. Change and transformation of emotional energies.

Knee: Erotic signal. Also, agility or rigidity of one's own point of view. Uncompromising pride or humility. An injury to the knee is often part of a nightmare, particularly in situations of running away.

Astrology: Relates to the sign of Capricorn.

Knife: Seeking power. Aggression and symbol for masculinity. However, the knife may also point to security and protection. Often internal suffering and passions are being addressed, pointing out innermost secrets that you want to hide. Ask how to call up the unconscious strength that could bring results. Are you able to show your wounds and acknowledge your injuries? Can you see that acknowledging your wounds and your vulnerabilities could make you more human and likable? To acknowledge pain eliminates your fear of weakness, making aggressive action to protect your boundaries unnecessary. According to psychoanalysis, in the case of women, the desire for total abandon.

Analysis and differentiation, as in the Sword in the Tarot.

According to Freud, a phallic symbol; but today it is rarely seen in that context.

Folklore: Betrayal and deception.

Knight: Adventurous, immature masculinity, but also responsible and honest. In a psychological sense, you are protected by the armor and are unreachable, which can both make sense and cause problems.

Knot: Symbolizes complications, unsolvable problems, and entanglement. Warning of being emotionally tied in knots. Undoing knots means the end of entanglements (Gordian knot).

Laboratory: The place where we experiment—with life. This dream image represents the way we deal with our emotions and where we do our emotional work. How do you deal with your emotions? Is your life too planned or deadened by too much technology?

Folklore: Danger and illness.

Ladder: Overly organized development. A symbol of the connection between the unconscious (below) and the conscious (above). May point to Jacob's Ladder, leading into heaven. Are you confronted with new tasks? Are you climbing up or coming down? How many rungs does the ladder have? See the symbolic meaning of numbers. Some people get dizzy when they climb too high. According to Freud, the rhythm of the motion of climbing up and coming down is symbolic of intercourse. See **Stairs, Career, Step.**

Lake: See **Water.** In the *I Ching,* the lake is the symbol for a happy and cheerful youngest daughter.

Lama (dignitary): Spirituality, the archetype of the wise man.

Lamb: Purity in the sense of patience and gentleness. See **Victim. Easter.** The Easter lamb also points to a new beginning.
    Folklore: Domestic bliss. See **Sheep, Aries.**

Lamp: This is an object often found in fairy tales. The

hero or the dream-self is emerging. Light is about to be shed on a problem, which will then be solved. Trust your own insight!

Lance/Spear: To break a lance for somebody means that you are standing up for that person. It may, however, also point to sexual tension, as well as religious themes (the Grail). Jung saw a connection to the fisher king, who was injured in the groin by a lance, and therefore relates the symbol to physical and emotional suffering. He claimed the task of the hero (Percival) is to address the question of empathy/sympathy in the face of this suffering. If empathy is not expressed, the king and his court will continue to suffer.

According to Freud, as with all other weapons this is a phallic symbol.

Landscape: Freud saw this image as a symbol for the human body.

Lantern: See **Lamp**. Symbol of the light of awareness; it usually points to the need for taking a closer look at your problems. In rare cases, it also reflects the electric power of love. A light shining in the dark attracts attention, like a moth attracted by a light.

Lap: Return to mother, longing for one's childhood, or fears from childhood.

Large: Anything that grows in size during a dream should be paid attention to.

Lark: Singing bird. Good perspective, because the "lark" flies high in the air. Joy.

Laughing: Usually seen in a very difficult situation, where laughing is the last thing that you'd like to do. Laughing is a form of relaxation. Sometimes it is also an expression of the search for freedom and emotional peace.

Laundry: See **White**. White laundry and white clothing are considered the symbol of innocence and purity. White laundry is, according to Freud, a symbol of femininity.

Folklore: Quarrels, separation, and loss.

Laurel: Striving for success and acceptance. This may be a warning not to be addicted to approval and fame.

Folklore: Luck and money.

Lava: An important dream symbol, pointing to inner, psychic energies. Uncontrolled release of tension.

Lavender: A symbol for woman.
Folklore: Positive omen.

Lawn: See **Grass, Meadow.** Hope and well-being.

Lawyer: See **Attorney.**

Lead: Physicality, heaviness (clumsiness), but also relative softness; it is durable, but melts and mutates easily. Lead is poisonous and has been associated with a curse as early as antiquity. Are you "poison" for somebody, or has somebody been malicious toward you? Also, weighing down, complaint, center of gravity/main focus.
Astrology: A symbol of Saturn.

Leader: Symbol of authority, as in **Father** and **Wise Man.** One who is free to move, a symbol of freedom. See **Mountain Guide.**

Leading: Motivation to pursue advancement. Or loneliness. Life needs to be better organized. This is a dream that almost always calls on your inner guide, or how you are guiding others. Can you lead and still let others lead you?

Leaf (of a Plant): Being subjected to changes, or **Letting Go.** Similar to **Abyss, Brook/Stream,** and sometimes **Parachute,** only in more playful terms. A wilted leaf means troubles. A green leaf means rejuvenation, fulfillment of a wish.

Leaf (of Paper): Are you being challenged to take note of something or express something? In what sense do you see yourself as a blank piece of paper, and in what sense as a piece of paper that has writing on it?

Leak: Emotional isolation and separation is breaking up.

Leather: Symbolizes toughness—tough as leather—aggressive tendencies, fetishes, but also soft, "smooth as silk," indicating tenderness.

Leather clothing: Isolation and promiscuity, but also a search for invulnerability and sensuality. See **Animal.**

Leaves: Emotions and thoughts the dreamer has. The

condition of the leaves is important—what time of year is it? Green leaves mean joy, fun, and growth; dead leaves mean disappointment and failure, but also, in time, maturity and insight.

The interpretation in antiquity was Joy.

Leaving (on a trip): Wanting to leave, often because of stress, overwork, and marital conflicts. Desire for irresponsibility. Also a sign that, having assumed power in order to move out of the situation, you have freed yourself.

Lecture: As with everything that is performed publicly, it refers to a portrayal of the Self, as in **Theater** and **Concert**. If the dreamer is the speaker, it indicates a desire to make a statement. The task is to serve the interests of all the listeners and to find and make clear to them your point of view. There is a desire to solve present situations intellectually. See also **Puzzle**. As far as the speaker is concerned, the issue is to combine emotion and logic, intellect and consciousness. This dream symbol almost always includes aspects of self-understanding. It might also encourage you to become a better listener, as in **Ear** and **Mouth**. And, last but not least, this dream symbol also represents your inner voice.

Leeches: Feeling of disgust for your own body. The feeling of being sucked dry, as in **Vampire.**

Folklore: Symbol of luck, since leeches were used for healing purposes.

Left: The side where the heart is, the emotional area of the dreamer, and also the feminine aspect. It rarely has political meaning. Sometimes, it is injustice. According to Freud, it is perversity. See **Right.**

Leg: Foot. Symbol for setting things in motion on your own initiative, in contrast to being in a vehicle——**Auto, Car.** It is also a symbol of your attitude toward life and, particularly, to being grounded.

In psychoanalysis in the past, the leg was considered a sexual symbol: a beautiful leg meant satisfying intercourse; a broken leg was a symbol of adultery (today this is probably less appropriate).

Lemon: See **Fruit.** You are "sour" and/or feeling funny. This might also point in part to the body's need for more vitamin C. On the other hand, it may refer to an intrinsic worthlessness, as in the car that is a "lemon."

Folklore: Bad luck.

Leopard: Vitality, elegance, drive. In case of danger, a leopard points to your fear of erotic entanglement. See **Cat**.

Folklore: Difficulty.

Letter: Being connected with a loved one, news, communication with the outside world. A message that has not yet reached your consciousness.

Liability/Guarantee: You have been made responsible for something; or you are making a promise to yourself.

Library: Symbol of intellectual life, as in **Book**; great knowledge. A warning of too much one-sided intellectual activity, as in **Balcony**. Often a challenge to look for a more holistic education and character formation.

Lifeboat: One way to extricate yourself from "oceanic emotions" and/or escape from the storms of life.

Light: See **Lamp**, **Lantern**, **Lighthouse**. Symbol for consciousness, intellect, reason, clarity, hope, and joy. The image of the center of life—as the sun is the center of the universe—the spark of the soul and the longing for a much sought-after object. The light is the opposite of depression, doubt, darkness, and illness. Light means creative spirit. However, keep in mind that light and darkness contradict as well as enhance each other. Negative meaning: Blinding, bright, or dying light.

Lighthouse: See **Lamp, Lantern.** Helpful for orienting oneself in difficult situations. Problems that you are not aware of are made conscious. Well-known phallic symbol.
Folklore: Luck.

Lightning: If lightning is only illuminating the sky—a sudden idea. On November 16, 1619, Descartes had a dream and, among other things, saw lightning, which showed him that he now had found his own method of understanding.

Lightning as a natural occurrence indicates a repressed effect, denial that wants to be expressed or lived out through sudden aggressive action; an uncontrolled release of great energies. Fighting ("lighting into somebody").

According to Artemidorus, the 2nd century dream interpreter, a good omen.

According to Freud, a phallic symbol. Jung also stated that everything that strikes something has to be interpreted as a phallic symbol.

Lilac: Love, tenderness, and romance. It is also a warning against arrogance and witchcraft.

Folklore: Finding love.

Lily: A symbol of purity, innocence, and naturalness. In France, a symbol of power.

Limping: Emotional injuries are making it difficult to get ahead in life.

In myth, the most famous limp belonged to the Greek god Hephaestus, husband of Aphrodite. Ares/Mars, with whom Aphrodite has an affair, is seen as being Hephaestus' shadow side. Hephaestus is considered the personification of **Fire.**

Linden Tree: See **Tree.** Healing; a power place where energies are renewed.

Folklore: Romance.

Linen/Sheets/Pillowcases: The color is important.

Folklore: Good omen.

Lion: The king of the animal kingdom was often used as a symbol in the Coat of Arms: the British lion, the lion of Judea, Christ as a lion, the red lion of Wales. It stands for spirit, courage, awareness, and power. It is the symbol of transformation in alchemy, and represents the essence of the masculine and feminine. In antiquity it was the symbol of the creative power of the **Sun**, since in the summer the constellation of the Lion in the night sky is at the highest point. In the history of the Rosicrucians, initiation ceremonies included taming a lion. The lion is the fire of the libido and thereby of vitality. If not tamed, this energy will devour and destroy.

The lion as a Christian symbol stands for the domestication of the non-believers. In Northern Europe, the lion was replaced by the **Bear**. According to early Christian and medieval imagination, the lion used his tail to erase his footprints so that he could not be followed and found. It has also been said that lions sleep with their eyes open. And when a lioness gives birth, the young are initially born dead until three days later, when the male lion appears and blows in the face of the young. This gave rise to the idea of the lion as a symbol for awakening and vitality. In Christian fables, it is also depicted as the cunning animal. See **Dragon, Sun, Heart**. The evil spirit Utukku is depicted with the head of a lion.

Lips: Erotic desires, communication.

Liquid manure: Inferiority complex, disgust; less often, fertility.

Liquor: Relaxation or troubles.
Folklore: Be warned—somebody wants to cozy up to you.

Liver: First, make sure that you do not have real, physical complications involving the liver. If you don't, this symbol refers to restlessness and irritability—something is galling you. Also, it is a symbol of vitality and productivity.
Folklore: Eating liver leads to good health.

Lizard: Usually a harmless miniature **Dragon** will bring you luck.
Folklore: Betrayal.

Llama (spitting animal): Take chances—just once try not to be so proper.

Lobster: *Folklore:* Luck.

Lock/Padlock: This is the image of inner, psychic tension between openness and retreat (isolation), between risk and security.

Lock/Sluice: A symbol for regulating the level of **Water**, meaning the emotions. Here the level of the water is adjusted to the needs of the traffic, and in that sense it raises the question of the need to regulate and adjust your emotions to the needs of everyday life. Are you holding your emotions in check, or allowing them to flow? What is restricting you?

Locomotive: See **Train**. Collective psychic energy; life's journey as seen through the eyes of society/community. Moving forward with energy and power, or being pulled forward.

Lodge: **Town**. Power and isolation, but also the symbol for the center. As a **Mother** symbol, protective, inclusive, or nurturing.

According to Freud, castles, lodges, and forts are always female symbols.

Logger/Lumberjack: See **Wood**. Since in the past the forest was thought of as a dark place and, therefore, the place of the unconscious, the logger is seen as creating order in an area of chaos. Here, the harshness of nature is transformed into something more refined, as the wood removed is put into the service of people in the form of firewood and building material. If the wood is not split, cutting down trees may also mean a loss of energy. On the other hand, chopping wood may also be seen as aggressive action against one's own aliveness and health. The logger may stand for being wooden and unrefined, resulting in a stupid and dull position or attitude. In the case of a city person, there could be a romantic longing for a simpler life, as in **Farmer** and **Craftsman.**

Folklore: Great effort without gain.

Loneliness: Inner longing for social contact, as in **Invitation.** You let yourself down (become unfaithful to yourself). Tendency to become too self-absorbed. Independence; you must stand on your own two feet.

Look: See **Eye.** Perception. What is it that you should take a closer look at? Who is it that you wish would look at you more often?

Loom (weaving): Time and fate, the thread of life. Longing for a "simpler life." Often a sign that much spiritual work is being done.

Folklore: Small financial losses are about to occur.

Loss: Fear of loss, or joy over separation.

Lottery: This image warns against risks of any kind. You have wishes and desires; take a good look at them.

Louse: Lack of cleanliness; leech, as in **Vampire**. Disgust.

Love: You are longing for love. A desire to be able to love as well as to be loved. Pay special attention to the quality, emotions, and circumstances in the dream.

Lower Body: Be sure that no actual stomach problems exist. See **Sexuality**, **Toilet**, **Stomach**, **Belt**.

Luggage: See **Suitcase, Pocketbook, Backpack, Package,** and **Box.** All symbolize a burden (everybody carries his own baggage) or, less often, energy and making plans. Energy reserves. Possibly a reference is being made to dowry and inheritance, which could be a burden as well as an opportunity. What talents are at your disposal? What tasks are connected to them?

According to Freud, a symbol of sexuality.

Lung: Feeling restricted, needing more space and **Air**, as in **Cage** and **Elevator (Lift).** A symbol of power that has been achieved through clear thinking and personal judgment.

Lying: A symbol of falsehood; it often points to a bad conscience. You are leading a double life. You are not honest. However, if you discover in your dream that you have been lying (including to yourself), you are now aware and have gained important insight. Be glad that you have found the capacity for self-criticism.

Machine: Lack of meaning in your work; stupidity. The type of machine is important. Is the dreamer a machine (a robot)? Also, it may be an image of the internal work your soul is undertaking.

Machine (Vending): Boring daily routine, dependency, and indifference. A need to act with more passion and conscience. In a stressful situation, it often calls up the irrational dream of a life of leisure. However, this image can also refer to how to make a work routine better, a prerequisite for working more creatively and independently. When you see yourself as a machine, you are made aware of some as yet unconscious habits. Pay particular attention to how details in the dream are presented.

Madonna: The big woman. Release from guilt and pain; self-elevation or self-denial. Also a sexual symbol and a symbol of self-sufficient, independent femininity. The image of the madonna may also be pointing to sexual repression and a bad conscience, because of the dreamer's attitude about his or her own sexuality and/or femininity.

Maggot: Greed and laziness.
Folklore: Domestic quarrels.

Magic/Magician: In the past (but still relevant today), the image of supernatural power that you wish you had. This dream symbol frequently appears when one is feeling worthless. Today, it refers more to the dreamer himself and his magical qualities. A magician represents the integrated whole and the individuality of the dreamer—that's the reason why the magician in the Tarot was assigned the number One. This integration and uniqueness is what makes him magical. The message here might be that the dreamer ought to concentrate on his "magical powers" and know that they contribute to success on his life path. But no personal magic will make itself known unless the dreamer chooses to pursue his own path. If he doesn't do that, everything will seem jinxed. He will not get ahead and a multitude of obstacles will get in his way. On the other hand, this dream symbol may also point out that too much emphasis is being put on the individual at the expense of the collective. See **Witch**.

Magnet: Strong force of attraction and personal success. Sometimes a symbol for one's own center, **Love,** and a lover. Pay attention to what is fascinating to you and what is attracting you. According to theorist and teacher G.I. Gurdjieff, great danger may lie in the powers that are attracted to you.

Magpie: The **Bird** that combines black and white, as in

Birch in the plant world. Light and shadow are to be integrated in your inner life, as in **Marriage, Intercourse,** and **Bride/Bridegroom.** The magpie is a thief; something is being taken from you, as in **Burglar.**

Mailman: See **Post.** Carrier of information, communication.

Mall/Market/Marketplace: Points to the dreamer's social connections. This image shows how you behave toward the outside world, what your connections are to that world, and how you are dependent upon it. If it is a lively marketplace, it means public contact, commerce, nervousness, chaos. An empty marketplace points to loneliness. Possibly, it is also a mirror of your inner, personal relationships, or your particular awareness of the world around you.

Man: See **Companion.** In the case of a woman, this dream may be pointing to a father figure or ego ideal. A strange man in a man's dream always means his own unknown side, the shadow. An older man represents the father figure in dreams of men as well as women, or he may represent the dreamer himself. A naked man means openness.

Mandala: A symbol of wholeness, aiding us to find our center. Points to personal development.

Map: See **Atlas**. As in the case of **Crossing**, this image points to finding direction in your life. A plan for your life. See **Book**.

According to Freud, it depicts the human body.

Marble: Steadfastness, luxury, but also toughness (biting into stone). A sense of beauty, but also a lack of feeling, up to and including frigidity.

Maria: See **Virgin**, **Madonna**.

Marketplace: See **Mall/Market**.

Marksman/Hunter: In mythology, the marksman/hunter is often depicted as a centaur, the wild rider. Today he would be seen as the cowboy in Western movies. In antiquity, the feminine equivalent was the Amazon. Human enthusiasm and concentration is part of the dream image that is integrated with the intensity of the animalistic "fire." The hunter craves a goal, which can refer to nostalgia and wanderlust; however, the goal is always also "he himself." See **Arrow**, **Goal**.

Marmalade: Enjoying life—the sweet life—or "preserves."

Marriage: Union of contrasting parts of yourself (often your feminine and masculine sides). Longing for a permanent bond.
Folklore: Unfavorable omen, because after the so-called "happy ending," "things" are just getting started.

Marriage Ring: Separation or longing for a relationship.
Folklore: Separation.

Marriage/Wife/Husband: Compensation and reconciliation of differences, melding of male and female energies. Usually, the dreamer's own characteristics are indicated. Longing for partnership, particularly in a divorce or separation situation; or fear of marriage and commitment. Are you able to accept the **Other**? Are you able to preserve the space between yourself and the **Other,** and experience it as positive? However, you also ought to ask yourself if you are expecting your partner to fulfill all your desires, or are you willing to work for them yourself? **Transference.**

Mask: That which we would like to present to the

world around us, or what we would like others to view as being real. A weak sense of self, inferiority complex. Hiding from the truth. But also fun, lust, and erotic adventures. Being misled, false impressions, and temptations. If the mask in your dream is visible, this is also a sign of your ability to look behind the scenes (including your own). See **Curtain**.

Folklore: Always negative.

Massage: Enjoying erotic and relaxing experiences. This image in a dream often expresses the need for more bodily contact, or a need to "save one's own skin." If bodily contact is present in the dream, it may point to emotional contact.

Masses (of people): Often a fear of social contact and agoraphobia. Here, you find the social contact you need and a place where you see yourself apart from—*and* also a part of—a larger whole. So in a sense, this dream image poses a question about your social adaptability on one hand, and on the other, your sense of what is yours and what you have taken on from the outside world. Do you have contact with many people, or none? Do you feel socially overwhelmed, or accepted? Does your dream express a need for liberation?

Mast: In psychoanalysis always a phallic symbol.
   Folklore: A long journey.

Master: See **Chief**.

Master of the House: One who has provided well, who keeps order. A frequent dream symbol for the conscience. Often points to the fact that you should take better care of body and soul.

Match: See **Fire, Flames, Light**. Did you set something on fire? Or have you burned your fingers?

Mattress: See **Bed**. Eroticism, sexuality. The place of birth and death.

May: Youth, eroticism, and growth; a productive time; and a favorable outlook.
   Folklore: Bad omen.

Maze: From a mythological point of view, the image of the maze is closely tied to the Greek hero Theseus and to Ariadne, who loves him. As legend has it, in order to slay the virgin-devouring monster in the center of the maze of Crete, Ariadne gives to Theseus a magical red thread that will help him find his way out of the maze after he has slain the monster. The maze symbolizes the womb of the Earth Mother and the cosmic order, which each of us has to create within ourself. And that is your task! The path is like a maze; after many twists and turns you finally reach your goal, where you can fulfill your obligations and responsibilities, find your shadow, and come to terms with it. Every time you dream about a maze you are challenged to come to terms with the monster within yourself.

On the other hand, the image of the maze points to a mother complex: if you cannot let go of the feminine, you are lost in it, which means the masculine in you loses its identity. And if this masculine identity is devoured by the feminine, the feminine cannot find its own identity because it doesn't have access to it, and you cannot find your way out of the maze.

The symbol of the maze probably goes back to observations made about how the sun or the moon is traveling across the sky. In the center of the maze resides death, where the sun and the moon are at their lowest point. After we have met death, we leave the maze in the same way as Theseus. Our modern world, the metropolitan big city, the asphalt jungle, where people are easily getting lost and feeling trapped, is often compared with the maze. What is addressed here is the idea that our lives have become so complex that it is difficult for us to find our way. See **Food (stored)**, **Thread**, **Dragon**.

Meadow: A large meadow points to growth and joy. The condition of the meadow is important.

Mealtime: Receiving psychic and emotional energies. What food you are eating is important. It is a symbol of the type of energy you will receive.

Meat: See **Sausage**. Physical, usually sexual, energies. A frequent image when you force yourself to follow a vegetarian eating style before you're ready for it.

Raw meat points to raw physical power, passion, and creative power. Cooked meat points to addiction to pleasure. Rejecting meat indicates chastity.

According to the Indian tradition Jaddeva, lust for power, or the desire to have many offspring.

Medal: Competitiveness and being externally oriented. You want to be praised, accepted, and rewarded. Also a symbol for wanting to belong to a certain group— almost always a group made up of men.

Medical Assistant: Erotic, helpful woman.

Medication: Apothecary, Pharmacist. Fear of illness, need for help, bitterness, emotional or physical neediness. Fear of disappointment, pain, poverty and/or old age. Often a hint that one can heal oneself. You have to "swallow" something.

Melon: Erotic symbol, luck in love.

Memento: A hint that something needs to be remembered. Do not repress your feelings. Remember vacations or other memorable events.
  Folklore: A wish is not being fulfilled.

Menopause: Primarily a woman's dream, pointing either to menopause about to take place, or other general and long-term changes.

Menstruation: A dream about menstruation is usually based on a real event that is either announcing itself or is starting up. Fear of pregnancy. In addition, we also have to look at the symbolism of bleeding, which usually indicates fear of injury, but is also a sign that we are coming closer to understanding the secrets of life. Blood stands for the vital and the real. Female bleeding always is a reminder of the vitality and passion that is able to create life.

Menu: Important is the symbolic meaning of the foods that are listed on the menu.

Mercury: Speed, nervousness, agility, and poison. Symbol for the planet Mercury.
Folklore: Having fun.

Mermaid: A magical water spirit who has much in common with the spirits of the forest, but who lures young men into the depths, where they drown. The dreamer will recognize in the mermaid his desire for and fear of the feminine. Also addressed is a man's desire to identify with femininity and his fear of doing so. The water spirit mermaid is enticing men to follow her into her kingdom, where, "under a glittering surface, are hidden inexplorable depths," according to C. G. Jung, who saw the realm of the water spirits as a symbol of the unconscious. So the mermaid is a symbol of life and inner maturity, a spirit who "walks" along boundaries. Young men dream about mermaids when they reach manhood; young girls, when they become women. In another sense, the mermaid is without a soul and therefore is after the soul of humans. According to Jung, the water spirit is at the instinctual stage, the pre-stage of the feminine being, or *anima*.

Also, the mermaid is a being in need of liberation: since she lives in water, she is drowning in her emotions—and she has no sexual organs.

Male water spirits seldom appear in dreams. (They are usually cruel, ugly, old, and comparable to goblins.)

Messenger/Carrying a Message: Are you playing the role of an intermediary? Are you satisfied with that role or would you rather take care of your own affairs? What message do you have to transmit? Is the messenger coming to you—are you receiving an important message? In any case, important news.

Metal: Success, prosperity, wealth, consistency, and toughness. Also, iron will, weighed down by fear. See **Iron, Gold, Silver, Fire,** and **Earth**.

Metal Worker: What has been close to you is opening up.

Meteor: Brainstorm, idea. A messenger from heaven.

Microphone: Challenges you to internalize something. You need to speak your mind, announce something publicly. Also, self-talk.

Midday: See **Light**. Awareness, midpoint of life.

Midnight: The darkest hour and the hour of ghosts. The beginning of a new day.

Midwife: Wishing for a child or fear of pregnancy. Desire to bring something to light or fear of its coming to light. A new phase in your life. A new idea or new behavior needs help in order to be accepted.

Military Duty: Self-affirmation, possibly also self-punishment, authority, fleeing from an inferiority complex, immature masculinity, and repressed aggression. In women's dreams, often the desire for aggressive sexuality and devotion.

Milk: See **Cow**. Food, security; a symbol for the original mother. Paradise is the land where milk and **Honey** flows. Something needs to be nourished with milk—with femininity. It might point to a tendency toward regression. Drinking milk means to increase knowledge and insight (*alma mater*, the nourishing mother is a name for the university attended). Sour milk means trouble and uncertainty. According to ancient Norse mythology, the cow is one of the oldest beings; it nursed the ancient giant Ymir.

Mill: Working, daily grind, but providing well and success.

Millet: Grain.
Folklore: Great fortune.

Mine: Depth of body and soul; highly self-absorbed; but also good news.

Minister/Clergyman: See **Priest**. **Father** figure and guide for the soul. Indicates too much or too little self-confidence. It points to good support, a perfect disposition of life, and an accepted portrayal of the Self to the outside world. Be more open, not only in matters of faith, but also in matters that deal with society in general.

Mirror: Insightful intellect that reflects reality. A common allegory for self-observation. We are looking into a mirror in our dreams in order to confirm our identity. If, in a dream, we are looking into the mirror and do not see our own but somebody else's image, it is always a sign that we are living in a fantasy world. It is also possible to see an actual person in the mirror.

The mirror is considered an attribute of the **Fool**, always pointing to vanity as one of the classic seven sins. Fools have often been depicted with mirrors. The image of a mirror in a dream is a very important event, and should be analyzed in detail. For the Greeks, a mirror appearing in a dream meant the death of the dreamer, since what he saw in the mirror was considered a look-alike. In fairy tales, a mirror represents hidden and future events, and the image of the soul.

According to Jung, the mirror is usually considered magical; it is "a knowing mirror," as in *Snow White and the Seven Dwarfs*. Using a mirror often transforms us into a mythical state. In Lewis Carroll's *Through the Looking Glass*, Alice enters another world through a mirror. In Cocteau's film *Orpheus*, the mirror is the entrance to the underworld. The image of a mirror also points to a tendency to inflate emotions and lose touch with our grounding.

Miscarriage: Abortion. May point to what is actually happening in the body. One is letting go of unproductive qualities. Or something new you started is not working out—this may be a warning dream.

Miser/Tightwad: Might be a suggestion to be more generous, open, and flexible. Or can you never be satisfied because your needs are not met? See **Vulture.**
Folklore: Bad omen for lovers. The way you treat money is the way you treat your lover.

Mist/Haze: Lack of clarity, as in **Darkness,** only less severe. Other than that, see **Steam** and **Fog.**
Astrology: Symbol of Neptune.

Mistake: Usually points to the need to deal with mistakes made during waking hours. Something is missing.
Folklore: Success.

Mistletoe: A symbol of the Druids and of consciousness. According to English custom, everybody is allowed to kiss a person who is standing below a sprig of mistletoe. The mistletoe stands for the healing power of love.

Model/Fashion Model: Conflict with conventional norms, accommodation, and vanity. Due to an inferiority complex you are trying to create ideal beauty; or emotional certainty about your own beauty.

Mole: Usually unconscious drives. You would like to or should go deeper and look at your secret drives and aggressions. The activity of the mole is always connected to subversion and you should always ask yourself: What is going on deep down inside and how is it affecting me?

Money: Rarely connected to financial problems. Dreaming about money points to your behavior in matters of love. It is probably the most frequent symbol of sexuality and power. A coin generally points to success and security. Are you always weighing every situation and thinking through a plan for every situation? Are you afraid of losing control over yourself or over a situation? Often such a dream is telling you to open yourself up to life and allow your wild side to surface. Passion for life is suggested here instead of control.

According to Freud and Jung, money is a symbol for the libido—silver coins indicate an attraction toward women; gold coins, an attraction toward men. For some modern psychoanalysts, it is a symbol of creative power.

Monk: Discipline, self-restraint and self-determination; but also losing oneself. See **Abbey**, **Cloister**, **Hermit**.

Monotony: See **Boredom**, **Uniform**, **Rhythm**.

Monster/Mythical Creature: Beast. Your animal nature is becoming too strong, too frightening, meaning that you are afraid of your own strength and drives. It could also indicate a person (**Father** or **Mother**) who appears overly powerful.

Talk to the frightening monster in your dream, have it out with him and observe him.

Mythical creatures, like dragons and ocean monsters, point to moral conflicts that may cause personality disturbances. Seek therapeutic help when these images appear often and include a great amount of fear.

Monument: Success, reward for efforts or trouble, seeking power——as in **Sword,** but not that aggressively.

Moon: Femininity, mother and woman. In a woman's dream, it is her own femininity that needs to be accepted. Mood, moodiness, and emotions. In Greek and Roman times: Luck with a beautiful woman.

According to Freud, the symbol of the buttocks (particularly a woman's buttocks). According to Jung, the moon is the "place of departed souls." He also sees it as the shadow side or the unconscious, a symbol of the libido. See **Cat**, **Night**.

Moor/Heath: Prudish restraint, emotional tension. Naturalness and asceticism.
   Folklore: Luck.

Moor/Swamp: See **Swamp**, **Mud**. Physical desires that are being repressed, that are dragging you down. Fear of death or fear of life. You are unable to move forward, and are being held back—pulled back—into the unconscious through fear of the feminine. On a positive note, the wild side of the character can be helpful in healing.
   Folklore: Obstacle dream.

Moped: As in **Motorcycle**, only less powerful.

Mosaic: See **Picture**. A mirror of the experiences of life; many parts create a whole. See **Concert**, **Puzzle**.

Moss: As with all plants, the *vegetative* in human beings; quiet, and equilibrium.

According to Freud, the symbol for pubic hair. An erotic symbol.

Moth: Subversive emotions and feelings. See **Light**.
Folklore: Difficulties ahead.

Mother: Your own nature, the archetypal feminine—life-giving, nurturing, devouring, protecting, that which is fruitful and fertile. When the mother in the dream is your real mother, it points to a bad conscience because of past behavior toward her. When the mother in the dream refers to the internal mother, it points to a desire for psychological support that is often not provided by a partner. The mother in a dream, as well as in fairy tales, is often the helper whose strength, in a negative as well as positive sense, reaches beyond death. She is the **Witch**, the Wise Old One, who gives correct advice, the **Earth** and the goddess of the earth. The symbol of the mother also addresses the task of self-discipline. Be a good mother to yourself and thereby become productive.

According to Jung, the mother is the archetypal symbol of "the secret, the hidden, the dark, the abyss, the temptation, the poisonous, and the inescapable."

Motor: Energy, power, and mobility.

Motorboat: Moving powerfully through your emotional landscape. See **Water**, **Ship**.

Motorcycle: Getting ahead and doing it alone. Individualism, the Self, psychic energy. Sitting on the "hot seat" represents vitality and drive.

Mountain: See **Hill**. Protection and consciousness. Overview, standing above a given situation, as in **Bird**. A difficult time in life's journey is beginning. Romantic notion about nature and solitude, flight from the city and culture. Climbing a mountain is facing an important problem. Encountering obstacles or troubles on the way points to actual difficulties. What did the mountain look like?

According to Freud, the mountain is a symbol of the male sexual organ.

Mountain Crystal: The treasure that is growing within us. The reward for discovering this treasure is the ultimate in purity of the soul. On the other hand, it might also be a warning of confusion, inadequacy, and idle fascination—particularly when in the form of jewelry, such as **Amber** and other crystals.

Mountain Guide: Authority, know-how and judiciousness; guidance and support on the way to the summit.

Astrology: This symbol is connected to the sign of Capricorn.

Mountain Ridge/Crest: See **Mountain.** Initial successes.

Mouse: A symbol of control *and* lack of control that you have over the small things in life. The "small" or unimportant things can also mean those that are invisible.

Mice are often "signs of death" (**Death** is meant in the sense of completion). They are symbols of nagging thoughts and a nagging conscience. When they become a plague, they are a bad omen. In Goethe's *Faust*, mice appear in the form of ghosts that nibble at the Pentagram that is supposed to ban the devil. Gray and black mice in a dream point to bad luck. The gray and the black mouse may also be a symbol of the shadow, since gray and black are shadow colors.

The positive meaning of this symbol lies in the fact that parents sometimes call their children "little mouse." It is also the language of lovers who use such endearments."

According to Mohammed, the mouse represents the

"little sinner," the adulteress. When Faust dances with a witch, a mouse jumps out of her mouth. White mice are believed to be the souls of children and of the poor, and also fever demons.

According to Jung, the mouse is the animal of the soul, the image of a difficult-to-understand reality, the relationship of the dreamer to sexuality, fertility, and the devil or witch.

Folklore: Always has an erotic meaning. The mouse is the penis escaping into the hole.

Mouth: Contact and communication, erotic kissing and relationships.

According to Freud and Jung, it represents the female sexual organ.

Moving. Changes.

Moving Out (of Home): Like **Emigration, Giving Up/ Getting Out**, and **Foreign Country**.

Mud/Sludge: See **Bog.** Fear of sinking and of stagnation. Being a mixture of water and earth, this image refers to emotions flowing and needs realized.

Mug, Cup, Beaker, Goblet: First try to establish if, in your sleep, you are really thirsty—see **Drink, Water.** That which is giving, that which is mysterious. But also zest for life, advances, and luxury, as in **Oysters, Balloon, Champagne.** A warning sign of alcoholism. What is the goblet made of? What is in it? Possibly something poisonous? The next question would be what kind of poison.

Classical symbol in depth psychology for female sexuality.

Multiplicity/Variety: If such symbols appear frequently in your dreams, like a street full of water puddles, for instance, or a sky filled with birds of the same kind, it is thought to be a sign of extreme distractions and psychological splitting. If such dreams are common, it would be a good idea to see a psychologist.

Multiplicity is the essential characteristic of all life events that register in the unconscious—the deeper in the unconscious, the more pronounced the multiplicity.

It is connected to the sympathetic nervous system, where whatever is happening is telegraphed to every cell in the body. Multiplicity has a destructive connotation, because it dissolves the unity of consciousness, occurring often where there is a conflict between the ego, the many different I's, and influences in the environment. This dream may also point to conflicts and prejudices that are a hindrance.

According to the theorist Gurdjieff, the person who is not free always depends on many egos, and they make themselves known through such dreams. Other people suggest that the many egos of a person are what bring out his or her creative potential.

This dream often occurs during illnesses that are part physical and part psychological—delirium tremens, for example, where hallucinations involving many **Mice** are not uncommon.

However, multiplicity might also point to an early stage of a new awareness.

According to Freud, the frequency, or the accumulation, of symbols or facts in a dream indicates that they are real and will also appear during waking hours.

Mummy: A long life. You want immortality and have a tendency toward grandiosity. The mummy may also indicate an age-old burden, something that died long ago but still influences and fascinates you.

Murder/Murderer: See **Shot**, **Funeral**, **Corpse**. Warning: A very important part of your emotions have been severed: unused talents, relationships to other people, the ability to love, and so on. These are frequent dreams during depression, and reveal repressed drives, as in **Ashes** and **Abyss**. This, however, is only one, although it is the most important, interpretation of this dream symbol. On the positive side, it is very healing that you are "murdering" something in the dream and thereby putting a radical end to it. You are standing by your aggression and thereby expressing a very important part of you. As in a detective story, murder can be stimulating as well as tragic and have a purifying effect.

Museum: Usually represents the dreamer. What is being exhibited there?

Mushroom: Something is growing out of the depths. It may be poisonous or nurturing. Drug-induced, ecstatic religious or sexual experiences. In addition, a symbol of the hidden energies of the earth and the importance of things that are very small.

According to Freud, a phallic symbol.

Music: Emotions, feelings. Important are the feelings that come up when listening to the music. Are there words to the music?

In ancient Egypt, music meant a joyful heart.

Mussel: A female sexual symbol—and not only according to Freud. A closed mussel means virginity or frigidity.

Mustache: See **Beard**, **Hair**. Symbol of creative power.
  Folklore: Unimportant squabble.

Mustard: Sharp; hot; spicy intellect, irony, cynicism.
  Folklore: Your talk is getting you in trouble.

Nail: Similar to **Needle,** or "hitting the nail on the head."

Nail File: Something needs to be smoothed out. Vanity. According to Freud, male genitals.

Naked: Often the dreamer fearing the truth. Or, naturalness, honesty, and openness, but also poverty and impertinence.

Narrow/Crevice: Great struggles await you on your life's journey. You feel restricted, as in **Siege, Amber, Trap,** and **Village.**

According to early depth psychology: female sexual symbol.

Native American: In the past, adventurous and immature, fleeing from reality and the world. This symbol, in a man's dream, is similar to the **Hero.** Today we interpret this image in terms of wholeness: we all live in one world and all of us are dependent, collectively, on Mother Earth.

Navel: Center, or egoism. The center of the person or the body. In the case of men, often bonding to the mother.

Navigation: This is usually a reference to the kind of life the dreamer is living. Also a symbol for the mental task involved in orientation.

Neck/Throat: When dreaming about a sore or painful throat, make sure that you are not being bothered by a real health issue, like a cold. Other than that, people you deal with, or annoying situations, may give you a "pain in the neck."

As the neck is the connection between your body and your head, you are either too intellectually engaged or not engaged enough. The throat is the place where "words get stuck."

A sexual connotation may also be indicated, when people are "necking." Or the idea of a close finish—as in a horse race: neck in neck.

Needle: Emotional and physical pain. Sometimes a symbol for an awareness that is driven to an extreme. It may also address "sewing together" single parts of what the consciousness is working with. It could also be— and not only according to psychoanalysis—a phallic symbol. See **Thorns**.

Neighbor: Suggests the usual characteristics of the dreamer, of which he or she is relatively aware. Here are the parts of the ego that are fairly close to consciousness. Or, responsibilities and sympathy toward others.

Nest: Motherhood, protection, longing for security, family, and home. Also, a projection for every type of positive feeling about life.

Net: You want to catch somebody or understand something. Loss of independence, temptation, and possibly something threatening about sexuality. Also, systematic entanglement of emotions and needs, thoughts, and insights. Points clearly to networking and, in that sense, a meaningful connection to others.

New Building: A challenge to find new directions.

New Year: A new beginning and fun.
  Folklore: Be careful of a rival!

Newspaper: Often a suggestion to pay more attention to the outside world. Emotional news.

Niche: Secrets, or a chance.

Night: The unconscious and unknown—the other world. Often also that which is frightening. End-of-the-workday, **Darkness**, **Evening**, **Moon**.

Nightingale: Harmony. Hoping to be lucky in love.

Nine: With the number nine you have reached a level of completion, which is also expressed in the nine-point configuration the enneagram, the system that explains the world, according to theorist and teacher G. I. Gurdjieff. In all Indo-Germanic languages, the number nine is connected to the adjective "new." Nine refers to renewal.

Noise: It might be real noise that is reaching you in your sleep. But it might also be that you want to create excitement or that you do not have enough excitement in your everyday life.

North: "Top" of the map—therefore, the intellect, cool, clear, and distant.

Nose: A phallic symbol—probably the reason why the long nose of the **Fool** is so popular. To have a good nose means to have rank and fame, intuition, and instinct. It is also a symbol for being nosy—sticking one's nose into other people's business.

Nosebleed: Loss of strength and a symbol of injured

sexuality. In the dream of a woman, it is often a symbol for the loss of a partner; or it may be a menstruation dream.

Folklore: Be careful.

Notes: Pay close attention. Remember what came into your mind and remember your feelings.

Notes (musical): See **Music**. Sensuality, desire for harmony and accord (particularly in relationships). See **Concert**.

Notice-of-Intention-to-Marry: Positive friendship or longing for a solid relationship. See **Bride/Bridegroom**. Looking for understanding and security, as in **Anchor**, **Family**.

Novel: The title and content are important.
Folklore: Danger in matters of business.

Numbers: When dreaming about numbers, pay attention to their symbolic meaning—often the sum of the digits is meaningful. Numbers always represent an ordering principle in the world of the dream. Jung suggests that when dreaming about numbers that have no noticeable meaning, you think about whether they might refer to a year or any other time or date.

Nun: See **Virgin**. Chastity and disappointment, the longing for a spiritual life. Problems with one's shadow and repressed desires.

Nurse: Femininity and motherliness. You either need help or you don't want be helped.
Folklore: One of the best of all omens.

Nut: A symbol of wholeness. Also represents the **Head** and particularly the brain and thereby thinking. Points to toughness. Ancient Egyptian interpretation: Expect a gift.
If there are two, see **Genital Organ**.

Nutshell: Narrowness, protection, and security.
Folklore: Advancement at work.

Nut Tree: Strength, fertility, wealth, and abundance.

Nymph: See **Mermaid, Virgin**. Similar is nymphomaniac, who also has sexual limitations.

Oasis: An erotic symbol. Relaxing after the troubles of the day, wanderlust, or memories of travel. According to Jung, it is the place that has water in the ground, which he interprets as contact with the unconscious and the possibilities of redemption.

Folklore: Solutions to problems.

Oath: Truthfulness. You want to have willpower and be dependable in times of (inner) insecurity. Relationship and commitment to something.

Oatmeal/Granola: Health and strength, new energies. You would like to eat healthfully. Also connected to soul food and "alternative" ways to eat on a daily basis.

Oats: Grain. High spirits. "Feeling your oats" means you should show the world what you can do! "Sowing your wild oats" points to pleasure, usually sexual and promiscuous, after which time, presumably, you "settle down" to a more responsible lifestyle.

Obedience: An indication that more discipline is necessary, or the opposite.

Obelisk: Phallic and power symbol.
Folklore: Procession.

Obstacles: Obstacles in life. Resistance to obstacles that need to be overcome. The positive side of this symbol is that unknown obstacles are made clear and become conscious, which is the prerequisite to overcoming them. The type of obstacle is important.

Ocean: (Latin: *mare* = Maria = Mother). Emotions, archetypal energy, power, food. It is a symbol of the collective unconscious. Traveling across the ocean represents courage, new beginnings, and new **Shores**. A longing for freedom and independence.

Odyssey: The wanderings of Odysseus or Sinbad represent the very fundamental desire of human beings to search, learn, and grow. Jung talks about the "hero's midnight travel at sea." Such a dream is often an indication that the dreamer has no clear direction and no concrete goal. Also, such dreaming could pose the question of how well you control your feelings or how much you are being driven by them, and particularly by your fears. Usually this is a matter of finding the right balance between chaos and order, and remaining true to yourself.

Office: Professional activity, work, feeling of comradeship. One's own office points to your working habits; somebody else's office may refer to the fact that you are looking to others for guidance in your work.

Office (Bureau): Dreaming of holding an important position expresses the desire for achievement. Are you too ambitious—or should you be more ambitious? Rigidity, stubbornness, and social protocol. Cooperation, need to be more factual.

Officer: For man and woman, a symbol of authority and masculinity.

Oil: Wealth, "striking oil." Fuel produces energy, as in **Coal**. The image of oil today also refers to environmental pollution. In addition to something dirty and destructive at work here, oil also has a capacity for healing: the ritual of oil offered to the dying, for example, a cleansing and strengthening function. We also think of oil change in a car, where clean oil is said to make for a more efficient engine. The dream image, therefore, stands between pollution and cleansing. This is particularly appropriate, since "oil and water do not mix."

Do we need to pour oil on **Water** in order to smooth out the waves of emotions?

Olives: A sexual symbol, erotic adventures, or travel memories.
Folklore: Peace, prosperity, and luck.

One: Unity. See **Circle, Ball.** That which is indivisible, the self.

One-Way Street: Being one-sided. Also, a sense of feeling trapped, and a sign of focusing on a goal.

Onion: Vitality and health, but also false tears. The onion is the hot spice of life.
Folklore: Good Luck.

Opal: Life that glitters in many colors! Opals also have the reputation of being unlucky.
Folklore: Extremely favorable omen.

Open Hearth: See **Fire.** Domesticity, protection, as in **Parents' House,** as with symbols of **Cooking, Baking, Roast.**

According to Jung, transformation process in alchemy; something wants to transcend.

Opening (of an Exhibition, etc.) Well-known symbol for new beginnings, as in **Baby, Birth,** and **Child.**

Is it a store or art gallery that is opening? What is being shown or sold? The kind of objects that are on display point, symbolically, to the kind of new beginning that is to come. A bookstore, for instance, might point to education and intellectual subjects; an art exhibition might point to creative/artistic self-development.

Opera: A warning of too much vanity, pathos, and self-absorption. Danger of overdramatizing, but also joy and vitality.

Operation: Emotional problems and their elimination. The type of operation is important. It will show what is disturbed and how it can be remedied.

Optician: Clear insight and objectivity are suggested. The way you see things is being questioned. See **Eyeglasses, Eye.**

Orange: A sexual meaning. When dreaming about two oranges or two apples, they symbolize women's breasts. See **Fruit, Sun.**

Orange Juice: Usually a sign that you are actually thirsty. See **Orange.**

Orchestra: Usually points to a desire for harmony in relationships or with people at work. You would like to unite many voices within yourself, or you experience many voices and run the danger of losing yourself. See **Concert, Mosaic, Multiplicity**.

Orgy: Points to boredom or undefined sexuality. This insight is only the beginning of the process of forming your own erotic sexuality.

Orient: Longing for beauty and to possess wealth. A symbol of that which fascinates us; but also that which we do not understand. Secrets and eroticism.

Origin: Purification, composure, prayer, devotion, and deep emotional feelings.

Other (Things and Persons): Usually points to too much egotism. Overcoming egotistical notions. Encounters with "others" (either in the form of strangers or the self) are the beginning of building self-awareness and self-knowledge. Often the task at hand is to become consciously aware of oneself. In most cases, the image in the dream is that of a stranger or foreigner who is representing a part of the self. On the other hand, what you believe to be normal (in your own life) is questioned, and you are challenged to seek self-knowledge and to re-examine your lifestyle.

Ouroboros: See **Phoenix**. Here is the tail eater, the serpent that bites its own tail. It represents the original state where there is neither beginning nor end. According to Jung, this is a symbol of the state of becoming aware, of completion, with the energy finally creating the higher self (**Circle, Zero**). The Ouroboros marries itself, impregnates itself with its phallic tail, and then kills itself, only to raise itself again. The tail eater is also a dragon, and a sexual symbol. Of interest, too, might be the famous dream of the chemist A. Kekule von Strodonitz (1829-1896) about the Ouroboros. He came up with the key to understanding the benzol chain and said it was the dream of the Ouroboros that gave it to him.

Oval: You are approaching the **Circle** and completion. See **Ellipse**.

Oven: Heat, urges. You are "cooking" something up; something is brewing internally. Romantic flight into the so-called "good old days."

Warm feelings. A cold oven refers to emotional coldness. Points to the state of your relationship.

According to Freud, female sexual symbol, uterus.

Owl: Symbol of wisdom. Owls can see in the dark and for that reason are said to have greater perception. One feels found out.

Ox: Energetic, stubborn, and clumsy. When stifled and overwhelmed, a search for relief and a lighter workload.

Oysters: Luxury, social advancement. Desire for material excess. According to classical depth psychology a symbol of female sexuality, and often seen as an aphrodisiac.
Folklore: Troubles.

Package: Troubles, worry, and burdens that you have to carry, but also gifts. The image of opening a package often has to do with self-awareness.

Package (large): See **Package**, **Container**. Often points to the unknown or to repressed emotions, obstacles, burdens, and complications that you carry with you. See **Gift**.

Pagoda: Wanderlust, travel experiences. You are looking at your own body and soul as a temple.
Folklore: A trip is cancelled.

Pail: See **Container** that wants to be filled or that has been filled. A full bucket always indicates that you have much to give. Female sexual symbol. Something is being ruined, thrown away into a pail!

Pain: Being sensitive or overly sensitive. It points to either the necessity of grieving or a new beginning.

Paintbrush: Stupid person. Art and harmony. In psychoanalysis, a sexual symbol.
Folklore: Your wishes are granted.

Painter/Artist: Creativity and a sense of beauty.
Folklore: Luck.

Palace: See **Castle**. An archetypal symbol for Mother. Emotional security or imprisonment. Compare this to "castle in the air."

Your own self as well as your own body; megalomania and freedom.

According to Freud, this image symbolizes the female.

Paleness: Fear, illness, or being blasé.

Palm: A phallic symbol, and also one of friendliness and peace. Exuberant vitality. In a man's dream it may also indicate an unsatisfactory sex life.

Pants: Vanity, self-portrayal, trying to hide shame (getting "caught with your pants down"). If a pair of pants is seen in the context of "I am the one that wears the pants," particularly in a man's dream, it represents a picture of self-determination and gender identity. For both men and women, this dream symbol may also be, at the same time, an overemphasis on one's masculine side. See also **Container, Genital Organ, Leg.**

Paper: Book. Something you are aware of, which is long overdue, needs to be resolved. A clean, white sheet of paper also symbolizes innocence as well as "empty consciousness." In a positive sense this could mean a creative emptiness. In a negative sense it indicates a lack of awareness. It is also a symbol of the spirit. Paper with writing on it is the same as a book, meaning you need to pay attention to the text.

According to Freud, paper is a symbol of femininity.

Parachute: Not a dangerous fall; letting oneself fall gently. Sexual connotation, as in **Falling**, **Brook**, and **Leaf**. You are letting yourself glide through the air, which symbolizes an associative, creative, and playful intellect. This dream symbol also points to more general situations where you are letting yourself go, and you will like it. When in fear of **Flying**, the parachute usually does not open.

Parade: Are you looking for honor and fame? Your emotional strength is being displayed; or you are looking at your own potential. If you are marching in the parade, you are displaying the dynamic of your inner strengths—with either too much or too little internal coordination. Spoiling somebody's parade is an expression of aggression.

Paradise: Possibly a symbol of running away from difficulties, or a "big dream" that points to important life goals and desires. A desire for quiet, relaxation, and peace—to be enjoying life and productivity. A conscience that is at peace with "God and the world" and that has recognized the Self. Release of what was repressed. See **Bird, Parrot, Hell**.

Paralysis: Feeling handicapped in a mental or emotional area. Feeling the need for quiet and rest. Should you be less active? See **Illness, Invalid**.

Parasol/Cap: See **Umbrella**. Old symbol for power, protection, and keeping your distance.

According to Freud, phallic symbol in the process of erection.

Parents: Father, Mother. You are seeking help from the outside, as in **Physician, Medication,** and **Pharmacist**; however, the danger is not that great. Often an expression of considerable immaturity in adults. "Dream parents" are a hint that you need to be a good father or a good mother to yourself. Are you a mother to yourself? Are you a loving father to yourself?

Parents' House: Separating from **Parents,** a new beginning (particularly when leaving home). Security in the **Family, Notice-of-Intention-to-Marry, Sidewalk,** and

Bureaucrat. Suggestion of helplessness. In this case, ask yourself how you experience your childhood. How are these feelings connected with your life today? In addition, the question of parenthood comes up. What do you want to bring into this world?

Park: A symbol of nature controlled; pointing to the dreamer's repressed wildness. At the same time, however, it is also a symbol for culture, beauty, and graciousness. It points to the connection between nature and intellect.

Parking: See **Car/Driving**. Coming to rest, becoming rigid, standing in one place. But also having found a goal and purpose.

Parliament: Points to your social abilities and desire for advancement. An indication of coming to terms with other people and the voice inside you. It is a symbol of governing and points to the need to coordinate your own qualities. How are you putting together your emotions and intellect? How do you "rule" yourself and others?

Parrot: Highly confidential secrets are being given away by close friends. An eccentric person glittering in many colors. Either dependency and immaturity, or a challenge to be more unconventional, exotic, and colorful.

Folklore: Unfavorable gossip is being spread about you.

Parsley: Strengthens the heart. Success.

Partner: Symbolizes your own often unknown characteristics. Or, it may be connected to the partner in your relationship.

Party: Pleasure after work is completed, social exchange, and communication. Well-being, fun, and joy in the dream, as in life, always mean to search for or to have found your center. Your personal characteristics are getting stimulated and recognized, and that is the meaning of "party," too.

Folklore: Bad omen.

Pass/Passport: The dreamer himself. Wanderlust; often also saying good-bye to old habits. In addition, it may mean fleeing from something, or indicate an inferiority complex, because you have to legitimize your identity.

Password: See **Pass**.

Path: As in **Street**; a frequent symbol of life's path. See **Wagon**. Your personal path is laid out for you. You are walking your own life's path. Or, difficulty on the path.

Payment: If you receive money, you are receiving energy. If you have to give money, energy is lost. Always make sure that you pay attention to the direction of the flow of energy: where it is coming from and where it is flowing to. Of course, in addition to the symbolic meaning, this dream might also represent an actual financial situation that might cause apprehension.

Pea: Female sexual symbol (clitoris). Easily irritated, or positive sensitivity (as in the fairy tale "The Princess and the Pea"). In another fairy tale is the incident of "counting peas," which could mean either pettiness and being a stickler for details or being precise and careful when dealing with small items.
   Folklore: The promise of happiness, only—be patient!

Peach: An erotic symbol. Romantic relationships. According to Freud, a symbol of the female breast.
   Folklore: Since the Middle Ages, a peach has meant reunion with a lover.

Peacock: Vanity. A symbol of narcissism and arrogance. But at the same time it may represent the beauty of the soul and the diversity of one's own personality. In alchemy it is a symbol that points to changes in life. Also, a symbol of rebirth. See **Phoenix**.

Pear: Symbol of female sexuality (as with all fruits); possible dream at the beginning of pregnancy.

Pearl: A symbol of the mature soul and completeness of the emotional experience. Also a female sexual symbol (clitoris), and a general symbol of women, loved ones, something precious and complete. Pearl also refers to domestic help and "the good soul." If a pearl necklace breaks, trouble and worries due to a loss.

Folklore: Happy marriage.

Pencil/Fountain Pen: News, notes. Appears often in dreams when something is in danger of being forgotten that needs to be remembered (better write it down).

According to Freud: phallic symbol (particularly a fountain pen filled with ink).

Pendulum: The ups and downs of life. Fixing on the

point "above," which means **Heaven**. In that sense the pendulum is a symbol of faith and eternal law.

Folklore: A big journey.

Penis: Symbol of masculine power. See **Genital Organ**.

Penitentiary: A dream about obstacles, as in **Prison, Cage**—only more severe.

Pension: Quiet and relaxation.

Folklore: A decision.

Pepper: Refers to "hot stuff."

Performance: Publicity, end of secrecy, vanity, and superficiality. Show your colors. You may be getting too worked up about something, showing off too much. See also **Arena** and **Amphitheater**. What is playing at the theater/movie?

Perfume: Wanting to look good and be seen in positive terms, loved, and accepted. Addresses the power of attraction and subtle radiance. Like the fragrance of a perfume that evaporates quickly, your understanding of yourself and others is difficult to maintain. On the other hand, making a definite statement (with a fragrance) about your presence, the scent of the perfume expresses sexuality and fantasies.

Period: See **Rhythm, Haste, Step, Menstruation, Nosebleed**.

Person: Any person in a dream can represent you yourself. Particularly when important persons—like father, mother, lover, and children—are recognized clearly in the dream, it is truly yourself that you are dealing with. In addition, every person in a dream may point to some of your own characteristics and tasks in life, or may symbolize something impersonal. Less often, a person in a dream might be a reminder of another similar person.

Pest/Vermin: A symbol that points to unmet sexual desire or fear of unwanted pregnancy. In antiquity it was a symbol for foolish gambling.

According to Freud, it often points to children or siblings.

Folklore: Good luck.

Pestilence: Emotional disturbance and, at the least, great insecurity.

Pets: Either "back to nature" or damaged nature. The tension between the animal and civilized nature.

Pewter: See **Metal**.
Folklore: Satisfaction.

Pharmacist: See **Alchemist, Chemist.**

Pheasant: The pheasant was brought to Europe during the Middle Ages, where over a period of time it became wild. It is a symbol for the power of nature and beauty (similar to the astrological sign of Leo), but also of the inability to make decisions. It has been considered a reluctant and decidedly stupid bird.

Do you have trouble making decisions, thinking that all possibilities will always be available? Are you afraid to follow your own desires and needs and, for that reason, are you dismissing many possibilities right from the beginning? What if you took a chance and followed your feelings? In China, the pheasant is a symbol of wealth. It was the emblem of the Emperor Yü. In Japan, the pheasant is the female symbol of mother-love and protection.

Phoenix: See **Peacock**. According to the most widely

read book of the Middle Ages, *Physiologus*, the phoenix of India is more beautiful than a peacock. After 500 years, and at new moon, the phoenix flew to Heliopolis, presented itself to the priest, and then burned itself on the altar. What remained was a worm from which wings began growing, and the phoenix was reborn. A symbol of resurrection, rebirth, and transformation.

Photo/Photography: The past of the dreamer, memories of past events (also in the sense of wanting to hold on to them and idealization). Playing with **Light** and **Shadow** (with so-called light and dark places), which means seeing life according to your own imagination. You want to focus on seeing clearly and recognizing what you see. You are working with the camera lens, which is a hint to be more objective.

Photo-Collage: Photography, but with the main emphasis on creative aspects. Here, it is a question of putting the puzzle of your own life together. It is important what is being assembled, and in what way.

Physician (male or female): Comfort, sympathy, fear of pain, **Illness**, and **Death**. Anticipating problems ahead and looking for a way out, for advice and help. May also stand for general improvement and stabilization. A symbol of masculinity, of a wise man, wise woman, or an emancipated female. Authority and wealth. Try—in the dream—to talk to the physician and ask questions about the situation. The answers can serve as an important clue, not only to your health. If the dreamer is the physician, he or she wants to have control over life and **Death**.

According to Freud, also a symbol for eroticism. The physician is a person that we stand before naked.

Piano: The scale of the emotions, intensive feelings, culture, and harmony. Being spiritual and intellectually alive.

According to Freud, because of its rhythm when being played, it is a symbol for intercourse.

As with all musical instruments, according to psychoanalysis it symbolizes the body of the woman. See **Grand Piano**.

Pickaxe: A symbol of aggression in a sexual context, but also, the other side of the axe—used to loosen and penetrate hard surfaces.

Picnic: Eating always points to the natural and intimate.

Picture: Portrait. Not the real thing! Being either ego-centric or self-reflecting. Search for a relevant world-view or your true self.

Pie: Enjoyment.
Folklore: Domestic joy.

Pig: See **Greed**. Sexuality demanding to be set free, but also rejection of physical sexuality. Symbol of luck, natural sexuality, intellectual power. Fertility. According to Moses and the Koran, pork is considered a forbidden food. It is the symbol of something low and primitive—"casting pearls before swine"—laziness, wallowing in dirt; but also comfort.

According to Freud, a sexual symbol (in the *Odyssey*, Circe transforms men into swine; she frees their animal side in order to bind them to her).

In the East, a symbol of the unconscious.

Pigtail: This image refers to taming.

Pill: Bitter truth, illness, but also searching and finding. Fear of pregnancy. *Uppers:* a suggestion that you have to find happiness in yourself and not expect it to come from the outside. *Downers:* You need to "work" for relaxation and not expect it to come by itself. *Drugs:* You are seeking deeper spiritual insights, but in a regressive way. One has to learn to find experiences of freedom without drugs. *Birth control:* The dreamer is longing for sex, but there is fear involved.

Pillar: Support. According to Freud, a phallic symbol.

Pillow: Rest, relaxation and domesticity, as in **Baking, Roast, Cooking, Flowerpot, Iron, Porcelain, Apron, Hen**.
   Folklore: Difficulties.

Pineapple: Being a juicy and sweet **Fruit**, it is a sign of self-confidence, enjoyment of life, and sexuality. It is a female sexual symbol (as are all fruits, except bananas).

Pinecone: Phallic symbol.

Pipe: As with cigarettes, it often points to difficulties. Or, a symbol for relaxation and enjoyment.
   Astrology: Related to Neptune.

Pipe (water/sewage pipe): A sexual symbol. If you are crawling through the pipe yourself, it is a symbol of birth. If the pipe is clogged up, it usually points to a problem with freely expressing your feelings. See **Constipation**.

Pirate: Freeloader. Longing for freedom and independence and living out the masculine in man and woman. Opposite, and a complement to, **Admiral**.

Pistol/Gun: Masculine sexual symbol, and a symbol for aggression always connected to power and achievement. The dangers and the potentialities of self-determination are emphasized here. It also means: come to the point; hit your target—or better not hit it—and conclude something or begin something new.

Place: Often your own center, especially if the place is round or square. Or, in a public place, becoming aware of something.

Plain/Plateau: Boredom, but also being in balance. Good foresight and perspective, similar to **Bird**.
Folklore: Material rewards.

Plane/Slicer: A very focused attempt to create order,

smoothing things out at any price. This dream often indicates a process of elimination.

In its connection to "airplane," see **Flying** and **Parachute**. Also, may indicate a concern with how people judge you and how you want to be seen.

Planet: For an interpretation of the meanings of planets in dreams, look up books on astrology, or better yet, read Greek mythology. A symbol of your own **Star**.

Plant: See **Tree, Flower**. A plant often represents a part of the dreamer. It is a symbol of growth, naturalness, but also that which is slow and logical.

This dream image often suggests the need to plant something, pointing to the development of the dreamer's talents and abilities.

Plaster: Stabilizing, bonding medium. Being steadfast or stubborn. **Heat** that needs to cool down.

Getting stuck, being glued to something (in reference to relationships, work, etc.). Something may be smoothed out with plaster, as in **Ironing**. Plaster is used to make a copy of an original. What are you copying? Falsehood.

Folklore: Being wrongly accused.

Plate/Dinner Plate: Social advantage or hunger for life.

Plateau: Perspective, as in **Skyscraper/High-Rise, Hiding Places,** and **Bird.**

Platform (at the train station): See **Railway Station.** The symbol for taking a trip and for waiting. Also, meeting other people.

Platform/Cockpit: See Pulpit.

Playing Cards: Happenstance, luck, and skill.

Pliers: Are you feeling squeezed? Often a hint to be more decisive in a given situation; or, are you trying to force something? This dream often points to a complicated situation, perhaps "Catch 22," and requires your finding a different approach, another level of communicating, a different attitude.

Plow: Changing and loosening up one's lifestyle. According to Freud, and also most other dream interpreters, plowing means intercourse (see also **Furrow**). Plowing, as well as **Sowing,** is one of the many late-medieval sexual rituals. See **Fools.**

Plum: A female sexual organ. In the Orient, it means luck, and is also an erotic symbol, suggesting domestic bliss.

Plumber: This image refers to **Pipe (water)**; in other words, guiding the emotions. In addition, the matter of sexuality should not be dismissed, since the plumber does install a **Pipe**.

Pocket/Bag: See **Container, Suitcase**. Indicates the ability to carry a load and, if necessary, the ability to take action. It is a symbol of that which we carry around with us (purse, attaché case, etc.), that which we own. It is also a symbol of what we are made of (what is in our pockets symbolizes what is in ourselves—what moves us—because the pocket is inside our clothes).

According to Freud, female genitals. The apron pocket, according to Jung, is the "pocket" the woman or girl carries within her body. In the case of a man or a boy, the pocket refers to the region from which sexual desires arise.

Pocketbook: Property. A female sexual symbol that appears frequently in women's dreams. On one hand, a pocketbook stands for personal **Luggage** (or burden).

On the other hand, it points toward a notebook, as a symbol for memory.

Poet: Longing for creative activity, fantasy, and inspiration. The belief that creative work is the result of suffering is an often quoted meaning of this dream symbol. In the end it comes down to condensing one's existence, compressing it, intensifying it, and living in a more focused way, according to one's personal essence.

Pointer: See **Cane/Baton**.

Poison: Cruelty and aggression. Often, poisonous thoughts and feelings. It may represent everything that is a contradiction within the dreamer or, on rare occasions, medicine.

Poisonous Snake: See **Snake**. Well-known symbol for a deceptive woman. Dangers in matters of the heart and erotic issues. See **Enemy**.

Pole: See **Rod**. Masculine sexual organ, and not only according to Freud.

Policeman: Father figure, authority, and person of

respect—in short, a symbol for the superego. A feeling of oppression and dissatisfaction, possibly a sign of immature masculinity. This dream image points to the danger of an impersonal and abstract consciousness. It challenges you to find out if you have a mind of your own or are strictly submitting to an authoritarian direction. Does law and order play a big role in your life? Or would you rather be a friend and helper? Maybe you should bring more of your own personality and opinions into the game. Take a chance, be more liberated and more responsible.

Pond: Stagnant water, often symbolizing erotic feelings. If the surface is calm, a balanced emotional life. As indicated in the saying "Still waters run deep," it is also a symbol of deep feelings. If the water in the pond is cloudy, it is often a symbol of sexual conflict.

Pope: See **Bishop**.

Poppy/Flower: Intoxication; more awareness is demanded. Losing oneself as either a dangerous or a positive sign.
   Folklore: Temptation.

Porcelain: See **Marriage**, domesticity, culture, and lifestyle, as in **Iron**, **Flowerpot**, **Hen**, **Pillow**, **Apron**, **Baking**, **Cooking**. Sometimes, but very seldom, it points to luxury.

Porcupine: Withdrawing because you are too sensitive and too easily injured, while at the same time being "prickly" and ready for some cunning attack. According to early Christian understanding (the most widely read book of the Middle Ages, *Physiologus*), the porcupine is lovable and loves children. It kills **Snakes.**
   Folklore: Your friendship is being taken advantage of.

Porter: Someone who is carrying the burden for others. Is it you or is somebody else carrying your burden for you?
   Folklore: Slander.

Portrait: You are getting a clearer picture about yourself or somebody else. Calls for creative vision and actions instead of logic alone. Portraits almost always show characteristics of the dreamer. Every picture is a self-portrait and a reflection of one's personal or broad and universal attitudes. See **Picture.**

Post/Post Office/Postcard: Sending or receiving important information from the unconscious. Increased awareness, communication.

Post/Stake: A post driven into the ground is a symbol for intercourse and it usually starts a spring flowing.

Pot: Container. A symbol for virginity. Pouring liquid out of a pot points to devotion. See **Container**, **Frying Pan**, **Soup**.

Potato: The food of the poor, particularly in the 19th century, which thereby connects this image to fear of social decline—note Van Gogh's painting *The Potato Eaters,* for example, where dark and somber colors convey the mood of poverty.

At the same time, the image of the potato refers to groundedness, since it grows underground. As a root plant, the potato addresses the rootedness of the dreamer. As a tuber, the potato has a peculiar androgynous shape: it could represent a phallic symbol as well as typically feminine shapes. As one of the basic food forms, the potato also represents the nurturing female as well as the power of Mother Nature.

Potter: Shaping life. Creating a way to express emotional energies. Romantic longing for an activity that is perceived to be simple.

Powder: See **Mask**. Inferiority complex, disguise. You want to pretend you're something that you are not. On the other hand, completion, the final touch.

Folklore: A festive occasion.

Power: The game of power is always playing with fire. This image points to your passionate vitality. At issue here are the energies that are available to you and how they are being used. The image of power addresses your shadow as well as your strength. How are you using your power? Against others? Or is somebody's power being used against you? Are you feeling powerful or powerless? See **Ruler**.

Indicates luck and health, or it may be pointing to weakness. More important is how the energy is being expressed—through the heart, the soul, the mind, the body, or the character.

Prayer: Often points to a dreamer's childlike behavior. Often a hint to become more active, or to turn more inward. On the other hand, praying is also connected to the practice of asking and giving.

Precious Stone: The treasures within you, the higher self. Points to the fact that something very precious has been growing within you. Steadfastness, faithfulness, dependability, but also pride. The shinier the stone, the greater the emphasis on pride and vanity. Pay attention to the color and the type of stone. Stones that are damaged have a negative symbolic meaning.

Predator: "Every woman at some time dreams about a predator." So it has been said in the past, but the same holds true for every man. Points to sexual feelings, animalistic ones that could be enjoyed or that you are trying to repress.

Presentation: Showing something off, as in **Undressing**. Wanting to be cultivated or sophisticated or at least appear to be. Self-portrayal, as in **Arena, Performance**.

Price/Payment: You must pay for everything. Or do essentials come as a gift to everybody? May or may not have to do with transformation of energy.

Priest: See **Minister, Bishop, Professor.** Ancient Egyptian interpretation: You are offered a prestigious position.

Primeval Forest/Jungle: A place that is generally inaccessible, representing the unconscious and physical drives. A symbol of strength and vitality, but also the danger of falling prey to drives and urges. It may point to more discipline, or challenges to live out physical urges more clearly. See **Maze.**

Prince/Princess: Always you yourself. Often refers to your own magical spiritual dignity—either negative or positive—new emotional independence, and ability to express yourself.

Prism: Points to a situation that has many facets, as in **Crystal** and rainbow, **Multiplicity.** A symbol of unity and of collecting what is scattered.

Prison/Being Imprisoned: May symbolize restrictions and dependency in many forms. Usually, it expresses a need for more space and freedom, as in **Crowds, Shackles,** and **Cage.** You feel limited (often because of a relationship or situations at work) or awkward. In rare cases, it refers to a "blind spot" or a sore point you're saddled with.

Freud dreamed in his youth about a prison in the shape of a **Box,** which to him was the symbol of a uterus.

Prisoner: See **Prison**. Strong guilt feelings, to the point of feeling unconscious restriction. But by recognizing this feeling of apprehension and imprisonment in the dream, you can change it. Often this dream image is about recognizing that it is not necessary to punish yourself.

Procession: See **Parade**.

Professor: Intellectualization and advancement. Or, life is too one-sided intellectually. Somebody who pronounces something publicly, defends, and teaches. See **Minister/Pastor**.

Prostitution: Men or women who sell themselves. Repressed drives, as in **Breaking Up, Attack, Electricity, Defloration, Flames, Violence, Greed, Harem**. Also see **Skin rash** and **Wire (High-Tension)**. The dreamer is dissatisfied. In the case of a woman, a symbol of courage and independence, but also of sense-less and thoughtless sexuality. This dream symbol often points to an aversion toward sexuality and everyday life.

Protest: Self-determination and establishing boundaries.

Pub/Saloon: Restaurant.

Public: Self-portrayal or lack of it, depending on whether, in the dream, you have an audience or you are the public.
Folklore: Social advancement.

Public Transportation: A limited but sensible way of moving about collectively, not individually. See **Train**.

Pudding: Is what you eat unhealthy? Do you think you are too heavy? See **Ice**, **Cake**, **Jellyfish**.

Puddle: Dirty **Water** and emotions.

Pulling Teeth: Something that you cannot or are not supposed to have. ("Getting the information is like pulling teeth.")

Pulpit/Cockpit/Platform: In dreams these terms take on different meanings. As a pulpit in church the symbol might point to increased problems and hypocrisy. It is either your bad conscience that is speaking to you or a suggestion that you are following moral standards too rigidly.

As an airplane cockpit, and as a politician in government, these images also stand for leadership. Among others, they represent personal skills. Often there is a hint to guide yourself more forcefully toward your goals.

Folklore: Bad omen.

Pump: Sexual symbol, fertility, flowing emotions.

Punishment: Bad conscience and masochism. Moral problems, similar to **Confession.** It is also possible that you will be asked to consider taking responsibility for somebody, or that you need to forgive somebody.

Puppet: Numb, childish, dependent, insensitive (a child projecting its psyche on the puppet). It is important to look at how these symbols are connected. They may point to a rediscovery of childlike emotions, or to the necessity to say good-bye to them.

If you are the puppet, you see yourself as without a soul, as only a pretty plaything.

Until the late Middle Ages, the puppet was considered a defense against evil ghosts or as possessing magical powers. Such beliefs are still mirrored in the practice of having mascots.

Puppet/Puppeteer: This symbol addresses your nervous system, where the wires of the puppet are your nerves. Often you cannot see the puppeteer directly, but he is the one who is "pulling your strings," symbolizing the power that is hidden behind the curtains. This symbol questions how you could "better" coordinate your intellectual resources and nervous system. What is pulling you? And where?

Purple: Purple is the color at the border of the visible spectrum. You are seeking awareness and transcendence. This is also a symbol of conservative religion (the aristocratic cardinals in the Middle Ages wore purple). It is also a symbol of royalty, and of woman's emancipation.

Pursuit: A dream symbol that appears rather frequently. Something that you have repressed is trying to make itself known. Subconsciously, sexuality is perceived as bad.

According to Freud, drives and urges are haunting you. But in contrast to Freud, this dream may indicate that the dreamer is pursuing that which is rightfully his, which are his ideals.

In so-called chase dreams, according to Jung, something is trying to reach you. What has been split off and repressed wants to be united again. If this is the case, don't put up defenses, rather invite in what is trying to reach you. If the dream suggests that a good-bye is necessary, resist what is chasing you.

Putrefaction: In alchemy this image is part of the process of blackening and a symbol of total unconsciousness, of decay. A frequent symbol in nightmares. The decay usually points to your own characteristics that have died and that you either need to let go of or revive. Fear of illness. Challenge to be more self-critical and more self-confident

Putty/Cement: Holding together (against the outside world).
Folklore: Hard times.

Puzzle: See **Riddle, Mosaic**.

Pyramid: According to Jung, the graves of kings who were honored as gods are a symbol of the idea of resurrection. Egypt is not the only place with pyramids; they have also been found in Mexico and in China, where the idea of resurrection is expressed through the choice of the place where they were built, between mountain and valley. A pyramid stands between heaven and earth. Pyramids also refer to wanderlust and travel experiences. Also, they are signposts. The pyramids served as enormous mirrors, due to their polished surfaces, making them a source of light. Given their foundation, they are also a physical mandala. Know your own light—your strengths and talents. The pyramid stands for those who elevate their own fire and light, growing beyond their personal world. See **Square**, **Triangle**.

Pyre/Stake: Guilt feelings have piled up.

Quarantine: Warning of isolation and illness. Something is troubling you and you are dealing with it in the emotional arena.

Quarrel: Inner conflict and contradictions.

Quarry: Is your rigid attitude crumbling? Is your heart—that seems to be made of stone—softening?

Quarter/District: This image is always a part of the dreamer himself.

Queen: See **King/Queen**.

Quicksand: Getting lost in emotions. Treacherous dangers, lost insights, insecure emotions. See **Dunes**.

Rabbit: See **Hare**.

Race: This image almost always refers to career issues, addressing primarily the question of winner and loser, because such dreams usually deal with emotional energies. Are you running ahead? Are others behind you? Or are you running behind the pack? Different people taking part in a competitive race in the dream represent the many different sides of the Self.

Racing: Wanting to reach the goal in a hurry. **Haste.** That holds true for your external as well as internal goals. Racing—whether it is a marathon, an auto or horse race—is always connected to stamina and not "getting out of breath." This dream symbol appears often during stress situations. On the other hand, racing is also an image of ecstasy.

Radio: Communication, information, messages about emotions, internal dialogue. To listen to a radio in a dream is to listen to your own voice.

Rags: Desire for advancement, or fear of poverty, as in **Charity**, **Asylum**, **Beggar**. Also a romantic desire to let things go and break with convention. A protest against success and self-portrayal.

Railroad Car: See **Railway Station, Platform**. A frequently appearing symbol for travel. What is important is whom you meet in the railroad car.

Railway Station: See **Train.** A frequent dream symbol. Changes in the present life situation. At the train station, we often find out where our life's journey is taking us. Also an image of rushing ("It's high time"). Waiting for something or "being thrown off-track."

The conductor might be a symbol for our better-informed self. Is the train coming, are we on the right train, where and to which train are we changing, the waiting room: all these symbols can easily be a reflection of our own emotional situation.

In depth psychology, the train represents our unconscious, which is trying to get us on the right "track."

Rain: See **Clouds.** Longing for deep relaxation. A symbol of fertility. Also, a longing for mental/intellectual inspiration.

Rainbow: A symbol of wholeness. The **Fire** of the sun and the **Water** of the rain come together; contradictions are united. The connection between desire and will. The rainbow has also been a Christian symbol for the bond between God and human beings. Today, it is often a symbol for creativity and fantasies.

According to the *Talmud* and *Kabbala*, we are not allowed to look at a rainbow, because it leads back to

God. In some African mythology, the rainbow is a devouring animal. According to Jung, it is the bridge leading into the next life.

A rainbow can also be seen as a **Circle**; it contains every color and meaning, every quality.

Raisins: Money, but also romantic feelings.

Ram: See **Buck**.

Range/Cooking Range: See **Oven**. In the past, the central place for family events, eating, motherliness, woman, and marriage. Similar to **Cap.** Today, a range does not display an open flame; but the transformation of food from a raw to a cooked state is emphasized more. The oven, like the **Kitchen,** is one of the most frequent symbols of transformation. Danger lurks when the fire is going out.

According to Freud, the symbol for women and the female body.

Ransom: Emotional expenditure; an attempt to free oneself.

Raspberry: See **Berry**. Happy life.

Rat: Warning signal in a dream—nagging thoughts and doubts. If this is a frequently occurring dream and is accompanied by fear, it would be a good idea to seek therapeutic advice.

Raven: See **Bird, Crow.** Supposed to mean bad luck, or a messenger of bad luck. At the same time, however, the black bird is a symbol of creativity and femininity. In Germanic mythology, the raven is the bird of death. According to Mohammed, the raven represents the sinner.

Folklore: The bird of the soul.

Razor/Razor Blade: Analytical thinking, the need to smooth something out.

Folklore: Warning of troubles and quarrels.

Rebel: How do you deal with your real emotions? See also **Protest** and **Pirate.**

Receptacle: See **Can, Container.** According to Freud, female sexual symbol. According to Jung, symbol of mystery ("Pandora's Box," which when opened will set loose all the troubles of the world).

Recipe/Prescription: Dreaming about prescriptions often points to real healing. A kitchen recipe generally means new plans.

Recluse: Hermit. Being one-sided, grief, longing for social contact, but also wisdom (see the Tarot card of "The Hermit.") The hermit is lonely, or alone in the sense of being one with oneself, being a person who can be trusted and asked for advice. If you remember your hermit dream, talk to the hermit, ask him your question, and you will get an answer that comes from your own center. Since time immemorial, the hermit has been considered a signpost, guiding you through everyday troubles and darkness. The hermit can bring you warmth, affection, brilliance, and wisdom.

Recuperation: You are healing—body and/or soul.

Red: A positive color, representing vitality (fire) and activity, love and passion. Red, however, can also be a sign of aggression, rage, and vengeance. According to alchemistic tradition, red is the color of the spirit, of gold, and of the sun. It is a warning of danger. For the Hindus, red means vitality and expansion. For the Mayans, red meant victory and success. For the

Chinese, red is the color of luck. In alchemy, red is the color of emotions, of **Blood**, and **Fire**. The colors of heaven and hell are red. Red is the color of overwhelming emotional upheaval and in a dream often points to a situation that is packed with intensity.

Reduction: See **Telescope**. Inferiority complex, devaluing the Self. Taking small things too seriously. Possibly a suggestion to expand your frame of reference and thereby grow in awareness. See also Lewis Carroll's *Alice in Wonderland*.

Reed: Be careful—quagmire and mud. Either it is difficult to get ahead or the reed points to protection; you can hide in the reeds, and you can also cover your roof with them.

Referee: This image refers to fairness in contact and dealings with the world and the Self. The image points to the inner, psychic authority of the Self that judges you as well as others. It suggests you take on a more neutral and detached attitude toward life. Observe your own "games" a little more closely.

Refrigerator: Hiding place for physical drives; repression and isolation. What do you want to preserve? Or are you expressing here a need for "staying cool" or for "clarity"?

Rejection/Refusal: Longing for closeness; or distance. Feeling of social isolation, of being closed off or refusing to face up to something, or refusing to take action. Often, however, the opposite meaning—being accepted, though fearing rejection.

Relative: Usually points to sides of the dreamer himself, such as well-known characteristics and qualities. When a relative is rejected in the dream, a side of yourself is also rejected. According to Freud, sexual organs.

Rent/Tenant: Using something without owning it. Everything we use we must pay for.

Report Card: See **School**. Expression of old fears of failure or failure of performance. The dreamer is evaluating his own life, his actions, and his performance. It is either validation and acceptance or a reprimand and criticism.

Reptile: See **Snake** and **Crocodile**. According to Freud, male sexual symbol.

Responsibility: Are you overtaxed? Do you feel you need more balance and more appropriate tasks?

Rest/Quiet: You are usually longing for it.

Restaurant: Enjoying contact and communication; but there is also superficiality here. A longing for social contact and diversion. Eating and feeling comfortable in public points either to being open or lack of a private space.

See **Food, Eating.** It is important what type of restaurant and what is happening there. How do you feel being there?

Folklore: Good omen, if you see yourself in the restaurant. Watching yourself eating points to small pleasures; watching others eat suggests poor emotional health.

Resurrection: Developmental process. Something has to die, needs to be let go of, as in **Ashes, Funeral,** and **Phoenix.** A new beginning, perseverance. For Christians, this image is always connected to "The Last Judgment" (fear of death, overcoming death).

Folklore: Long journey.

Retirement Home: See **Age, Harvest**. This dream symbol is often connected to an invitation for self-acceptance—to just be, and to pursue appropriate goals.

Revolution: See **King, Government**.

Revolver: See **Pistol**.

Rhythm: Your own vibrations. Rhythm in a dream often has to do with scheduling time. Are you following your own rhythm or are you feeling pressured?

Rib: According to the Bible and Mohammed, this is the symbol for woman.

Ribbon/Twine: Connecting, restricting. Also, untangling a situation in one's life, as in ball of yarn.

Rice: See **Grain**.
Folklore: Plans may go awry because of wrong advice.

Riddle: Search for an answer, search for freedom.

Riding/Horseback Riding: Controlled (reigned-in) eroticism and energy, power, and movement.

According to Jung, a symbol for intercourse, especially in women's dreams.

Rifle: The dreamer wants to impress others through power and strength—or may be intimidated by it. Fantasies of omnipotence are a symbol for aggression. It may also be an expression of fear, as in **Helmet, Bomb, Bayonet, Shot.** By far the most famous sexual symbol in classical psychoanalysis. it retains that meaning to this day.

Right: The masculine side. Being active. The logical and rational side. What is right, correct, fair—in contrast to the left (unfair).

According to Freud, "the normal," in contrast to the left or perverse sexuality. Possibly a political symbol. See **Left.**

Ring: See **Circle.** A symbol for commitment or a bond. A symbol of wholeness that may also point to vanity.

Riot: Changes and action; fear of political unrest. See also **Assassination.**

Ritual: On the surface, it points to habitual behavior, even though rituals are important and bring deeper meaning to life. This symbol can be pointing to something that has become rigid, as well as to something lively and meaningful. See **Rule, Wealth**.

Rival: Usually the enemy within.

River: Stream, Water. In the stream of life and time, **Flowing**. A trip on a river often symbolizes your life journey. A raging river predicts difficult obstacles connected to physical urges and bothersome emotions. Pay attention to how the water is moving!

Roast (as in oven): You are planning something at work and it has to be successful. Desire for domesticity, as is frequently the case with symbols like **Eating**, **Baking**, and **Feast**. Often an expression of lifestyle and enjoyment. But be careful: Don't let it burn!

Robber: See **Thief/Stealing, Pirate**. What has been stolen? Have you been robbed, or are you the robber?
According to Freud, fear of sexuality.

Robot: See **Computer**. What is missing is a lively spirit. A repressive atmosphere has taken over. On the other hand, a robot is also doing work for us.

Rock: See **Boulder**.

Rocket: Courage; fleeing from life and everyday burdens. Sexual symbol. In danger of losing the ground under your feet, or of wanting to lose it.

Rock Music: Lively, erotic movement. Business, star-cult. Possibly also emancipation of the unconscious and expression of the "wild side" of the dreamer. Who is singing? What song? What message? What emotions?

Rod: Well-known phallic and power symbol (a rod of the chieftain, the magician, the king, or emperor). It points to a search for personal freedom.

The shepherd's rod refers to the responsibility for drives and physical urges. The animals that the shepherd is guarding are the symbol for the animal side. See **Wood, Fishing Rod**.

Rodent: Usually points to nagging problems. Less often, it points to domesticity and fertility—as with all small animals.

Roof: Security, protection, head, and intellect. Area of conscious mental activity. We are talking about having "a roof over our heads," and very often "roof" is a metaphor for a higher intellectual capacity. Are you asked to gain more new insights? Roof also stands for the whole **House**.

Folklore: Well-being and prosperity.

Roof Tile: Security, protection, as in **Roof, Gable,** and **Arch**.

Folklore: Advancement at work.

Room: The room of your soul, the dreamer's inner space. According to Freud, points to woman.

Rooster: Dreaming about masculine vitality. Ever since the Middle Ages, the **Buck** and **Rooster** have been considered symbols of lechery, at the same time as they have meant a desire to be taken care of. On the other hand, a symbol for maturity in the sense of awareness and dependability.

Roots: See **Tree**. Being grounded and rooted. Ancestors. Possibly a symbol for a lack of decision and a lack of ego-identity.

Rope (general)/Cable: Reliable help that, if received

often, is an aid when descending from a tower or a high building. Aid when one is fleeing. But also a symbol for bonding as well as being tied up. Dreams about a rope always have something to do with security, similar to **Anchor** and **Buoy**.

Rope/Cord. Obstacle dream; or desiring or needing to connect with somebody/something. Despair (the rope that you hang yourself with, the rope of the gallows).

Rope (nautical): See **Cord**. Connection and security.

Rosary: Comfort. See **Prayer**. Praying the rosary means comfort. See **Rose**.

Rose: A symbol of Venus—love and devotion. The contradiction of blossom and thorn. The rose plays the same role in the West that the lotus plays in the Orient. Both blossom, producing many thousands of petals, and represent the highest stage of consciousness. The rose is often a symbol of the self. As a well-known symbol of love, it points to the dreamer's feeling of security and suggests that he should be more open to love. The Greek word *rodor* for rose came from the ancient Greek word for "flowing," which may have been coined to convey the flow of fragrance from this flower. But this never-ending flow of fragrance from the rose also shortens its life, causing it to wilt rapidly. Because this magnificently flowering, fragrant blossom wilts so fast, it is also considered a symbol of death.

The rose also points to the world beyond, which is the reason that the Catacombs in Rome are decorated with garlands of roses. The rose also is the harbinger of death in the *Oracles*, and it is reported that a few days before their death, bishops would find a white rose on their chair. The belief in the death-announcing rose has influenced customs in England and Germany, where people have been reluctant to bring roses to a sick person. And if a rose bush produced a green rose—that is, when the petals turned green—as English folklore had it, a family member would die.

It is not only in England that the rose is connected with death. As far back as ancient Rome, every year a festival of the roses was celebrated where the dead were honored. Graves were decorated with wreaths made from roses.

Since time immemorial, what happens in the presence of the rose is not talked about. In antiquity, when a rose was suspended above the table, the meal was taken "sub rosa," as it was called then, which means that absolutely nothing from the conversation was repeated after the meal. The early Christians took up this symbolic tradition: the presence of a rose indicated that silence was to be observed when heathens were among them. The rose as the symbol for silence continued into the 18th century, when, for instance, wooden roses were carved into the woodwork of the confessional and roses were also included in the stucco of the halls of the court. The rose, like the lotus, is considered the perfect flower, which is one of the reasons why the Christian Church declared it to be the image of wisdom. This was instrumental in the rose becoming a symbol of Christ. Mary is also depicted as a rose, but a rose without thorns, because in Christian symbolism the thorns of the rose indicate sin, and Mary was free of sin.

The rose has something very mystical about it. Praying the rosary is considered meditation. The Sufis pray with a drop of rose fragrance dabbed on the area of the "third eye," because it is said that the rose cleanses and strengthens the spirit. In ancient Greece a wreath of roses was already thought to strengthen the mind. The Roman Emperor wore a wreath of roses for the same reason. Romans wore wreaths made from roses during decadent outdoor feasts, because they hoped the roses would minimize the effects of too much drinking.

The rose as the image of a *clear mind* was also known to the alchemists, who connected the rose to the idea of deliverance. In Dante's *Paradiso* the small group of saved sinners is pictured in the form of a white rose above which angels circle like bees. That the way to salvation is possible only through love is perhaps the most important lesson of the rose, the flower originally dedicated to Aphrodite, goddess of love. But that the rose also symbolizes flesh and blood is seen in the fact that Dionysus also claimed the rose to be his.

Time and again we hear about a rose bush that never stops blooming; about rose branches in a vase that for 70 years produced white blossoms; and about how the food for the poor that, in the basket of saints, is transformed into roses.

For those interested in the magic of the rose, we might also mention the *Pentagram* of the Rose. If you connect the center of each petal with the center of the petal that comes after the next, you will form a pentagram, the foot of the Druids, the old magic figure that Faust wanted to use to overcome Satan. The Greeks considered the long-lived, five-leaved rose bush, with the imprint of a pentagram, to be the symbol of the cycle of the Cosmos, which, according to Aristotle, is determined by the five elements (fire, water, earth, air, and ether). Also, the Rosicrucians see the rose as a symbol of hidden wisdom, using it as a symbol in their cross.

The color of the rose is also important. A wilted rose is a sign of a relationship gone bad. According to Jung, the rose is always the symbol for wholeness, representing, in the form of the mandala, a symbol for the order of the world.

Rose Garden: The garden of the soul, representing great beauty, but also thorns, which represent work. The rose garden is the image for paradise on earth, a place of mystical transformation, magic, and wonder. See **Paradise**, **Heaven**.

Rowing: Heavy work, moving under your own power. See **Ship**, **Boat**.

Rubber: Smoothness and adaptability.

Rudder (in the sense of steering): You need solid direction, a goal. Determination.

Ruin: Pay more attention to your health. Or, the sign of a new emotional beginning—from ruins grows something new.

Rule: Here lies the tension between habitual and pioneering thinking. Are you making up your own rules? Or are you following the rules others have made? Do you follow them or break them?

Ruler: Self-determination and self-rule. To be the ruler in your own home. See **Dictator, Leader, Pulpit, King/Queen.**

Rust: Impermanence, a sign of the times. What is rusting?

Rye: See **Grain**.
  Folklore: Good omen.

Saber: Repressed aggression. According to Freud, it is a male sexual symbol, as are all weapons that penetrate the body.

Saddle: Being upright and well established (sitting securely "tall in the saddle").

Safe/Security Vault: Security. Fearing for the safety of possessions, or being either locked up too tightly or not tightly enough (from the Self and others).

Sailboat: You are driven by intellect (the wind) and are carried by **Water** (emotions).

Sailor/Voyager: Male sexuality, restlessness and wanderlust; also adventuresome and immature masculinity.

Salad: Longing for nature and health. Sometimes also a hint to eat more healthfully.

Salamander: A magical animal. See **Snake**. Symbol of the movement of the unconscious.

Salmon: May be a phallic symbol, but, as with all fish symbols, it usually points to the attitude of the dreamer toward his emotions.
Folklore: Family squabble.

Saloon: See **Pub/Saloon**.

Salt: Intellectual spice. Grounding ("the salt of the earth").

Salve: See **Medication**. In a dream, also emotional injuries.

Sand: This image represents the transitory—as in the hourglass—and the fear of getting stuck and sinking into the sand. The saying "throw sand in people's eyes" means deception. However, the sandman also throws sand in people's eyes so that they can get a restful night's sleep. In addition, sand also points to the element of earth (in a more delicate form), and in that sense again points to the dreamer being grounded.

In the form of sand on the beach, this image points to vacation and relaxation and, in addition, the gentle waves of emotions that over time smooth out that which is rough and tough (stone). If this dream takes place in a sandbox, your unconscious wants to give you a plan that you can use in your everyday life.

Sanitorium: The place for health.

Satan: See **Devil**. Symbol for logic, but without a soul. Also undefined nature. An archetypal symbol for darkness, but also a symbol of creativity and resistance.

Sauna: Cleansing, as in **Bath** and **Shower**. Openness and eroticism.

Sausage: See **Meat**. Phallic symbol, specifically the sausage in the hand of the **Fool**.

Savings: Energies that you can reach back for (in the sense of reserves and inner strength). It might also imply that you are withholding energies that could be put to better use. In addition, we are talking here about savings, which could mean hoarding as well as keeping a thrifty, good house. At times it might be connected to fear of poverty, as in **Asylum** and **Beggar**. However, here it is not so negative, and more like **Food** and **Coins**.

Saw: Something drastic is happening. A well-known symbol of differentiation (analysis) and intellectual work. The saw is changing something rough into something more precise that the dreamer then can use. In many instances, this dream image has something to do with willpower that can be used to bring success.

Scaffolding: New beginning, helping yourself, support.

Scale: Power of judgment. The dreamer's weight in terms of personal influence and significance. Assessment, judgment, balance, and order. Where is the center of your life? What is important? Vocal complaint about life's ambiguity and what is unknown and unclear.

Scar: Great misfortune and injuries from the past, which can now be overcome.

Schedule: Working efficiently; order and discipline. Also often refers to the feeling that thoughts and work have become inflexible; you are "caught in a cubby hole mentality" (organizational blindness). See **Rhythm.**

School: Learning, as in **School Work** and **Tests.**

School Work: See **Tests**. Something you still have to do.

Science: Indicates feeling intellectually or mentally secure. What does knowledge mean to you? What does knowledge do for you? What are you doing with the knowledge you have? See **University, White, Temple.**

Scientific Instrument: See **Laboratory**. On one hand, a place for the unnatural and artificial; on the other, the receptacle for intellect, or the place where connections are made. In alchemy, a reference to the uterus.

Scissors: An intellectual process and separation (something is being cut off). Also it often points to the repression of aggression. According to psychoanalysis, the scissors, like all stabbing objects, are a symbol for masculine sexuality. Scissors may also be a more threatening symbol against masculinity, since they are used to cut something off—castration.

Folklore: Warning false friends.

Scorpion: Sexual danger, death, and rebirth. When it comes in dreams, the scorpion represents a powerful positive symbol for the transformation of vitality. It is related to the symbol of the **Phoenix**.

Even so, the scorpion, is considered a negative symbol. Dreaming about a scorpion almost always suggests that something old that has caused great suffering is being dissolved in order to make room for something new. The body of the scorpion is very delicate. At the end of its body is a poisonous sting that is used not only for sudden attack, but also to kill itself. This dream image always refers to life with all its tensions, sufferings, death, and liberation. Here is the question of whether or not you are willing to let go and open yourself up to something new.

Scoundrel: Dishonesty, a warning against taking financial risks.

Scream: Warning dream. Desperation, but also experiencing and waking, as opposed to the image of **Sleep**.

Screen/Movie: The symbol for your inner screen, the soul, which is a mirror of your internal and external situation. You are asked to look at what is playing on the stage of life.

Screw: Sexual symbol. Here the relation between two people or two situations is emphasized. What has to be connected here? Or, experiencing increasing pressure.

Sculptor: Creatively accomplishing something in the face of obstacles. Negative: Shying away from accepting oneself and things as they really are. Maybe fear of not presenting a good "image." Positive: You are working to get to the core of things and to find the essence of yourself.

Scythe: Ability to achieve. **Harvest**, aggression, and **Death**.

Sea: See **Ocean**. Important is how the water and the weather are; sometimes a symbol of obstacles.

Seal: "Under the seal of secrecy"; or, you are locking up something, closing off something (usually yourself). You are taking yourself very seriously.
  Folklore: Insecurity.

Seat: Resting and relaxing. Whatever you do, take your time.

Second Story/Second Floor: See **Attic, House**. Awareness and perspective. A frequent symbol when your life is too one-sided and you are engaged intellectually either too much or too little. According to Jung, the intellectual area and consciousness are challenged.

Secrets: Denial of the truth or, just as likely, a hint that we also need our own secrets.

Seed: Psychic energy, creativity, and productivity. See **Rain**.

Serpent, Cosmic: See **Ouroborus**. In the lore of many cultures, this serpent laid the eggs out of which the cosmos grew. It points to the unconscious and the necessity to organize one's energies. Here the dreamer is made aware of the importance of life's energies and vitality (the Kundalini "serpent"), and it usually suggests that the dreamer pay more attention to physical drives and urges.

The Indian god Vishnu, after having concluded the creation of the world, rests on the back of the cosmic serpent and watches over the preservation of the cosmos.

Servant: As in **Chauffeur,** points to the fact that you must either be more humble or that orderliness is lacking. Symbol of one's own reason and intellect; or a sign of laziness.

Seven: A holy number that connects the masculine with the feminine, since it is a rational number (masculine), which is needed to explain the irrational number Pi (female) as $^{22}/_7$.

According to Jung, seven always characterizes time.

Sewage/Waste: Going with the flow, but there is a certain amount of stain connected to it, in contrast to the image of **Brook, River**. Often a symbol for the shadow or underworld (as in underground sewage pipes). Need for cleansing (see **Toilet**). It may also be a sign of concern for the environment (see **Environmental Pollution**).

Sewing: Fertility, growth, emotional and intellectual maturity. Traditionally, sewing symbolizes intercourse.

Sexuality: Often unfulfilled desires. Generally, a symbol of meaningful contact and development of Self. The male *animus* and the female *anima* are what the dreamer needs or wants to be connected with. Sexuality in dreams often refers to the secrets of life, such as birth, marriage, death (also life and the Devil). One of the strongest symbols of creativity.

Shackles: Usually points to a situation at work or with your partner. You are bound to something or somebody and are unhappy about it. On the other hand, shackles also hold something together, keeping you from running away immediately. See **Shadow**.

Shadow: The shadow is, first of all, that which is invisible. If it becomes visible in your dream, a very important step toward increasing awareness has been taken.

You are beginning to become consciously aware of your "dark side." The reason for the shadow in a dream is a sign that you are in the process of becoming aware of your Self. So, there is no reason to fear your shadow or try to avoid it.

The shadow is usually connected to the past or the future: old injuries are casting their shadow onto today's behavior and emotions, and creating fear for the yet unborn reality of the future. Coming to terms with the shadow is necessary in order to understand life here and now. It brings intensity, wealth, and imagination to life.

If you are standing in somebody's shadow, or are put into a shadow by somebody, this refers to low self-esteem. You have an inferiority complex—want to appear to be more than you are, want to be more accepted. The shadow follows us but is not easily seen; it also provides protection.

Jung sees the shadow as an underdeveloped structure in people.

The shadow is one of the original definitions of the soul. The chieftain of some Polynesian tribes loses his *mana* (power), if somebody steps on his shadow. In southern European countries midday was considered the ghost hour, because the shadow would then be its smallest and retreat. Behind this superstition was the fear that the shadow would disappear altogether and with it the soul and its relationship to the earth.

Shaft/Well: A symbol of the level of the unconscious, and for descending into the world of the mothers and the past, into one's own darkness. A vaginal symbol, according to Freud.

Shame/Ashamed: See **Shadow**.

Shares (Stocks): See **Bank, Money**. Are you taking too many risks? Are you looking for great riches and easy money? Are you looking for security (See **Family, Bureaucrat**, and **Sidewalk**) that is not necessarily available? Or do you simply want to be part of something? What is it that you want to (or feel you should be) part of?

Shark: Vitality and aggression, brutal violence. Projections of all kinds of fears (as in the devastating film *Jaws*).

Shawl: Warmth, protection, and deep devotion.

Sheep: Patience, stupidity, romanticism about the

country, but also devotion and innocence. The **Wool** of the sheep refers to warmth, protection, and the need for loving care. See **Lamb, Aries.**

Folklore: Luck.

Shelf: Storing. You are hanging too much on something.

Shell/skin: Superficial and tough, but something soft is hidden underneath the toughness. See **Person.**

Shield (protective): Protection. Something behind which one can move freely and organize an attack. It is also a place to which the soul can retreat.

Ship: See **Boat.** If you are in the boat yourself, you need to rethink the direction you are taking. A distancing from emotions: you are not in touch with the **Water.** Also, if the ship is far in the distance, a longing for femininity. Different types of ships characterize your personality.

According to the Koran and the Bible, the ship is a symbol of rescue.

According to Freud, it is a symbol for woman.

Shipwreck: The image of a shipwreck is often connected to the feeling of failure, as is the **Breach** in a dike; while, on the other hand, it may point to a positive development. The distance to the **Water**—meaning to feelings and needs—is removed. A shipwreck can also mean an outburst of emotions, where the dreamer is acknowledging his passions.

Shirt: The image that you project to the outside world—how you would like to be seen—the role you play. This often is an indication of your economic state—the garment you wear when you're dead and being laid out; or losing your shirt—meaning all you had left has been taken away.

Shoe: Being grounded and protected against the powers of the earth. It also points to the place where the dreamer is standing.

According to Freud: putting on a shoe symbolizes a sexual act. Compare this to **River**.

Shoemaker: See **Shoe**. Being grounded.
Folklore: Bad luck.

Shooting: On one hand, a reference to your setting

your sights on a goal. Are you meeting your goal? On the other hand, aggression and a hunter's instinct. See **Arrow, Pistol**.

Shooting: Murder. Something is being killed (violently): a relationship, an emotion, an unused talent, or any number of things. On the other hand, just as often, it may mean a courageous act of liberation that is freeing emotional energies. A frequent dream symbol to have at the end of a depressive phase, because now, after being liberated, you can search for a new beginning. Such dreams always set in motion something symbolic and by no means refer to the real danger of death.

Shop: The place of the emotional, spiritual, and libidinal work of creativity and production where energies are mobilized, where things are exchanged. You want to be served and choose the right thing. Can you serve yourself? Serving oneself always refers to self-sufficiency. Are you buying or are you selling?

According to Jung, this is the place where you get something that you don't have and that you have to pay for. See **Businessman, Cash Register**.

Shore: "Land in sight," and everything will be better

soon. The shoreline is the seam between land and water and, in that sense, the connection between body and soul.

Shoreline: The intellect that guides and thereby limits emotions, in contrast to **Water**, the emotions. The shore is sometimes the image of the outside reality, while water represents the emotional reality. What condition is the shoreline in? Reaching a new shore often represents new insights.

Shot: In a sense, this image represents two different situations:
1. Out of the "starting gate" like a shot.
2. Fear of wars, as in **Helmet**, or more generally, fear of aggression. See **Explosion**, **Lightning**, **Marksman/Hunter**, **Fireworks**, **Shooting**.

In classical depth psychology, a sexual image: emission/ejaculation dream, sexual aggression. It can symbolize the aggressor as well as the victim. This aggression is not necessarily negative, because it can also express sexual freedom, reaching the goal (gratification, orgasm).

Folklore: Illness.

Shovel: Repressed feelings or memories need to be

uncovered; something needs to be remembered; it is necessary to do some work.

Shower: Desire for cleanliness, as in **Bath, Soap, Sauna,** but the sense of not being clean is not as negative as in **Abortion, Abscess,** or Sewage/Waste. It is more a desire to gain new energy and more zip (emotional rejuvenation). Relaxation.

See **Rain, Fear.**
Folklore: A setback.

Shrinking: A frequent symbol when the dreamer is feeling inferior. As in the story of *Alice in Wonderland*, shrinking means entering a new reality. A suggestion to become smaller, more childlike.

Shrubs: See **Bush.**

Siblings: See **Brother, Sister.** All are different parts of self. According to Freud, this is very often a symbol for genitals. Older siblings, according to Jung, point to more developed parts of the self, that which is wanted and admired.

Sickle: See **Scythe, Moon.**

Sickness: See **Illness.**

Sidewalk: Almost always indicates security that one is longing for in order to get ahead, as in **Shares, Bureaucrat.**

Siege: Confinement and narrowness, as in **Amber, Trap, Elevator, Village, Cage.** Fear of war, as in **Bayonet, Shot,** and, more specifically, **Atom Bomb.** What reserves are at your disposal during the time of siege?

Sieve: Something is draining away, but what counts remains.

Sign/Nameplate/Advertisement: The meaning of the image depends a great deal on what is written or depicted on the sign. If there are names on the sign, pay attention to the writing: small letters, elegantly written letters, ornate letters, or letters written in color. If the sign has a picture, look up its meaning.

Signal: Advice and help.
   Folklore: Wishes are being fulfilled.

Signature: If it is about the dreamer's own signature, it points to his identity. What was signed and what effect did the signature have? If it is the signature of somebody else, get to know that person better.

Signpost/Crossroads: The crossroads is a place where one must decide which way to go. It points out to the dreamer which road should be taken in life. See **Cross**, **Fork** (as in fork in the road), **Division**, **Ouroboros** (as a counterimage).

Silk: Ruler; well-being and luxury. See **Caterpillar**.

Silver: See **Metal**. Emotions, a symbol of the moon and femininity.

Singing: Emotional release, peaceful times, harmony, balance, and unburdening.

Sinking: Fear of sinking into the world of the emotions and/or instincts that need to be dealt with. An opportunity for self-knowledge. See **Submarine, Swamp, Diving**.

Sister/Nurse: See **Illness** and dependency. The feminine side of the dreamer, the emotional side.

According to Steckel and Freud, breasts.

Six: Usually a symbol of sexuality.

Skeleton: Clear thinking, lack of emotion, asceticism, and death.

Ski/Skiing: You are doing well, everything in life is going smoothly.

Skin: As a mirror of the soul, the skin points to the state of the dreamer's nerves and emotional condition. Isolation from the world around you. A person's protection.

Skin Rash: Emotional tension, repressed urges, and aggression. The external and internal states are out of balance. The boundaries to the outside world are not intact.

Skirt: See **Clothing**.

Skull: A reminder of **Death** and the meaning of life. This symbol often points to a feeling of spiritual emptiness. On the other hand, it also addresses the shape, structure, and essence of spirituality and, in that sense, of life itself. (See the skull of Yorick in *Hamlet*.)

Skyscraper/High-Rise: Usually the same as **House.** Great perspective, loss of restraint, individuality—but also elevation.

Slap in the Face: Carelessness, punishment, and lack of appreciation.

Slaughterhouse/Butcher: A place where your animal side is killed. The symbolic meaning of the animal being slaughtered is important.

Slave: Dependency.

Sled: The image of letting go with abandon, in a positive sense, as in **Brook, Leaf, Parachute,** and in part also in **Flying.** It might also express aggression.

Sleep: Something important is not being understood. A lack of clarity, and consciousness, avoidance of problems. The need for rest.
  Folklore: Negative omen.

Slippers: Domesticity in all its different meanings. Sluggishness and insecurity.

According to Freud, female genitals. See **Shoe**.

Folklore: A small gesture of friendliness is royally rewarded.

Slipping: Behaving badly or not being centered. Fear of falling (due to lack of attentiveness), or a desire to have "a slip," to *want* to behave badly. Not behaving like everybody else but rather finding one's own way of being. Have courage to live according to your beliefs. See **Fool**.

Falling suddenly in a dream often happens when there is too little or (rarely) too much humility.

Smell: See **Fragrance**. A bad odor symbolizes aversion ("I can't stand the smell of____"). Pleasant smells symbolize affection. Furthermore, the expression "having a nose for news" may play a role in this image, pointing to the fact that you can either trust your intuition (do you "smell a rat"?) or that you should trust more.

Smith/Blacksmith: A symbol for great misfortune or stroke of fate; or of becoming the master of transformation. See **Anvil**.

Smoke: Something dark; but also something light rising out of your unconscious. Where there is smoke there is **Fire**, transformative power that comes through your energy. Dissipating smoke indicates relaxation. See **Steam**.

Smoking: A frequent dream symbol when the dreamer has stopped smoking. Otherwise see **Pipe**, **Smoke**.

Snail: Retreat, being overly sensitive, inhibition and lack of contact. This dream symbol appears often when one's shyness collides with the desire for an energetic lifestyle. Are you facing risks with courage? Or retreating into your shell? This dream symbol is also a challenge to make life a little easier and to follow your own **Rhythm**. According to Freud, a sexual symbol.
  Folklore: Lack of moderation.

Snake/Serpent: See **Poisonous Snake.** More than anything else, this is a symbol of fear. It is also often a sexual symbol, and a symbol of wholeness, transformation, and rebirth, as in **Ouroboros.** A symbol of the dark feminine and deception, it also represents wisdom and cunning. Almost every woman dreams about serpents at least once in her life, which could mean fear of a rival or of the male gender. The serpent stands for physical drives. If something is not right in that area, snake dreams appear. The image of the serpent may also refer to the "water of life," since it comes from inside the earth where the healing springs originate. The Caduceus, the staff of Aesculapius, a symbol of the healing arts, shows two serpents winding around it. In the sacred temple of Aesculapius, serpents crawled on the floor of the sleeping halls. They were said to induce healing dreams.

According to 2nd century dream interpreter Artemidorus, dreaming about serpents indicates healing and the return to vitality. It is also a symbol of immortality (shedding of the skin—rebirth). The "Midgard-serpent" and the "Ferris wolf" in Norse mythology threaten the gods as the world comes to an end.

The serpent is also the symbol for secret wisdom and the revelation of the hidden. Snakes are quick, attracted by fire and the birth of energy. A snake steals from Gilgamesh (hero of the Sumerian epic) the herb of immortality, while he is taking a bath in a pond. In Greece, Gaia, the goddess of the earth, produces two half-serpents called Titans, who do battle with Zeus. For the Gnostics of late antiquity, the serpent symbolized the dark, deep, and unfathomable side of God. The serpent is also a symbol of Kundalini (the yogic life force). In ancient Greece, serpents were even honored publicly, because they were believed to be ghosts of the dead.

Snakes appear suddenly, out of the unknown, creating fear. It is impossible to have a meaningful communication with them; they are secretive and fear-inducing, as is the unconscious. Their poison is sin, their wisdom transformation and deliverance. According to Early Christian imagination, when a snake was attacked, it would only protect its head.

According to Freud, a phallic symbol. According to Jung, the image of the snake means that something important is taking place in our unconscious; it may be dangerous or healing. See **Eel.**

Snow/Snowing: See **Ice, Cold.** Emotional coldness, feeling of security, but also punishment, **Virgin.** White snow also symbolizes the **Leaf** of innocence. Customary and sharp distinctions lose their significance; the snow turns everything soft and white. In that sense it points to liberation from conventional attitudes and to a new orientation. See **White.**

Snowman: See **Snow.** Either emotional coldness or playfulness.

Soap: Symbol for cleanliness, as in **Bath**, **Shower**, and **Sauna**.

Folklore: Something is dissolving.

Soccer: See **Football**.

Solarium: See **Light**. Devotion, warmth, and relaxation.

Soldier: Aggression, but also camaraderie. If a man dreams about a soldier, it often expresses a longing for connection with other men. See **Military Duty**, **War**.

Son: This image refers either to the actual son, or to future ideas, creativity and something new. The son, according to Jung, is the absolute substitute for the father, guaranteeing the immortality of the father. Also, pay attention to the similarities between the words "son" and "sun."

Song: Happiness. The text of the song is important.

Soup: Whatever you have cooked up you must and should be allowed to eat. This is a reference to consequences. What we have "cooked up" is composed of what we have created through our actions, influenced by emotions.

Soup is also a symbol of strength and nutrition. The soup pot is a symbol of fusion and integration. See **Kitchen**.

Sowing: Well-known sexual dream in the widest sense—the urge to impregnate or be impregnated. The need to accomplish something. It frequently appears when the dreamer is feeling unproductive. May also be interpreted as a longing for a simple life in the country.

Space: Inner space.

Spade: Sexual meaning; attempted grounding.
   Folklore: Satisfaction.

Spark: See **Fire, Flames.** The so-called spark of the soul, the divine in us.

Sparkling Wine: See **Champagne**.

Sparrow: Secrets that are being given away. See **Bird**.

Spear: According to Freud, phallic symbol. Aggression,

being focused, and having success. Elias Howe in the middle of the last century had a very important dream about spears. He was captured by natives who pressured him to invent a sewing machine. The tip of the spears they brandished in front of his face had holes. This dream gave him the idea for the double-stitch sewing machine.

Symbolically speaking, this dream refers to the feminine and masculine side of the dreamer, presented here by the image of the needle or the specialized spear.

Specialist: Estrangement; intellect, but also stature. This symbol warns against one-sidedness of emotions and spirit. It is often a suggestion to become a specialist in your own important matters.

Speech: Emotions and/or needs are vocalized. The content of your soul is made conscious, expressed, and vocalized to the people around you. The content of the speech is important.

Speech (Giving a): A need for communicating something, getting somebody's ear, convincing somebody. Usually a sign that you are justified in expecting recognition. Fear of appearing in public or public speaking.

Wanting to arrive and be liked (see **Applause**, **Approval**). If a politician is giving the speech, it—almost without fail—has something to do with lying and egotism.

Speed: A typical symbol of stress. Take more time, or move faster in order to take advantage of your chance. However, it seems that stress can also be overcome with speed.

Sphinx: That which is mysterious. It was Oedipus, the hero, who solved the riddle of the Sphinx.

Spices: Sharpness, in the sense of intellect and wisdom. Emotional irritability, but also extravagance and finesse.

Spider: The image of an aesthetic or artistic person. One's own dark side. Intrigues are planned. In a woman's dream, indicates conflicts with the mother.

According to Freud, the fertile mother or fear of mother incest.

Spider Web: A certain subject has to be approached with great care. You are feeling trapped. See **Maze**.

Spine: The support that brings everything back into order. Honesty and civil courage. See **Stairs, Tower, Skyscraper/High-Rise.**

Spiral: Emotional dynamics and development.

Spit: You ought to spit out something, or has something overwhelmed you?

Splinter: Are you feeling injured? Inconsequential things are getting you upset. (In the Bible, one often sees a splinter in the eye of a neighbor, but not in one's own.)

Sponge: See **Water.** Squeezing out and soaking up. Let go of something.

Sports: Ambition, performance, and physicality. In a dream it is often a suggestion to be more playful in everything you do; or are you taking things too lightly?

Sports Car: See **Car.**

Spring (season): Generally well-known symbol for virility, fruitfulness, and **Youth. Easter.**

Spring (water): Symbol of fertility. In fairy tales it also symbolizes virginity—the dreamer's emotional energies. Positive psychic energies, dedication. Expressing purity. Fairy tales and myths also tell about clouded and poisoned springs; in that case, go back to the origin of the problem and work with your karma in order to clean up old burdens. See **Water, Bath, Environmental Pollution**.

Spy: See **Agent, Detective**.

Square: A symbol of wholeness. You are on the path of individuation and self-awareness. You are grounded and emotionally balanced. The idea of being grounded was particularly emphasized by Plato, who considered the square the original symbol of Earth, since the angles of the square are an expression of permanence, in the sense of its structural shape.

Squirrel: Fast, shy, smart animal that symbolizes ideas, plans, and hope. Longing to be in nature.
   Folklore: Hard work is ahead for you.

Stab: See **Needle, Sting**.

Stabbing: Shooting, Murder. Clearly there is a sexual component here, since it points to penetrating (the skin), **Thorns,** and **Blood.** The sting, as in the fairy tales "Sleeping Beauty" and "Snow White," points to the awakening of consciousness. One is opening oneself and something of oneself (blood) flows out. Such a dream often points to the dreamer having been injured. Where is your wound? Could you protect yourself from injuries? Were you stabbed or did you stab someone? How did it happen? From the front, in the back? As is the case with **Shooting,** this dream is also a symbolic reference to your inner strength, and never has anything to do with a real danger to your life.

Stage: Points to an important position at work or position in life. A desire to be more in the limelight, as in **Arena.** Are you outgoing? Do you share of yourself? What role have you played, or what mask have you been hiding behind? What piece have you forgotten?

Stains/Spots: Dark spots in the soul, being soiled and feeling guilty. Often combined with being embarrassed. There are also "erotic" spots, which, however, appear seldom. Usually it is a suggestion to become aware of a "dark spot."

Stairs/Spiral Staircase: Changes and transformation starting from below (the unconscious) and coming to the surface (consciousness), or vice versa. A frequent symbol in fairy tales and movies, suggesting personal growth and wholeness. The landings in a staircase correspond to the dreamer's energy centers (the chakras). Are you going up the stairs or coming down? According to Freud, going up symbolizes sexual union.

Stall: An image of one's drives that have become domesticated.

Stallion: Horse. Increase in strength, but also taming one's own strength.

According to Freud, a symbol of sexuality, particularly of repressed drives in men and women.

Stamp (as in rubber stamp): Putting your stamp on something. Desiring a higher position.

Stamp (letter): The value of communicating with the outside world. The value is important, as well as what is depicted on it.

Standard: Which flag did you see? Under which flag

did you join? The way the flag acts in the wind might possibly be a hint about your sex life.

Folklore: Good omen, particularly monetary.

Star: See **Light, Comet.** The inner core, the image of guidance and hope. In dreams and fairy tales, this symbol is always connected with the fate of the hero (he was "born under a good/bad star"). Just like the hero, you are also following your star, meaning following your inner desires and longings in order that life may be bright and shiny. To follow your star means to be clear and to know your own needs. Following your own desires, longings, and needs presupposes the courage to be unconventional, which in turn will bring about new insights and a more fulfilled life.

When the sun—the symbol of consciousness—has gone down, stars appear in the heavens, so in a real sense stars are the "light" in the darkness.

According to an old Native American dream interpretation: illness.

A falling star in a dream means birth. A star often points to the birth of an important person.

Statue: Who does the statue represent? If necessary, look in the encyclopedia to get information on the personage. Or is it a representation of yourself? In that case, this symbol is a warning about an addiction to approval and self-elevation.

Stealing: Greed and dissatisfaction.

Steam/Steam Kettle: Suppressed emotional energy, as in **Dam,** that wants to escape (letting off steam). You are under pressure. Or a jack-of-all-trades. If the steam is not under pressure, this symbol might also mean dissolving, solving, solution, resolution, and the pleasure of shedding, as in letting go. Steam is also the symbol of devotion and self-abandon. Steam as a combination of hot water (passionate feelings) and air (intellect) also points to conscious commitment.

Steel: See **Metal, Iron.** Toughness ("hard as steel"), determination, and will.

Steering Wheel: Independence and determination.

Step: Something new is arriving. A **Threshold** (obstacles) that needs to be overcome. Usually a sign of growth. See **Heel, Stairs.**

Steps (stairs): Reaching a stage of advancement—social and conscious. Often, stopping in order to gain a better view. Stairs also represent an interim stage between above and below—between head and belly, emotions and intellect, heaven and earth.

Step/Tread: Fear of social decline, opponents, and enemies.

Sting: The sting in our flesh symbolizes obstacles in our life that need to be removed, or may be a symbol of our desires. Other than that, the meaning is similar to **Splinter** and **Rose** (with thorns).

Stock Market: Risky business; you are speculating about something where the outcome is unsure. "Have-Mode" according to Fromm, as in: **Auction, Loot, Attaché Case, Shares;** usually refers to your finances.

Stocking: Being grounded. In rare instances, may also have a sexual meaning (particularly putting on a stocking).
Folklore: A light stocking means grief; a dark stocking means enjoyment; a stocking with a hole symbolizes loss; a silk stocking symbolizes wealth.

Stomach/Stomach Illness: First, make sure that there are no real physical symptoms. If not, this symbol may be pointing to the ability to digest and to metabolize, to be receptive, and to deal with intellectual and emotional "food."

A full stomach points to overstimulation and too much consumption. An empty stomach is an indication of greed; you feel short-changed.

Stone: See **Earth**. Merciless, tough ("a heart of stone"); durability.

Stone/Clay (floor): Points to the necessity of becoming more grounded, but at the same time it is what separates us from the "naked" earth.

According to Jung, it expresses darkness, as in **Forest**.

Stool: Elevation, as in podium, but also unsafe seat. You need more security, support, and grounding.

Folklore: To sit on a stool is sitting in a place of honor.

Storage Room: See **Food (stored)** and **Closet**. Here your energy reserves, your potential and unused abilities are being addressed. Pay attention to what is stored and what the individual items might symbolize.

Stork: Emotional strength, desire for family. Legend has it that it is the stork who "delivers" babies. It is also said that the stork never leaves its nest. According to Christian symbolism, the stork is the one who knows about the return of the Lord.

Storm: See **Hurricane, Wind**. An obstacle dream or possibly a symbol of breaking out, being liberated from or through intellectual efforts. Storm of emotions. Try to be either more or less emotional.

Stranger: Something new is announced. The image can also point to the shadow (the stranger within), rejected or unknown characteristics in yourself that you don't want to see. See **Shadow**.

Strangulation: Something is denying you the air to breathe; something has got you by the throat. "Spit out whatever is sticking in your throat," which means look at what is bothering you and get rid of it. Don't panic about this dream. The dream is giving you a chance to see what is holding you back!

Straw: Troublesome work or difficulties. Also refers to bed and camp/cot (in the past consisting of fresh straw or mattresses stuffed with straw).

Strawberry: Sexual symbol (like nipple). Marriage, becoming a mother, summer fun.
  Folklore: Sign of unexpected success.

Street/Sidewalk/Path: Life's path. What is happening on the street is normal and available to everybody. Important is the condition of the street and possibly the direction in which you are walking. Who or what are you meeting on the street? What is your destination? Intersections symbolize decisions, street signs are an aid in finding direction.
  According to Freud, sexual organs. According to Jung, the collective world of awareness.

Street Car/Trolley: As in **Train**. A symbol of collective forward movement. Do you need a trolley right now in order to get ahead?

Stretcher: Symbol for resting, particularly during times of stress. Support and help, but also fear of an accident or death.

String: See **Ribbon**.

Stripping (Clothes): Being open and refraining from pretense, as in **Bareness, Naked**. Enjoying fully the sensuous beauty of yourself or somebody else. Do you want, no matter what the subject, actually is, to bare yourself? A warning against lack of boundaries and being insolent. Shedding clothes, according to Jung, is always the shedding of parts of ourselves. See also: **Amputation**.

Stumbling: Something is out of order—a dream of obstacles or the opposite: you have found a new order, meaning that you have lost your customary rhythm.

Submarine: Wanting to hide and look at the world from the emotional side (**Water**). It suggests regression and a weak ego, or being submerged in oceanic feelings and being powerless over them. Even in the presence of great emotional turmoil, maneuverability is still intact. See **Diving, Fish**.

Suburbs: Not being quite inside and not quite outside. Boredom.

Success: Do you want to be successful?

Suffering: Fear of suffering and illness. Such dreams usually offer constructive advice on how to end the suffering in your life.

Suffocating: First determine if you had a *real* breathing problem while you slept—a cold, for example. Were you feeling constricted? Were you bothered by unspoken and ambiguous thoughts that took your breath away and which you denied, creating tension and stress? Here it is not a question of your being in danger of your life, but rather a desire to get more **Air,** as a symbolic expression for more intellect and greater mental clarity.

Sugar: Though sugar in a dream usually is not sweet, still you would like to sweeten your life.

Suit: The rigid, conventional side. Initiation into manhood. Wanting to amount to something in life. The *persona* in the Jungian sense (that which is presented to the outside) in contrast to **Naked**.

Suitcase: Container, Luggage. Burden and problems that you carry around with you; but also a reservoir of abilities and talents. Very important here is the weight of the suitcase. A heavy suitcase usually symbolizes unsolved tasks, unused talents, and similar burdens. A light suitcase is a symbol of talents and abilities that are being used.

According to Freud, it refers to the female body, as in **Oven**.

Summer: See **Sun**. Energy, vitality, and success.

Summit: The achievement of higher consciousness, spirituality. In another sense, a case of arrogance, career ambition, and lack of humility. What do you believe is your calling? What is the price you are willing to pay for achievements? In addition, here is also a connection to your inner center (and to God). Are you taking sufficient time for yourself? It is a symbol of the growth and maturity you have set as a life goal. Also, fear of depth and confrontation.

Sun: See **Summer**. Creative energy. If the sun is shining in your dream, it always refers to consciousness. If the sun does not shine, you are either approaching the unconscious or a loss of energy. The sun is also a symbol of the father, midlife, the danger of being dazzled.

Sunday: Rest.
Folklore: Changes.

Superior: The mirror or image of the dreamer's own tension over what life is presenting, tasks that are assigned. See **Chief**.

Superman: Comic book characters and those from science fiction and Westerns are modern symbols for the **Hero**. They often, however, also express immature masculinity, delusions of grandeur, and being all-powerful in situations where they are surely powerless. This dream image is about the antiquated ideals and unfulfilled goals of the dreamer.

Supervisor: Order and discipline, as in **Office**. Restriction, male authority; can also mean negative masculinity. Pressure at work, but also having a good perspective/overview.
Folklore: Promotion at work.

Surf: Accumulated urges, as in **Fire**, but with a more intense emotional depth **(Water)**. Waves of emotion, but also vacation and experiencing nature. In most cases, the surf is a surging soul that is expressed through the force of nature, but it can also address oceanic feelings that you are afraid of or longing for.

Surfing/Riding the Waves: Being carried away by emotions (**Water**), being transported by and giving in to the existing **Rhythm.** See **Sailboat.** Here the power of the **Winds**, as well as the intellect, is used for moving forward. This is also often an expression of fear about going under, in the sense that the **Head** would be submerged under **Water** (similar to fear of emotional chaos, as in **Swamp**). This is also a sexual and virility symbol ("Surfers do it standing up"). See **Captain, Admiral.**

Surgeon: By cutting off (forgetting) something, something needs to be healed. Being saved in times of distress.

Authority, often the male hero; or appearing in a dream of a contemporary woman, the limitations of the hero.

Swallow: Domestic bliss and **Spring**, announcing the end of winter. Great speed and mobility. According to *Physiologus*, the most widely read book of the Middle Ages, the swallow reproduces only once and possesses great knowledge about herbs.

Swamp: See **Moor**. Being stuck, afraid of being trapped in the unconscious. Fear of emotions, of being "devoured back into the feminine." This means that the masculine side in the man and the woman (*animus*) fears that consciousness—fought hard for—will be sucked up by the vortex of emotions and the unconscious. Expressed here is the desire for *and* fear of emotional chaos.

Swan: Swans are a symbol for family. They mate for life and raise their young together. Intellectual interests, idealism. A symbol of beauty.

According to Celtic tradition, swans and geese were considered messengers from another world and for that reason were not used as food.

The black swan is a messenger of bad luck or death.

Sweat: Trouble and work, but also success.

Sweets: Sensual pleasures, according to Freud. Often sexual pleasures; at least, desire for love. See **Paradise**.

Swimming: See **Water**. Relaxation, the world of feelings. It is often connected to liberation. Where is the swimming taking place and what is the condition of the water? According to Freud; urine and the life of the unborn. Also, a symbol of pollution.

Swing: Mood swings; the ups and downs of life—we either give in to them too much or we repress them too much. The symbol of the rhythm of life. Are you being "taken for a ride"?

It may also be connected to memories from your childhood. Playfulness. A sexual symbol.

Switch: Is the switch turned on or off? That would point to your vitality. It is in your power to regulate and switch things and modes.

Sword: Appears rarely in dreams. It is a symbol of power and intellect. See **Knight**. Seeking power, as in **Monument** and aggression. Frequent symbol for intellectual work since the sword separates and, therefore, leads us to make decisions. We use the sword to fend off somebody and it is, in that sense, a sign of distancing and individualism.

According to Freud, a phallic symbol, as is **Knife.** In psychoanalysis, separation or fear of separation, as in **Goodbye, Abortion, Corpse, Death, Divorce,** and **Funeral.**

Syringe: The male sex organ. Fear of a syringe points to sexual inhibitions. At present, the syringe is also a symbol of fear of AIDS, and fear of something intruding on you. Often a hint that you should be more open. If a diabetic dreams of syringes, it could be a message from the inner healer to think about the right dose.

Syrup: A symbol of everything that is sweet, or everything that is sticky.

Table. The desire for unencumbered connections to others, or a hint that whatever the connections are at present, you'd do better to accept them. Sticking together and belonging. Also refers to a noble attitude that is either to be adopted or has already been incorporated (Knights of the Round Table). See **Feast, Communion, Restaurant**.

Table/Desk: See **Furniture**. Vitality. The symbol of matter as well as Earth (world). Ancient Egyptian dream interpretation states that a table is an indication of the arrival of guests, and that they must be entertained lavishly.

According to Freud (as well as the Talmud), it is a symbol for the body of women.

Tablet/Pill: See **Medication, Pill**. Medicine.

Tail: Always a sexual symbol, but also symbol of the Devil.

Tailor: See **Dress, Needle, Thread**. The traditional meaning is cunning and being a coward. Vanity, as in **Jewelry**.

Folklore: In the case of a woman, marriage below her state.

Taking an Oath: Suggests you ought to make a decision in a particular situation, or that important responsibilities to yourself are being neglected.

Taking Apart: Excavation. Looking inward, understanding, and analyzing. Often appears as a dream image when living without much thought. Pay attention to what is being taken apart. What do the individual parts look like? See **Puzzle**.

Tank: Energy reserve.

Tank/Shell: An object of war as well as a protective shell, as in the turtle or lobster, for instance. Fear of war, or do you want to get your own way regardless of the consequences? Are you feeling overwhelmed? These are symbols of toughness, of protection of your emotional qualities.

Tape Recorder: A suggestion that something has to be recorded (documented) very precisely. See **Ear, Radio**.

Tar: This image refers to dependency (it clings) and the dark. See **Black**.

Target: Focus, the ability to assert yourself.
Folklore: Hitting the center of the target means good luck; missing it, bad luck.

Taste: The kind of taste determines the symbolic meaning. Taste is what is on the tip of your tongue, what is felt and should be expressed.

Tattooing/Tattoo: Courage, boldness, and masculinity. To display an eccentric and sensual Self in the skin.

Taxi: You are not in charge of your life journey, even though you have chosen the goal.

Tea: Stimulation. Practice patience.
  Folklore: Difficulties.

Teacher: Functioning as an emotional aid. Points to the times when you were in school. The teacher is an archetypal figure of authority. Bad conscience, often connected to sensuality. Teachers are almost always the leaders that guide us into adulthood. This may also be an initiation dream. The inner guide teaching about maturity and self-discipline. On the other hand, there may be the tendency to preach to oneself and to others.

Tears: Similar to **Drink**. The **Water** of life is able to flow. It is a sign of solution and resolution. See **Crying**.

Teddy Bear: Usually an expression of a desire for security and simplicity. A teddy bear may also indicate the desire for children.

Teeth/Loss of Teeth: Vitality, relatives, friends, and lovers; but this image also has a predatory and destructive side. See **Vampire**.

As far back as Greek mythology, teeth were said to refer to children. The reason probably was that, during pregnancy, mothers experienced the rapid loss of their teeth ("Each child will cost you a tooth").

In mythology teeth are considered similar to seed corn, comparable to dragon's blood. In addition, teeth symbolize the oral qualities of the dreamer. The possible reason for this might be an eating and biting urge, or the repression of it. And, last but not least, teeth, like **Mouth**, are used to take in food. See **Beauty, Face, Bones, Bite**.

According to Jung and Freud, teeth are often a phallic symbol; and according to Freud, dreams about toothaches are considered masturbation dreams.

According to the newest dream research, women often dream about teeth during menopause.

Telegram: See **Letter**. Something important and urgent.

Telephone: Frequent dream for men, suggesting good connections. It also symbolizes contact with the other side of the self. Important is whether you have reached your party or not. Not reaching the other party could be a sign of difficulty in making/maintaining contact. Once the "busy signal" is removed, the dreamer can improve communication with the outside world. Pay attention to the style of communication, especially in relationships.

Telescope: Should you take a closer look at something? Or, do you need more distance?

Television: Openness, enjoying contact, or lack of contact; mindlessness, superficiality, and diversion. Possibly a mirror of the dream.

Searching for orientation. Are you appearing on TV yourself? Or what are you watching? It is important to know what kind of program is running—the program mirrors your mood.

Temple: One of the luckiest symbols, meaning completeness, zest for life, getting ahead, and always finding your way to the center of things. The temple is also a symbol for Mother, and in that case is usually an idealization of mother. See **Priest**.

Ten: A new beginning, after having reached the goal. In the Egyptian tarot, the Wheel of Fortune. And a "10" is, of course, the perfect woman.

Tent: Adventure, something momentary and temporary. Wanderlust, being in the mood for a vacation, longing for a more natural life. See **Snake, Home, Roof, Skin.**

Termination: 1. In the sense of ending—ending something, or longing to end a relationship or a situation.

2. In the sense of demolition (such as demolishing a house), it points to the need to be aggressive; or fear of aggression. It is usually based on feeling either destructive, disappointed, or both.

Confrontation with **Death**, if a house is being demolished, similar to **Funeral**, and **Grave**. Often it indicates underlying desires that are being repressed, as in **Attack, Fire (Surf),** and **Violence.**

Terrace/Patio: Tentatively moving into a new, usually public area, and presenting the Self to the outside world. Relaxation and free time.

Folklore: Reaching a higher position due to an inheritance.

Terrorist: Breaking out of rigidity, necessitating change. See **Adventure** and **Hero,** who is dissatisfied with the social situation or who is a social outcast. When images of rebellion and protest appear repeatedly, ask yourself what your goals are. Often in such dreams we are looking for the **Leader** in us or for a sustaining principle.

Test: See **Exam/Test**.

Theater: Take life a little easier and don't be so dramatic. Vanity, and the need for acceptance, but also a symbol of personal dreams and ideals. The theater/stage is in some ways the model world for the dreamer. See **Actor, Exam/Test**.

Thermometer: This image is always a barometer of the dreamer's moods.
Folklore: Much excitement is in store for you.

Thief/Stealing: Fear of loss, particularly in personal relationships, or you want to "steal away" from a relationship. Is something being stolen from you or are you the thief? What is being stolen?

Thirst: Often you actually *are* thirsty. Restlessness,

dream of obstacles. It is important what you are thirsting for; often a sign of emotional longing.

Thistle: Work, troubles, and fighting. According to 2nd century dream interpreter Artemidorus: problems and difficulties with a man.

Thorns: Spine, Thistle, Rose. According to dream interpreter Artemidorus, obstacles and difficulty with a woman.
   Folklore: Poverty.

Thread: Fleeting ideas, spontaneous thoughts, or making meaningful connections. The red thread of Ariadne (in the Labyrinth) symbolizes life's journey and life itself.

Three: Three is tense, dynamic, rhythmic, and complete (the Holy Trinity). Three is a symbol of the spirit, since it is assigned to the third stage of human consciousness (after the physical and emotional). In the Middle East, three is considered a holy number. It is always connected to time: past, present, future. In ancient Rome the Fates almost always appear as three goddesses. Since ancient times femininity has been seen in three aspects: the virgin (Artemis), the woman (Hera), and the old woman (Hekate). Faust calls out three times until Mephisto appears. Peter denies Christ three times. Doing the same thing three times has magical effects— it represents the connection to reality.

According to Freud, refers to male genitalia. Jung considers three a mystical number; the three servants of the Queen of the Night in *The Magic Flute*; the three witches in *Macbeth*; the three wishes that are free. All this relates back, as do many god-trinities, to the original trinity: father-mother-son. It is the male child, since the number three, according to Western tradition, is uneven and, as a prime number, a genuine male number. In this tradition, the male child is seen first in terms of male fertility.

According to Jung, the number three is connected to the diabolical. The den of craving in alchemy is depicted by a three-headed snake. The three-headed snake in mythology is always Satan. Also, according to Jung, three belongs to the young; and in ancient China and the Greek patriarchy, it points to masculine attributes and their function.

On the other hand, Three as a feminine number is part of the tradition in the area of the Mediterranean, through the veneration of Mary in Catholicism and the rediscovery of the matriarchy. Also, Goethe's play *Faust, Part II*, ends with a prayer to the great goddess appearing threefold: "Virgin, Mother, Queen."

Threshold: See **Step**. Crossing over to something new. Separation. Also the connection between two or more worlds. See **Buckle**, **Bridge**.

Throat: Inexhaustible and unquenchable.

Throne: Desire to rule. Have you elevated yourself to the throne? Are you the heir to the throne or have you been asked to abdicate? Are you the power that stands behind the throne? See **Chair**, **King/Queen**.

Thrush: As with all **Birds,** connection between heaven and earth, between the gods and humans. Perspective and overview. According to a medieval interpretation, the thrush in a dream means new acquaintances for women; for men, unexpected affection.

Thumb: Indicates male and female productivity (also seen as a symbol of male and female genitals). Symbolic expression of creativity. Often points to the dreamer feeling small. The position of the thumb can mean life or death, as in the fights of gladiators in ancient Rome. According to Freud, sexual urges.

Folklore: Obstacles are in the way.

Thumb Sucking: Flight back into childhood. In psychoanalysis, a well-known symbol for masturbation.

Thunder: See **Lightning.** Be more assertive and don't put up with everything. "Let it roar!" The task here is to shape your own personal world. According to the *I Ching,* thunder indicates excitement and, by implication, the firstborn son. According to ancient Egyptian dream interpretation bad news, anger, rage, aggressive emotions. According to Homer, Zeus, the jovial "thunderer."

That which destroys and cleanses. Thunder gives your aggression a voice.

Folklore: Great difficulties.

Thunderstorm: See **Thunder, Storm, Hurricane, Wind.**

Ticket: Pleasure of traveling, new plans for your life; changes.

Tie: An emphasis on masculinity. Either a hint that you

are conceited, or that the **Knot** on your **Neck** refers to self-control. Often also a phallic symbol.

Tiger: See **Leopard**. An image frequently dreamed about by women. Longing for powerful love while, at the same time, also being afraid of the experience. The tiger and the **Lion** are both symbols of vitality and passion. The tiger is more a symbol of female sexual energy, while the lion is more a symbol of masculine sexual energy. The tiger possesses great energy, and one of its main strengths when it attacks is the surprise factor. It is also the symbol of severe loss. In the Shinto (of ancient Japan), the tiger was considered a holy but people-devouring predator, the personification of horror and fear who stops at nothing. According to Jung, it is also the symbol for female compulsion, as in **Cat**, **Bear**, **Snake**.

Time: How you use your time is a hint of your stage of development and your personality. It symbolizes how you organize and plan your life. It is meaningful to know what time period your dream represents—noon or night? Summer or winter? Also the century could be important.

As happens in many dreams, time sometimes seems

to stand still (stagnation) or is passing quickly (stress). If time is standing still, it could mean it's time to slow down, to look at something more closely. Time speeding up—as in a time-lapse photo—often symbolizes expanded awareness.

Tin: Nonsense; malleability, of little worth.

Toad: See **Frog**.

Tobacco: Pleasures (sometimes with regrets), restfulness but also addiction. See **Sweets**, **Smoke**, **Fog**.

Toes (tiptoe): Suggests that you become much more careful in your present situation. Do you want to perform at the highest level? However, it could also mean that you are not resolute enough and lack wholeness. See **Dance**, **Thumb**, **Finger**.
Folklore: Warning of a lovers' quarrel.

Toilet: The zone of the root chakra, where the Kundalini resides. This image may point to the relief of undigested leftovers, problems one has worked with. The suggestion here is to "let go."
From time immemorial, the toilet has been seen as a

dark and scary place—in dreams, all places connected to natural functions are demonized. It is the place of forbidden sexuality—self-gratification and homosexuality—a place full of danger and frightening activities. It is a place where ghosts and devils do their bad deeds, and the reason why toilets in the past were always outside. It is a place of taboos, of secrets and forbidden things, a place where budding sexuality and puberty fantasies run amuck.

This dream image also expresses the finality of nature. On one hand, it addresses everything that is transitory and points out that everything material will pass on and has no value. On the other hand, it addresses the meaning of accomplishment, completion. It is, again, an example of the alchemistic idea that gold can be made out of feces. In one sense, the toilet is the place where products are transformed. Such dream images almost always point to a necessary change: you must let go of something, while, at the same time, you must produce something positive. In Norse fables, King Olaf warns his guests not to go to the toilet alone during the night, because they might end up in a dangerous adventure with the **Devil**. The toilet has also been considered the place of ghosts.

According to Jung, it is the place of the highest creativity.

Tomato: See **Red**. The tomato is a symbol of fertility. As a nightshade plant, it also has something scary about it. According to Rudolf Steiner, the tomato is the expression of eroticism and passion.

Tongue: Language, intellectual creativity, communication. The tongue always refers to the throat chakra and thereby to the honesty of your communication, or the lack of it. See **Speech, Giving a**; and **Lecture**

Tools: Used for and aiding work. According to Freud, all tools are symbols of the male organ.

Toothache: You are lovesick.
Folklore: Happy news.

Top Hat: In a man's dream, a desire for greater virility. In a woman's dream, often a wish for marriage. A top hat was worn only to very formal events, such as a **Wedding** and a **Funeral**. Pay attention to the symbolic meaning of the event to which the top hat is worn.

Torch: Once a symbol for marriage, because the fire in the hearth was lit in a ritual ceremony with a torch. Then it became a symbol of passing on psychic energies and ideas (Olympic torch); the light of reason and free-dom (Statue of Liberty). Today, however, it is more a symbol of light and consciousness that penetrates the dark (that which is not understood). Also, a symbol of honoring somebody (torchlight procession).

Torture: Something secret, monumental. It could be torturing somebody with suspense, but it is often con-nected to fear of pain. If you are torturing somebody else, it is usually aggression against your own habits, for which the Other is simply a symbol. If you are being tor-tured, you are harming yourself, revealing a tendency toward masochism, which we probably all have.

On the other hand, hidden behind such a dream might be a need for more tension or excitement in your life. An unconscious sadomasochistic attitude may be clamoring for release. Are you sure that what is called sexual lust is not part of a full range of sexual pleasure? In another sense, these dream situations might be an expression of tension due to repressed feelings of revenge. You may not be willing, except in dreams, to do to others what you feel is being done to you. Those are a few of the scenarios such dreams deal with.

Towel: You want to wipe something away, as if it never happened. Or, when you throw in the towel, you are giving up (usually on yourself). A wet towel is a sign of something unsuitable and dysfunctional.

Tower: A frequent phallic symbol, particularly in women's dreams. More perspective is needed (watchtower). A symbol of power (compare the similarity of the words "tower" and "power." Being locked up in a tower points to sexual inhibitions in women (Rapunzel), and also is an indication of an unusual and highly developed sexuality that has no outlet.

Town Hall: Office and honor. Points to an inner, psychic organization of your personality.

Toys: Childlike, childish, immature.

Track/Trace/Sign: You are beginning to understand your problems; you have discovered the signs and are on the right track.

Tracks/Train Tracks: The path of life is foreordained. Or it can reflect security and rigidity (everything running on track).

Traffic Lights: Traffic, stress, order, an indication of needing to understand the signs of the times, or to establish these signs. Green light: idea, insight, understanding. Red light: repressive dream.

Traffic Sign: Often a symbol for sexual behavior. What the traffic sign announces is important.

Trail: You are on to something, or you are on to yourself. You are looking for something.

Train: See **Railroad Station.** Vacation or business trip? Fear of "missing" the train; or it is high time (if you want to catch the train). See **Haste.** Developing one's personality, striving for success and being sociable. Fleeing from the present situation.

Are you observing the train or are you traveling on the train (you are either wanting to move or you are part of the movement). What is happening on the train and how would you characterize the action?

According to Freud, leaving on a train and traveling on a train means death. However, Freud suffered from a phobia about trains.

Train/Conductor: Enjoying contact and communication, travel. The conductor may represent the guide of the soul (travel guide and signpost). You know where your travel will take you.

Train (on a gown)/Veil: Something is dragging behind you. See **Shadow.** To take somebody in tow. But also dignity, splendor, and worship. Often this image refers to **Bride.** Sometimes it may suggest time is "dragging," addressing the subject of patience.

Transference: Since Sigmund Freud, a key term in psychotherapy. Besides the more technical aspects in actual therapy, the idea of transference in essence means that during everyday situations old and ancient content from the unconscious can be brought to the surface (if it has not been dealt with) through actual events. Anything that happened at a given moment could either have real objective meaning or has been "transferred" and has nothing to do with the present—it is rather something carried to the surface from the past. See **Television, Companion, Shadow.**

Trap: Difficult situation, being imprisoned; more prudence and caution is in order. Feeling of restriction, as in **Siege, Amber, Village, Cage,** and **Elevator.** See **Falling.**

Trapdoor: In contrast to **Parachute**, this is unpleasant **Falling**, as in **Abyss**, and particularly as in **Shooting**. See **Hiding Place**, but this image also accesses layers of your character.

Trash Can: See **Toilet**. Symbol for repression and cleansing.

Travel: The life's path of the dreamer. Rejuvenation of the psyche. You are moving, searching. What is important is the kind of trip and how it is proceeding.

According to Freud, traveling is usually the symbol of death.

Treasure: Something of value. You need to activate old and forgotten skills. Treasure symbolizes the goal of the search and represents either the beginning of or the reason for personal efforts and endeavors. See **Wealth**. According to Freud, treasure stands for the person we love.

Tree: Protection; archetypal symbol for life (tree of life, tree of the world, family tree) and for being human, rooted in the earth. The crown of the tree, like the head of a human being, reaches for the sky. Part of two worlds—

reality and obligation (earth) and spirit and freedom (heaven). Personal development and growth of the dreamer. Family situation across several generations. Connected to nature, as in **Field, Ear (of corn), Farmer, Farm**. Concern for the environment as well as personal growth.

Does the tree grow **Fruit**? In what season did the image appear? What is the condition of the root system (base of the root as a symbol for soul), the **Trunk**, and the **Crown**? Where is the tree and how does it stand—alone, in a small group, in the forest, in a park?

According to Freud, the tree trunk is a phallic symbol.

Tree (Blossoms on): Luck, fullness. A frequent dream symbol that appears during nocturnal ejaculation.

Tree-of-Life: See **Tree**. Growth. Connection between heaven and earth.

Tree Trunk/Trunk: Tree. Security, stability and productivity, similar to **Family, Notice-of-Intention-to-Marry**. It often has a negative connotation when the trunk is either split or cut off. However, the chopping of the wood may also point to warmth (food for the inner fire) and (allocation of) one's inner energies. Is the trunk straight and strong?

Trial: If you are the accused, pay close attention to what you are accused of. If you are the accuser, take a look at what injustice has been done. You need to be objective, focused, and fair in your everyday life. See **Attorney**.

Triangle: Spiritualization. It is a female sexual symbol if the tip points down; male, if the tip points up.
   Folklore: Triangles in relationships.

Trip (Outing/Excursion): Recuperation, fun, change of scene. Well-known dream symbol when overworking. Where are you going on your trip?

Trophy: You want to be recognized. See **Chalice**.

Trout: Fish. Enjoyment of life; you are able to move freely in the waters of your emotions.
   Folklore: Difficulties are disappearing; innate emotional balance.

Truck: You are carrying a heavy burden. Or are you the authority that is steering the truck? Important is the symbolic meaning of the products that the truck is transporting.

Trumpet: Attention-getting and trying to awaken energies that are asleep. The expression of powerful energies.

Trunk: See **Tree Trunk**.

Tub: Cleansing, as in **Shower, Bath, Sauna**.
Folklore: Hard times if the tub is empty, good times if the tub is full.

Tuber: Concentrated energies that now need to be used for further development, similar to **Bud**. According to Freud, a phallic symbol. See **Potato**.

Tulip: A dream of women, rarely men. Being connected to nature. As is the case with all flower symbols in dreams, the image of the tulip also has sexual meaning.
Folklore: Dreaming about a tulip indicates a quick engagement and secret marriage.

Tunnel: In most cases, this is a dream about birth—looking back to the starting point. A dream of rebirth. In a tunnel we often meet the unconscious.

According to Freud, a reference to intercourse, especially when **Trains** drive in or out of the tunnel.

Tunnel (as in a mine): That which is unconscious and from which inner treasures need to be brought to light.

According to Freud, symbol of the vagina.

Turtle/Tortoise: Hiding behind a character trait (according to Wilhelm Reich). Patience, wisdom; or hiding something essential.

Twelve: The number we use to keep time (hour, months), it represents completion, an end and/or a new beginning. Twelve apostles, twelve astrological signs, and so on.

Twig: See **Branch, Tree.** Growing and thriving. It is a symbol of your own foundation (don't cut off the branch that you are sitting on), your own growth and ability to branch out—to understand the outside world in its many different aspects. See **Y-Shape.** According to Freud, a twig with blossoms is clearly a sexual symbol.

Twilight: Romance, a transitional period. One is standing between two worlds and is not quite sure. Twilight indicates a moment of transition, in which everything seems undefined and undecided. Dusk is connected to fears, but in part it is also a symbol for new beginnings, curiosity (what does the new day have in store?) and openness. Morning sunrise and evening sunset are times of pleasure. See **Red**.

Twins: See **Two**. Talking to both sides within the Self, or one specific side—the side represented by the image of the twins. "The better half" and "the other self" (alter ego).

Folklore: Very bad luck.

Two: The opposites and contradictions that are in need of differentiation and balance. Your ambivalence is becoming known, which is a positive development.

According to Jung, two identical symbols refer to the unconscious, because two identical things cannot be distinguished from one another. Messengers from the underworld, for that reason, appear usually in twos.

Umbrella: You are rejecting insight and ideas; have no direct contact with reality; no contact with the water of the emotion. Or, the umbrella could mean flexibility—a **Roof** over your head.

Uncle: "Elder people" and authority.

Underground: One of the most frequent symbols for the unconscious. The task is to discover the unconscious and that which has been unconscious, and to become familiar with it.

Underground Garage: The place of the unconscious and everything frozen and rigid. See **Forest, Basement**.

Underworld: See **Underground**. Mythological symbol of the unconscious—the dark or shadowy gods of the deep.

Undressing: Openness, exposing oneself. What is underneath the surface (the clothing)?

Unicorn: Ancient symbol for innocence and purity. The unicorn places its horn in the lap of the virgin; it can't be caught in any other way. It is able to remove poison and its effects; it loves happiness. It may also be a sign of flight into an irrational fairy-tale world. Today, the unicorn also means hope of the removal of all differences, as well as fear of contradictions. Innocence and sexual urges are also connected to the image of the unicorn, and the dreamer is posing the question: How do I see my desires without feeling guilty? It is a question about the "purified animalistic self."

According to Jung, the symbol of self.

Uniform: Authority, self-affirmation, ambition, and seeking power; but also a lack of self-awareness and/or a weak ego. It may also be a sign of a lack of order or of too rigidly adhering to order. In the case of women, longing for or fear of a strong man. Uniforms also point to a lack of individuality, of repetitiveness.

According to Freud, nakedness that one is trying to hide.

Universe: The spiritual environment of the dreamer.

University: See **School**. Mother symbol (alma mater), but also a symbol of masculinity. It represents the intellectual side of life.

Uphill: The effort of **Ascension.** Succeeding in a task.

Urine: A magical liquid, as are all body liquids. Points to sexual or domestic problems.

Urn (container for ashes): See **Death** and impermanence.

Folklore: A young relative is being honored.

Uroboros: See **Ouroboros.**

Uterus: Fertility and inner wealth. With this image, are you remembering your own heritage, or something from a "past life"?

Vacuum Cleaner: Symbol of cleanliness and an orderly house.

Vagabond: Freedom, breaking with rigid convention. This dream usually appears in times of social pressure.

456

Valley: Low point, crisis, and turning point. Going down into the valley means either getting to the bottom of something, or descending into the unconscious. Pay attention to the kind of valley (its shape and what is growing there). If the valley is already in the shadows, it symbolizes dark areas. A valley that is shaped like a canyon symbolizes either female sexuality or sexual anxieties.

Folklore: Warning of an illness.

Vamp: Are you posing as a cunning female? Should you become sexually more provocative? In a man's dream, a desire to be more clever in sexual matters.

Vampire: See **Monster/Mythological Creature, Bat.** Guilt feelings, and the sense of being sucked dry. These dreams often appear during depression. The vampire image points to insufficient boundaries toward the world of shadows.

Vase: See **Container.** You are depending too much on external things. Also a suggestion that you are guided by sexual moods and feelings that are confusing. In women's dreams the demanding side of your sexuality needs to be lived out more fully, or in a way that causes conflict in a male-dominated society.

According to Freud, a symbol of the female.

Vault: As in **Cave**, a symbol for mother and security.
Folklore: Difficulty.

Vegetable: Stands for young people and children. See
Food.
According to Jung, usually a reference to eroticism.

Vehicle: Driving. Freedom of movement. You want to
get away. You want to keep moving. You would like to
arrive. The type of vehicle indicates whether you are
pursuing your own path and what progress you are making. Also, symbol for emotional independence and
momentum.

Veil: A symbol for secret. Something is being hidden—
something is being portrayed falsely. See **Virgin.**
Tearing down a veil symbolizes **Defloration.** But it also
refers to protection in the sense of having essential
emotional boundaries. Warning of, and emphasis on,
emotional immunity.

Velvet: Luxury and sensuality. The symbolic meaning of
the color is important.

According to Freud, pubic hair, as in **Fur**, and sexuality.

Vengeance: Should you be more aggressive?

Victim: Some emotions, characteristics, and behaviors need to be given up. If you are making a sacrifice in the dream, or giving something away, ask how easy it is for you to let go in real life. What you may have to let go of is symbolized by what you give away or sacrifice in the dream. On the other hand, giving something away shows how compassionate you are, and how much empathy you are capable of. If you are a victim, pay close attention to the perpetrator and figure out how you came to be cast in the role of victim and what kind of fearful or enjoyable emotions are connected with that role.

Victory: Desire for success and for the ability to achieve. Since our most significant arguments take place internally, this dream image refers to conscious development. You are now able to win over your own problems and blocks.

Villa: A symbol of wealth that one would love to possess. It is a wish dream, representing the popular belief that emotional emptiness can be filled with possessions.

Village: Symbolizes the personality of the dreamer: unsophisticated but well-balanced (at least as an ideal). But can also mean restriction, as in **Siege, Amber, Trap,** as well as a phony idealist. According to ancient Egyptian dream interpretation, peaceful existence, family, protection, belonging.

Vinegar: Insult, disappointment; you are sour. Something is getting ruined (turning sour).
Folklore: All your efforts are in vain.

Violence: Discipline is necessary. Or let go of too much discipline. Similar to **Obedience.** Repressed urges.

Violet (color): Consistency and perfection. It is the symbol of the search for transcendency (violet is the color on the edge of the invisible, the ultraviolet light). It represents the highest, almost delicate vibration of the spectrum, similar to inspiration and spirituality.

The color violet is very soothing. It depends on light, and under different light can take on very different shades.

Also, but rarely, violet is the color of passion. **Red**, as the color of the body, and **Blue**, as the color of the soul, combine to make purple—the body and the soul united. It is the most important color for the magic of love. As the witches' color, violet became the color of feminists. In Byzantium, violet was the color of power. Up to the 19th century in some parts of Europe, it was considered a color of grief and sorrow. In Roman Catholicism, it is the color of the robes of bishops. Violet is also used to stand in for black, the symbol of humility and repentance in the Catholic Church. See **Violet (flower)**, **Lilac**.

Violet (flower): Modesty, a pure woman or girl ("shrinking violet"). On one hand, the color violet points to emancipation. The emancipated woman is one who walks new frontiers. Violet, from a language point of view, is connected to the Latin word *violatio*, which means force and rape.

Violin: An idealization of the female body. Or wanting to "play the first violin." As with all musical instruments, harmony is addressed; and as with all string instruments, the image symbolizes the "string of nerves," as well as the mood and tension of a person.

The resonating power of a violin also points to how our inner world resonates. It could be interpreted as the "echo of the soul."

If a string breaks, it means quarrels.

Folklore: Domestic happiness.

Virgin: As with all strange women who appear in a man's dream, this image represents his own feminine side, which in case of a mother complex he is unable to integrate.

In a woman's dream, it represents her own unknown, often disowned, feminine side. It also reflects a strong connection to the father, egocentricity in love, and possible frigidity. See **Defloration.**

Something new should be undertaken. Also a warning about an action that cannot be undone. The action of the virgin in the dream points to unknown characteristics and behaviors of the dreamer.

Visit: Change, period of development and transition, loneliness. A longing for social contact, or too much of it, as in **Friend.**

Vista: A well-known symbol for perspectives and consciousness, almost always pointing to the future. The vista often appears in the dream as a mirror of the eyes and what the dreamer is seeing, meaning it is a symbol of the personal identity of the dreamer. What are you looking forward to? Are the choices good or bad? What do you see?

Vitamin: What is nutritious and good. Do you have to take more?

Voice: You need to make people to listen to you. Raise your voice.
Folklore: Bad omen.

Volcano: Drives repressed and drives released, stress or stress reduction. This implies a "test by fire." What is innermost comes to the surface. It might express a fantasy of merging in a relationship, or fusion of different parts of the Self in a developing personality. Also, what was hard is made to flow again.

Vomiting: Undigested concepts and emotions are being expelled, cleansed—similar to **Sewer, Toilet.** Letting go of unwanted emotions.

Vulture: Exploitation has become a way of life It may serve as an explanation of why you have difficulty with the world around you.

Folklore: Your enemies are a danger to you.

Waffle: Old and well-known symbol for female sexuality, domesticity, and enjoyment.

Wages: How are you handling your emotional energies? Are you getting what you want?

Wagon: See **Car.** A wagon symbolizes an important transitional stage in life. It also indicates the dreamer's courage in steering his own course and making his own discoveries. According to Jung, although the wagon is a means of transportation made by man, its wheels are a symbol of the wheel of the sun that symbolizes **Mandala.** It is a frequent dream symbol when making changes.

Wagon/Wheelbarrow: On one hand, this symbol points to difficulties ("pulling the wagon out of the ditch," for example); on the other hand, it is also a symbol of mobility. A wheelbarrow in a dream often points to the dreamer's body, as does the **Carriage.** In addition to checking the condition of the wagon, also pay attention to the condition of the road.

Waist: Those who want to lose weight probably dream about the waist more often than those who don't. See **Belt, Stomach.**

Waiter: Friendliness, help. Should you be more humble and think more about service? Similar to **Chauffeur.**

Walk: Often a dream of birth. A dark walkway may point to helplessness.

Walking: Making progress in life under your own power, slow but steady. Independence. How you walk is a clear indication of your present situation.

Walking Stick: Support. Symbol of a person that you can trust. Phallic symbol.

Wall: An obstacle dream, or support, protection. You should either be more open or have better boundaries.

Waltz: Symbol of love as well as **Rose, Circle, Dance.** *Folklore:* A secret admirer.

War: Real fear of war. In addition, confrontation between different parts of the personality of the dreamer: inner conflict. This dream image points to current confrontations with your own aggressiveness. Check to see if you are too aggressive, or if you should express your aggression more directly.

Warehouse/Department Store: Symbol of commerce or greed, but also may refer to an independent life and taking care of the Self. What is offered in the warehouse or department store refers to talents that are available.

Warmth: A frequent dream symbol when the dreamer is actually cold while sleeping. Warmth and devotion, but also demanding and feeling restricted. If the temperature is falling, feelings are cooling off.

Warning: A warning—even though it is only in a dream—ought to be taken seriously.

Warts: Symbol of witches. See **Witch**.
Folklore: Wealth.

Washbasin: As in **Washing, Tub, Shower, Bath, Sauna**. A symbol of cleanliness and purity.

Washing: A symbol for cleansing as in **Tub, Shower, Bath, Sauna**. In alchemy, being blackened is followed by washing; chaotic situations are followed by cleansing (from guilt feelings). Washing of the hands is a sign of innocence.

Wasp: Aggression and egocentricity.

Water: See **River, Sea, Ocean**. This dream symbol can be interpreted on five different levels:
    (1) on the sexual level

(2) on an emotional level where your own emotions are perceived as undifferentiated and flowing

(3) as a fear of flooding, being drowned by the unconscious

(4) as a feeling of going with the flow

(5) as a feeling that life is chaotic.

This symbol is also the desire for a totally new orientation.

In alchemy, water is connected to feelings; it represents the wild nature of the soul in need of being conquered. Water is the place where the souls of the dead meet the spirits of the water; it is a place of repression, of secrets with unknown depths and an element of rapture. It can tear us away and sweep us off, and it can be very frightening. Water is the symbol of what is changeable. Diving into the water means to seek wisdom. Whoever looks into the water always sees the Self.

Water symbolizes women, the process of birth and pregnancy. Running water means experiencing sexuality in a positive sense. Standing water means losing vitality and your very center. Or it might mean, as in **Pond** and the fountain of youth, that water is the carrier of life's energies and rejuvenation. Out of this understanding might have come the ritual of baptism.

Falling into the water means being swept away by

emotion; but this may also be a warning dream, pointing also to **Diving** and **Drowning**.

According to the Chinese understanding of nature, water is a symbol of the elemental, female force of *yin*. For the Taoist, water is the essence of life, its movement an example for a life lived in harmony with nature. The holy water in the Catholic Church and the water used for baptism represent the healing powers of water.

According to Freud, a water dream is often the memory of our life in our mother's womb. And again, according to Freud, to come out of water represents the image of birth. Water for him was always connected to birth. See **Baptism**, **Swimming**, **Bath**, **Diving**, **Tears**, **Drinking**, **Birth (rebirth)**.

Waterfall: See **Water**. A symbol for letting go.

Watering Can: Abundance, wealth. Or economical distribution of your energies, as in **Faucet**. According to Freud, this is a phallic symbol, because what flows out of the "spout" brings about fertilization.

Water Lily: The world of the emotions and a symbol for wholeness and completeness. See **Rose**.

Wave: See **Water**. An image of emotional excitement—tenderness, caressing, and sexuality. See **Surfing**, **Ship**.

Wax: Adaptability, steadfastness or the lack of it, and the power to shape. Symbol of temptation.

Wealth: The expression of a desire for a full and spirited inner life. In dreams, wealth and money always are connected with psychic energies. This is a warning not to be too modest, or to allow yourself to have false expectations. Your existence and your personal qualities are your greatest wealth. How you are dealing with the world—protecting what is uniquely yours and developing it—makes a decided difference. See **Price**, **Treasure**.

Weapon: Particularly in women's dreams, fear of sexuality. In the case of men, it is partly an expression of fear of the weapons of women. Fear of war. A weapon in a dream also symbolizes internal poison or corrosion. According to Freud and most of depth psychology, it is a symbol of masculine sexuality, since bullets penetrate the body. Today, this dream image is less relevant, because weapons so often totally destroy the body. This expands on Freud's interpretation, which sees it as an interesting tension between creating a body (sexuality) and destroying a body (modern weaponry).

Weasel: Symbol for speed.
Folklore: A warning of so-called friends.

Wedding: Marriage. Important and frequent dreams during times of marital and relationship conflicts. It is important how the wedding is celebrated. Also, gains, in a spiritual as well as economic sense.

Longing for a permanent relationship, security, and home. Today the image is often a symbol of being at the peak of your life, expressing the idea that peak experiences should be present more in your life.

In ancient Indian tradition, dreaming about a wedding points to impending death or pain.

According to Freud, a dream of desire. According to Jung, it always addresses the union of *anima* and *animus* —as in **Bride/Bridegroom**.

Weeds: Unorganized and unknown instincts and impulses that may be destructive *or* helpful.

Weight: Depression, burdened, as in **Luggage**. Or it

may be an admonition not to take things so seriously. May also refer to your ability to "weigh" the facts.

Well/Fountain: Strong bonding to the mother, regression, food, symbol of the female. If the dreamer is a man: passion, patience, true friendship. Rest and healing, as in **Breast.** Often the task is to become a "good mother" to oneself and to see oneself as "one's own child."

According to Freud, early childhood sexual symbol.

Wet Nurse: Food, comfort, closeness; in the case of women, often the desire for conception, pregnancy, and children. In the case of men, often the fear of the female and, specifically, motherliness (a nursing woman, because of the fear of her fertility, was once called a "milk-cow").

Whale: The feeling of being swallowed up by a task that needs to be completed, like Jonah in the Bible, who was swallowed up by the whale. Also a symbol of the endangered species in the world.

Wheat: See **Grain.**

Wheat field: Life's tasks, productivity, and success. See

Grain, Field, Seed, Harvest. Compare this also with the allegory about the wheat kernel that must die in order to bear fruit many times over.

Wheel: See **Circle** and **Mandala**.

Wheelbarrow: See **Wagon**.

Wheelchair: On one hand, restriction, suffering and the inability to escape from problems. On the other hand, in spite of a psychological handicap, moving forward. Often such dreams are a challenge, in a sense, to learn how to walk again.

Whip: Subjugation; the power of aggression. Masochistic tendencies that are lived out. Or, you are doing damage to yourself, and the dream is pointing that out. You need to find your Self.

Whirlpool: Sinking into emotions, into the unconscious. See **Diving**.
  Folklore: You are inheriting something.

Whistling: A rare dream symbol. You want to be noticed. As in **Scream**, a primeval outburst of psychic energy.

White: Cleansing and innocence, attraction, and openness. Symbol of virginity and innocence. A desire to go through life undefiled. The color white in a dream points to purity—the dreamer is either living a pure life or is longing for it. One is seeking cleansing, and probably is already cleansed in a certain sense, simply by having a dream about the color white. But it could also suggest exaggerated cleanliness, an addiction to washing and cleaning, etc.

On the other hand, white can also be an expression of fear, such as the white whale in *Moby Dick* and the great white shark. Here the reference is to a blinding white color. Ghosts, like those appearing as mice during delusional episodes (delirium tremens), are always white. The archetype of the wise man is usually clad in white (the guru, and also the physician). White is also the fundamental symbol for the *animus*; it addresses the male intellect and also male aggression (when white is experienced as blinding and gleaming).

The union of **Red** and white is that of contradiction: it is the symbol of the mystical marriage and Tantric sexuality (white semen and red menstrual blood). Here is where innocence meets the physical body and where heaven meets hell. Red and white are the colors of alchemy as well as the colors in the coats-of-arms of England and Switzerland.

Mabinogion, the ancient Welsh epic poem, refers to the white dogs of the underworld, except they have red noses and red eyes.

According to Freud, white always points to the feminine.

White Horse: Positive image of nature, energy, vitality, and purity. See **White**.

White Thorn: White thorn is the bush Viviane hides behind to put a spell on Merlin. The wood of the white thorn also is used to make magical wands. Considered a holy plant in Christianity, the white thorn grows in Glastonbury in southern England and is said to have been brought there by Joseph of Arimathea. It blooms twice every year.

Folklore: Good luck.

Widow: Loss of masculinity.

Widower: Loss of femininity, loneliness, brooding, grief. See **Death, Divorce**.

Wild/Primitive Man: Romanticizing the simple life. A suggestion to live more on the wild side and to dismiss prejudice and reservations. This means trusting the Self more, having the "courage to not be perfect." See **Fool**, **Lion**, **Tiger**.

Wilderness: The wilderness in dreams refers to the place where wild emotions and uncontrolled urges and drives reign, and suggests coming to terms with them. The wilderness, in addition to the so-called jungle characteristics, may also indicate a desert, meaning unproductive or unused talents within the Self.

Will: An attempt to bring order into one's affairs, gaining perspective about life already lived. Fear of death. Hoping for wealth without working for it. Coming to terms with a legacy, often in the sense of the dreamer's own past, talents, and abilities. The search for meaning. A desire for productivity and fulfillment, particularly after one period in life has come to an end.

Willow Tree: Flexibility, smoothness, but also sadness (weeping willow). It is a light in the darkness.

Wind: See **Storm, Hurricane**. Here the spirits of the air are being addressed. They personify intellect or spirit. The wind can also mean an idea or a new understanding. If it conveys a sense of fresh air, something new is going to happen. See **Air, Breath**.

Windmill: Intellectual powers. Intellectual or spiritual work. Battling with imagination, as in Cervantes' *Don Quixote*.
   Folklore: Small winnings.

Window: House. Here, almost always, internal and external references are being addressed. With this dream symbol, it is important to note what you see when you look through the window. In what direction are you looking? Is the window clean and clear or opaque? All this is of great symbolic meaning.
   According to Freud, this image points to the body's openings (the house is the body, the windows are the eyes).

Windowsill: According to Freud, projections from the human body—for instance, the breast.

Wine/Grape Wine/Vineyard: Intoxication and hard work; the juice of life and sensual enjoyment. *"In vino veritas"*—do you need to tell somebody the truth?

Wings (for Flying): You need to live an easier life, be

more open to playful energies, be more spiritual (soar). This is a direct challenge to think big and to have courage to do great things. This image fits the observation in the *I Ching*: "It furthers one to cross the great water."

According to Homer, wings symbolize thought.

Winning: In every instance, a symbol of success.

Winter: See **Ice, Cold, White**.

Wire (High-Voltage): Drives and urges must be guided sensibly. This image points to severe nervous tension—or exceptional strength.

Wire (High-Tension): Connection to somebody, to another place; or being informed and clever. It is a frequent symbol for nerves and intellectual connection. An electrical wire usually indicates the tension the dreamer is under.

Wise Man: An archetype of the wise old man as a guide for life's journey. Particularly in women's dreams, it is the expression of a longing for positive masculinity and "the better" father.

Witch: Hedge. A negative symbol for Mother, the overpowering, malevolent woman who is feared. Often points to a mother who does not care properly for her children (particularly in children's dreams). Less often, the image of a witch points to the wise woman (particularly in women's dreams) who exudes great magnetism. The witch is almost always a symbol of the power of the unconscious—**Magic.** In fairy tales as well as in dreams, the witch plays an important, archetypal role, because she separates the hero or dream-self from his (usually royal) origin, which can then only be recaptured after he passes a certain test.

Witness: What we have witnessed in a dream—what we have seen—should be taken very seriously and remembered as accurately as possible. You are feeling included and part of the event. Being a witness means being productive and possibly an originator.

Wolf: The male wolf is universally accepted as an image of Man, with reckless aggression and problems in sexual restraint. Considered a cunning, malicious predator, the concept of the wolf implies greed and hunger and, in that sense, physical urges and dissatisfaction. See **Greed**. The wolf often symbolizes the shadow of male sexuality. Be glad to have had such a strong dream. You are powerful; you do not need to kill the wolf, but you can dance with him.

In *Steppenwolf*, by Herman Hesse, the wolf becomes a symbol for the lonely seeker (and sufferer). Here it is not so much a reference to the meanness of the wolf, but rather the lonely search for the meaning of life.

In Christianity, the wolf is compared to the false prophet and heretic.

According to Jung, the wolf is wilder than the **Lion** and the **Dog**. Between 1910 and 1914, Sigmund Freud treated a patient who later would become famous as the "Wolfman." As a small child this patient suffered from terrifying dreams about wolves, which was the reason why Freud gave him this name. The earliest memories this man had about his nightmares involved six or seven **White** wolves that were sitting in a hazelnut tree in front of his window, and he was sure they had come to devour him. Freud here makes reference to two fairy tales: "Little Red Riding Hood" and "The Wolf and the Seven Little Goats." In addition, Freud sees the wolf as a father substitute. As a young boy, the patient had observed his parents having intercourse from behind, and according to Freud, the patient transferred his repressed desire for sexual gratification by his father to a fear of wolves.

The female wolf symbolizes the nurturing power of nature, like Romulus and Remus, who were both nursed by a wolf. This is also the essence of the fairy tale "Little Red Riding Hood," where the wolf is not only devouring Grandmother but he *is* Grandmother—the great mother symbol of wild nature.

Woman: If a woman dreams about women, it is almost always about her shadow and seldom about herself. If a man dreams about a woman, he is dreaming about his emotional side, which, in the end, is about his connection to his mother. In the case of a man, the behavior of the woman in the dream often gives insight into his unconscious life, his unknown characteristics, physical urges, and behavior.

According to ancient Egyptian dream interpretation, the image of a beautiful woman is always a warning that a task is too large.

According to Jung, a strange woman in the dream of a man is always the feminine side of the dreamer, his *anima*. Jung also thinks that a woman in a man's dream always represents his emotional "teacher."

Women also appear in many dreams as old and wise

(woman or hag), lecherous (threatening or liberated), imprisoned (like Rapunzel's trapped physical drive), ugly (as a witch), young (as a temptress), powerful (as the mother), and beautiful (the lover, the ideal).

Wonders: In dreams, wonders and miracles are "normal." They suggest forsaking limitations. The dreamer is living life too rigidly.

Wood: Symbol for mobility, warmth, and naturalness. Important is the condition and type of wood; for example, **Firewood** and **Ebony.**

In the *I Ching*, wood means gentleness, that which penetrates, like the wind, and it is related to the first daughter.

According to Freud, wood is a symbol for femininity. However, in the Tarot, wood corresponds to the wand which—according to traditional as well as modern interpretation—is connected to masculinity. This is an example of how contradictory meanings can be in the symbolism of depth psychology. At a certain level of consciousness, the difference between masculinity and femininity loses its importance. This higher level of consciousness is mirrored in everyday life where some symbols can be seen as typically feminine as well as masculine, in accordance with the present state of consciousness of the dreamer.

Folklore: Bad omen.

Wood Instrument: Music, relaxation, enjoying art, but also screaming silently. In most cases, it is an expression of great vitality.

According to classical depth psychology, a phallic symbol.

Work: Problems and burdens of the day are being carried over into sleep. Image of emotional work done in a dream.

Worker: Something is being accomplished; one must do something, be active. Social decline or social romanticism.

Worm: The **Snake** is often called a worm, a symbol of the lowest stage of the animal kingdom, often indicating bad conscience or troubles, usually with a sexual connotation.

According to Jung, worms represent the first movement of an unevolved soul, without "color," emotions, and reason—representing blind instincts.

Worship: Prayer, peace, meditation; centering is necessary. This is a frequent dream image when life is oriented too much to materialism.

Wound: See **Injury**. Painful emotional experience.

Wreath: Disappointment. A female sexual symbol, it may indicate the end of a relationship. In the form of a victory or funeral wreath, it is an expression of maturity and the completion of a task. Here you should check on the goals you have set for your life.

Wreck: Fear of going under.

Wrestling Match: You are fighting with yourself about something. It is important who the opponent is. Are you courageous, or do you feel like a coward? Meaning: Are you facing your problems or denying them?

Wrinkles: Experience and age.

Wristband: Bond/relationship; a feeling of one's activity being restricted, similar to the symbol of **Chain** or **Cage**. Also, an emphasis on independence. In the form of **Jewelry**, it implies vanity, but jewelry can also be an expression of pleasure in one's own beauty.

Folklore: Receiving money, or a love affair.

Wristwatch: Order in everyday life, rushing, stress, and time pressures. See **Clock, Time**. In addition, take a look at your own life span. How are you using time? The image of "time" in this context is closely connected to your personality. What have you achieved over the years? Are you satisfied?

Writing: Thinking, planning, and organizing. To account for something to yourself. But it may also mean an important message or tip. You need to turn to a particular person and discuss something important with him or her. Or, if you have an important question, this person may have an answer.

Yacht: Symbolizes spoiled and expensive women, and a longing for more femininity. If the sea is calm, luck is indicated; your ambitions are being fulfilled. A wild sea represents danger.

Yard: Points either to something hidden, as in **Backyard,** or the open side of the dreamer's personality.

According to Freud, the yard symbolizes the vagina, but today this meaning is only thought relevant if sexual drives are repressed. However, these interpretations remain in the imagination, because once a meaning has been culturally established, the human soul does not ever forget.

Yarn: See **Thread.** A relationship that should be kept intact. Red yarn is the red thread that Ariadne gives Theseus to help him to find his way out of the Maze.
Folklore: A joyful event.

Yarn (story): Untruthfulness, "spinning a yarn," or thoughts and feelings that are taking shape very slowly. See **Thread.**
Folklore: Prosperity. In folk tradition, dreaming about spinning a yarn is thought to bring luck in love.

Yeast: What drives us; the important, small things in life.
Folklore: Money that you have saved.

Yellow: Refers to intuition and intellect (also in the sense of awareness). Symbol for the color of the sun.

Yellow also stands for irritable feelings. It may also be a sign of mental illness that may be expressed, for instance, in the choice of yellow as a dominating color in paintings, such as those of Van Gogh. The term "Yellow Peril" warns of mental and physical illness. This is a classic example of how a political term with an archetypal meaning has over time led to new associations, regardless of whether others share the same political opinion. Advertising works in a similar way.

If the yellow seems to have a golden tint to it—abundant harvest, intellectual activities. Dark or muddy/dirty yellow, on the other hand, means envy, greed, jealousy, and betrayal.

In Hinduism, yellow symbolizes the light of life; in Buddhism humility and freedom.

Goethe wrote "[Yellow] is a happy, alive, gentle color, but it can easily become uncomfortable and with the addition of even the slightest amount of another color, it becomes devalued, ugly, and dirty."

Yoga: Body control and meditation. As a dream symbol, yoga usually suggests a more conscious way of dealing with the body.

Yogi: This dream symbol addresses the magical belief of

the yogi. Expression of hope that one can overcome natural law.

Young Boy: One whose life is in front of him. Start something new. It also points to weak masculinity and a poorly developed masculine side of the woman, as well as poor gender identity in a man. This is often connected to the aging process in a man. In the *Koran*, it means one whose wealth is increasing.

According to Freud, the male genitalia, often in connection with masturbation fantasies.

Youth: Primarily a symbol that appears in the second half of life. In the dream your life is seen in perspective, pointing to behavior that might have lead to problems (neurosis).

If such a dream happens to appear in the first half of your life, it usually points to undeveloped characteristics of the dreamer.

Y-Shape: The letter "Y" unites the masculine and the feminine. It also represents the dowsing rod that is used to find something hidden. The "Y" also represents a magical formula where one becomes two and two become one.

Zebra: Contradictions in life need to be better integrated or more clearly defined.

    Folklore: Differences among friends.

Zeppelin: See **Airplane**. Phallic symbol.

    Folklore: Unrealistic ambitions.

Zero: A sexual image, nothingness, triviality, less often also death, quiet, and completion. See **Circle**, **Mandala**, which, according to Jung, represent the Self as the anchor (center) of a person. See **Fool**.

Zinc: See **Metal**.
Folklore: Your future is secured.

Zipper: This symbol is connected with **Naked** and **Clothing**. It might also have to do with the joining of **Left** and **Right**.

Zoo: Are you looking at your own animal side? This image refers to the *animus anima* (and your masculine and feminine sides).

Dealing with Your Dreams

— Practical Advice —

Dream Diary

If you have decided to work systematically with your dreams, it is essential that you begin to keep a dream diary. Just the act of using one will allow you to remember your dreams much more often and more clearly.

What you should keep in mind if you start a dream diary:

1. Make a note about the date of the dream (use the date of the morning following the dream).
2. Start out by describing the events in the dream without any kind of interpretation and in the sequence you remember them.
3. Write whether the dream you remembered is complete or only a fragment.
4. Write how you felt before and after the dream.
5. Give each dream a title at the conclusion, one that best characterizes the content of the dream.

For interpretation, remember the following:

1. The attitude you adopted toward the dream. Were you a passive observer or actively involved in the event?

2. Which persons appeared in the dream and what your attitude is toward them, emotionally and behaviorally.
3. The mood of each individual scene and of the dream in general.

Your Personal Dream Symbols

An alphabetically arranged address book lends itself well to keeping track of the most important symbols in your dreams. First, make a note of the personal meaning and then the general meaning of each symbol. Choose those images that you consider most important, especially the symbols that continually recur. For each symbol, make note of the title and the date of the dream in which it appeared. A general interpretation of a symbol listed in this handbook should only be noted if it expands or changes your understanding of your *personal* dream symbols.

How to Begin

Most people who do dream work have found it helpful to establish a system that allows them to jot down the initial interpretation of the dream quickly. Such a system makes it easy to refer back to their dreams. The system should include the following:

1. Which persons in the dream could represent the *animus* (the masculine side—primarily in women but also in men) and/or the *anima* (the female side, primarily in men but also in women)?

2. Are there people in the dream whom you reject, whom you fight against or hate? Particularly when they are of the same gender, they are likely to represent your own dark and rejected side, the shadow.

3. What is the main symbol, and what is your attitude toward it? It is possible that there is more than one "main" symbol. Access to a clear understanding of the symbol is possible when you characterize it in one sentence.

4. Which objects are important in the dream? What is their objective function in your daily life? What is their subjective function?

5. Try to determine what, in yourself, each symbol refers to.

6. Go over the sequence of actions or situations in your dream once more and ask yourself: Where in my everyday life have such behaviors or situations occurred?

Only after going through these steps, should you attempt to interpret your dream in its entirety. Summarize each interpretation in two or three clear-cut sentences.

This type of system is for those who have very little time in the morning for any extensive and detailed dream work. It could well be called a system for the stressed-out city dweller, which however doesn't mean that it cannot be an effective and precise way for dealing with your dreams.

For those with more time, here are a few additional suggestions:

1. Before each interpretation, ask yourself: Where have I come from and where am I going? Examine your dream in that connection.
2. Look closely at each detail of your dream. The small things give important suggestions that are easily overlooked.
3. Look very closely to see if there are objects that appear in an unusual combination. Look for magical and fairy-tale elements: for instance, transformations, breaks in time, or other unusual incidents. This is often the case in short dreams that sometimes seem composed like a still life and where natural objects combine unnaturally to create a certain atmosphere. Arbitrary combinations

of familiar things always create unusual images or special atmosphere, and that is significant here. Begin your interpretation with this atmosphere.

4. At the end of each interpretation, ask yourself: Can I transfer what I have learned in the dream to my everyday life? It is best to have a plan on how to immediately integrate these "lessons" into your life.

The Attitude of the Dreamer

Never interpret your dreams intellectually! Reasoning creates distance. Such distance often leads us to misunderstand symbols and whole dreams. Symbols are dealt with by the heart and not by the intellect, because their effect lies in moving something emotionally. Dreams therefore must always be approached on an emotional level. We can often recognize intuitively—and very quickly—what a dream is trying to tell us. Bring a little bit of your heart to every dream analysis and you will gain a lot.

Afterword

As a therapist I had many reasons for *not* wanting to write a dream encyclopedia. Luckily, my publisher and my studies of the writings of C. G. Jung convinced me that, instead of one rigid sentence, a dream dictionary could stimulate the reader into finding many different possible interpretations of a dream symbol. As it turns out, such a dictionary is not only useful on a personal level for interpreting dreams, but it can also be of great help in a general sense. Because many different key words are listed for one dream symbol, readers are inspired to find many creative solutions, some of which they might not have thought about before. It is precisely that which interests me today in my therapeutic work and workshops: how, with the aid of our dreams, we may creatively solve problems in situations where our thinking has become rigid, preventing solutions. In other words, how can our dreams be used productively in dealing with everyday life and the working world? Allow me to introduce you to a dream a client of mine told me a couple of months ago:

I find myself in a medieval town with narrow

streets. The streets are already filled with people; they are rushing back and forth with their faces all muffled. All of a sudden, I see my mother and a very strong man, both of them with hands outstretched in my direction. I proceed to dismiss the man and walk up to my mother to say good-bye to her; very quickly we are separated by the mass of people and I don't see her anymore. Shortly thereafter, I find myself in the middle of a group of people who are trying to climb a high mountain. But first we must go down into the valley where, to my amazement, I am confronted with a maze of train tracks. And sure enough, a train appears and I am afraid, believing that this train would carry me even further into the valley. However, I am boarding the train, and to my great amazement the train is climbing up the steep mountain relatively quickly.

The client has been asking herself for some time now if she should end her relationship with her boyfriend or if it is worth continuing to work on it in order to improve the situation. Like so many of us, she is very indecisive in questions of relationships: Are further efforts to improve this situation a sign of "Work on something already spoiled" (*I Ching*)? Or is it just one more proof that she is unable to have good relationships? After all, she is 37 years old and already has two very unhappy marriages behind her. "Do I need a relationship at all, or am I just running after what convention expects a woman to do—meaning looking for a man"? This is a question she has raised several times even before this dream occurred. At the same time she is well aware of the irony of the situation since, by profession, she herself is a psychotherapist specializing in relationship issues. The dilemma that she is facing is of great interest to her. She had planned to write an extensive paper on the subject and submit it to a psychology journal for publication. But this is only one reason why she has given so much thought to her situation. Ever since this dream, she told me, she feels as if she is "at the end of the line, totally immobilized and at [her] wits' end."

Surprisingly enough, but also very typically, she does not know what to do with her dream. The same thing happened to the great masters of dream interpretation, Sigmund Freud and Carl Gustaf Jung, who each had great difficulties trying to understand their own dreams. It seems to be much easier to understand and interpret somebody else's dream—at least in general terms—than one's own, because an outsider does not have to deal with the emotional blocks and filters that we carry with us each and every day.

As my client began to take a closer look at her dream, she recognized the town as being an old part of Göttingen, Germany, where she had lived in a very old house during her studies at the University. She also remembered that, during that period, she felt very lonely and considered herself quite ugly. Every weekend while she was in school she took a train to see her mother, but never felt any better when she was there. The mountain she was dreaming about she saw as a huge obstacle, and as far as the man in the dream was concerned, she had absolutely no clue what that was about. "Maybe I felt so bad all the time because I had no sexual partner and I was always longing for one. Climbing the mountain in my dream seemed to represent just that: trying to reach a place where I could find a sexual partner." After a short pause, she continued, "And now I have somebody and he reaches out with both arms and I'm still not satisfied; even so, I'm climbing a mountain." And then she added that, somehow, she has the feeling that her interpretations are all wrong. In resignation, she said: "All of this is all wrong. I simply can't get anywhere with it. Every time a relationship question turns up for me I don't know what to do. It seems I can't think logically anymore, and worse yet, it feels like I'm going around in circles." And that indeed is the sense of being stuck. We simply can't find a way out of our situation and we suffer tremendously because of it. Our thinking is clouded, and no matter how hard we try, we cannot find a solution. Everything seems frozen, including our emotions.

In such a situation we might consider turning to our dreams and letting them challenge us to find new meaning in our present situation. This might just return life to frozen emotions, because the desire for a better and more creative way of life obviously exists. So why not reach for this handbook and look for ways to stimulate associations that have been blocked?

This is precisely what I suggested to my client. First, we looked at the subject "city," and she immediately took note when she heard that this is a symbol of protection and that the city is often a symbol of mother. This is something she had suspected, but had totally repressed. At the same time, it came to her with rushing clarity why she had to leave the city and say good-bye to her mother: it was simply a matter of needing to grow up and to find security and support within herself. No such motherly protection can ever come from a man, since it is not his job to replace a mother (or is it?).

If we take a closer look at the motions that the two people are making, it becomes clear that the mother as well as the man are the ones who need the dreamer: they both are stretching their arms out toward her. The dreamer, however, leaves the man standing there and says good-bye to the mother. Is the dream suggesting a new way for the dreamer to behave, as often happens?

Encouraged by what she has discovered so far, my client proceeded to look under "mountain." To her great surprise, she found the word "protection," and also the words "perspective" and "awareness."

"That is it! I must stop forgetting about myself constantly in all my relationships. I'm really not in need of this kind of protection anymore. What I do need is a better perspective and a more objective examination of my situation. And that is what I will find when I reach the summit, the cool, crisp air of clear thinking. And it has nothing to do with the inability to bond or with frigidity. The trip into the mountain does not render me without protection. On the contrary, it will give me new perspective and new insight."

A train, generally speaking, is a collective means of transportation, and my client is beginning to look at this as a means of being together with people who are in similar situations. Together with others with whom she is associating, it will be much easier to look at her unrealistic expectations of relationships and her childlike need for security. The maze of the train tracks, which at first glance looks like a very complicated path, might in reality become resolved, given the solid support of a group of people. Relationship problems, after all, are collective problems.

At the same time, my client realized how much she was longing for stability and still clinging to the rather childlike hope that changes would come by happenstance.

Of course, there are many more meanings to this dream; in subsequent visits we took a close look at the important connection between the mother and the strong man, *anima* and *animus*, both of whom were reaching out to her. To the *animus* she can neither say good-bye nor get involved, and that is exactly her dilemma.

Later on, we discussed the maze (the train tracks), and talked about the Greek myth of the labyrinth on Crete, where Theseus, as a young hero, is aided by Ariadne, who loves him. When, later, she is abandoned by him, she meets the wild god Dionysus, who loves her, satisfies her, and sweeps her off into heaven. In other words, this dream offers the dreamer a whole new way of looking at her problem, while her "thinking" got her nowhere and rendered her numb. In order to recognize this new way of thinking, we need either an extensive knowledge of mythology, fairy tales, or fables—or a good handbook of dream symbols that will open our eyes and allow us to see what we are either not able to see or do not want to see. In our example, my client was convinced that she would only feel safe and secure when connected to a man. To him she projected the protecting *animus*, even though he himself was one of the worst mama's boys. This woman was too fearful to recognize that many men offer insecurity rather than protection. It did not fit into her emotional view of the world.

Expanding one's view through a dream, as in this example, does not take place only with emotional problems. It also holds true in the scientific area. We often go numb when we are confronted with a problem that we are unable to resolve in spite of our greatest efforts. Mental blocks are very similar to emotional repression: We frequently refuse to see certain connections because they are challenging and question our own worldview. So we should not be surprised to hear that the 19th century German chemist A. Kekule von Stradonitz for the longest time simply could not imagine that molecules could arrange themselves in a circular form. It was a clear case of rebellion against the "father authority," when he discovered the circular organization of the Benzol rings, and all because of his dream about Ouroboros (see page 322).

Something very similar happened to Einstein, who, by observing his dreams and questioning the almost godlike authority of "objective natural laws," made the bold and revolutionary statement that the only objective view of the observer is a subjective view.

These are only two examples of the many we could cite where natural scientists particularly had their worldview creatively expanded through their dreams.

All of us could increase our creativity enormously simply by observing our dreams. One prerequisite, however, is that when we observe our dream symbols, we be willing to look at what, under normal circumstances, we would rather look away from. This is the so-called blind spot that we simply refuse to see under any circumstances. Such blind spots only become visible when we are willing to leave behind conventional associations. When set in motion these conventional beliefs only define our limits. And that, in essence, is the breathtaking adventure of dreams: they point out so many new, never-before-imagined ways of interpretation and association that these new insights set everything dancing. Our task as dreamers is to allow ourselves to be carried away by this dynamic process and jump straight into the whirlpool of creativity. In depth psychology, this adventure would be considered emancipation from the authority of the Father's habitual conservative attitudes, which have become paralyzed. A new idea appearing in a dream is awakened by the feminine side within us, the side that continually tempts us to look for new connections. This creative intelligence of the feminine was already known to the people of ancient Greece, and is the reason why the goddess Sophia was considered the embodiment of wisdom. A distant echo of this knowledge can be found in Christianity, where symbolically the female dove stands for the Holy Ghost.

So why not let our dreams tempt us to new creative thinking that will most certainly make our everyday life more colorful? Creative people, such as poets, painters, and sculptors, and also scientists and natural scientists, always took their dreams very seriously and through their dreams were able to see their world in a new light. It is my belief that our dreams represent the expression of our soul, and it truly would be a shame if we would allow, night after night, this creativity to go to waste. If you begin to pay attention to the creative and aesthetic side of your dream images and your dreams, you and the world around you will change. You will begin to recognize problems as challenges to your creative energy, allowing you to escape the widespread numbness that is nothing more than a thinly veiled attempt to feel "safe."

Inquiries, critiques, encouragement, advice, and information about seminars on this subject may be sent to the author via the publisher or at the following address:

Rhu-Sila
Cley-Next-the-Sea
Holt
Norfolk NR 257 UD.
Tel.& Fax: 01263-7440304—Great Britain